the

Seamless

Gospels

COMPILED BY
CHARLES ROLLER WITH CAROL MERSCH

the

Seamless

Gospels

THE STORY OF CHRIST

THE EVENTS OF THE GOSPELS
INTERWOVEN IN CHRONOLOGICAL ORDER

The Seamless Gospels
ISBN 0-7684-2302-3

1 2 3 4 5 6 7 8 9 10 / 09 08 07 06 05

For a U.S. bookstore nearest you, call
1-800-722-6774
For information on foreign distributors, call
717-532-3040
Or reach us on the Internet:
www.destinyimage.com

*Dedicated to those with an interest
in the journey toward Christ*

Endorsements

"The compilation of these New Testament stories, put in chronological order, is very well done. I trust that people who never pick up a Bible will read *The Seamless Gospels* for a better understanding and be blessed."

> Oral Roberts, *B.A., M.Div, LL.D*
> *Founder, Oral Roberts University*
> *Oral Roberts Evangelistic Association*

"The greatest possession in life is wisdom. Wisdom is the ability to apply knowledge effectively. However, it is impossible to apply what you don't or can't understand. Therefore, understanding is the key to wisdom. It is said that in all your getting, get understanding. *The Seamless Gospels* has taken a great leap in presenting the most important body of knowledge and truth in a people-friendly form. This is going to be a classic and will open the world of biblical revelation to a world in desperate need of it."

> Myles Munroe
> *BFM International, Nassau, Bahamas*

"The truth of God's Word sets people free. To have the Word of God presented in a sequential order is helpful in understanding the events and therefore grasping the true meaning of the scriptures. I pray the Holy Spirit will give you revelation in the knowledge of Jesus."

> Billy Joe Daugherty
> *Pastor, Victory Christian Center, Tulsa, OK*

"*The Seamless Gospels* is a flowing narrative of the most important story ever told. It is the King James Bible of old arranged in such a way that a grandparent can captivate the imagination and attention of even a young child as the good news of Jesus Christ is warmly shared. I found myself reading *The Seamless Gospels* as I would a modern novel, but the time I spent reading it will be measured not in hours, but in eternity. I highly commend *The Seamless Gospels*."

Wade Burleson
President, Baptist General Convention of Oklahoma

⁀

"The life of Jesus can be difficult to follow because His story is told in four Gospels. When we read the New Testament like any other book, it can seem like we're going in circles. The aim of *The Seamless Gospels* is to sequence the life of Jesus in an easier-to-read fashion. This approach can be very helpful to those who are being introduced to Jesus."

Dr. Tom Harrison
Senior Pastor, Asbury United Methodist Church, Tulsa, OK

⁀

"*The Seamless Gospels* is an incredible scripture text that has allowed us an opportunity to see scripture come alive. There are a number of Bibles that are open to us for reading, for application, for inspiration and devotion. But when a reader turns to the Bible, he is looking for a connection from one text to the other. *The Seamless Bible* has made this connection in a way that causes the scripture to come to life."

Èmile Hawkins, Sr., *BPS, ThB, MA*
Senior Pastor, Liberty World Outreach Church, Tulsa, OK

⁀

"The innovative presentation of *The Seamless Gospels* preserves all the integrity and richness of the King James Version, at the same time bringing the message of the gospel to 21st century seekers in a creative and meaningful way."

Rev. Penelope A. Black and Canon Elizabeth St. C. Stewart
Anglican Church of Canada, Diocese of British Columbia

⁀

"A great and scholarly job of bringing chronological order into the work."

Dr. Edgar D. Mitchell
Apollo 14 Lunar Module Pilot
Founder, Institute of Noetic Sciences
Author, "The Way of the Explorer" and "Psychic Exploration"

⁀

Table of Contents

THE JOURNEY OF CHRIST

To the Reader

The collection of lessons witnessed and recorded by the disciples as they walked with Jesus may well be the single most valuable guidepost to living that we have today. You have in your hands a powerful new presentation of the life of Christ, drawn from the original King James New Testament and recast in a refreshing narrative format that weaves all of the accounts of Jesus' life into one seamless story.

Over 25 years in the making, *The Seamless Bible* presents the entire King James New Testament arranged in sequential order, with special care given to preserve and blend the original King James text into one continuous flow of events without translation or interpretation. The King James Version of the Bible, first published in 1611 and revised in 1769, was chosen as the basis of the work, as it remains the most beautiful and widely accepted translation of the Bible in the world today.

The *Seamless Gospels* is an abridged version of *The Seamless Bible* with concentration on the four gospels in the New Testament. From this translation the Books of the New Testament are used to create a biblical biography of unique simplicity that details the life of Jesus. In the first section, "The Journey of Christ," the text of the Gospel authors—Matthew, Mark, Luke, and John— are woven together into one complete narrative of the life of Jesus in a consistent flow of time from His birth to His resurrection.

The result is a unique presentation of the most time-honored Book in all literature, meticulously arranged in order of time and true in every detail to the original King James text. Every available reference was researched and studied in the compilation of this book, including other versions of the Bible, Bible reference, and related scriptural texts.

The most memorable phrases of Jesus are inset in the margins and all text quotations from the Old Testament are noted in italics. Outdated words in the original version were carefully researched and replaced with their modern-day equivalents so that the lessons given by Jesus so many years ago can be clearly applied to our lives today.

The column of paragraph numbers in the margin of each page serves a unique purpose. As you study this book you may find it useful to refer to your favorite passages quickly by page and paragraph number.

The reader will realize that *The Seamless Gospels* does not contain the traditional chapter and verse. *The Seamless Gospels* is the New Testament gospels arranged in chronological order, without chapter and verse as in the original text, to allow a more undistracted reading of the Word. The cross-reference index in the back of the book can be used to trace a specific chapter and verse to its location on the associated page and paragraph.

Included in this narrative are some of the most respected words that exist in print—an endless stream of Jesus' experiences, words, and deeds that reveal God's love and provide spiritual guidance for every hungry heart.

Thus, following in the footsteps of time, page by page, *The Seamless Gospels* leads you alongside Jesus and His disciples in a journey through the greatest story ever told. Its sole aim is to carry the story forward in a more inspiring, vital, and meaningful manner so that you, the reader, might apprehend and apply its message more fully in the world today.

The Events of the Gospels Interwoven in Chronological Order

PART 1

BIRTH AND CHILDHOOD

The birth of Jesus was foretold long before He made His appearance on earth. His coming was revealed to many people in many ways hundreds of years before His birth. Throughout time, angels were the messengers sent by God to deliver His word to those chosen to do His calling. It is important, therefore, that we start at the true beginning of the story—with the prophecy of angels.

> THE ANGEL GABRIEL WAS SENT FROM GOD UNTO A CITY OF GALILEE, NAMED NAZARETH, TO A VIRGIN PLEDGED TO BE MARRIED TO A MAN WHOSE NAME WAS JOSEPH, OF THE HOUSE OF DAVID; AND THE VIRGIN'S NAME WAS MARY.
>
> (LUKE 1:26-27)

CHAPTER 1

THE GREAT ANNOUNCEMENT

The Proclamation
Luke 1:1-4

1   Inasmuch as many have taken in hand to set forth in order a declaration of those things which are most surely believed among us, even as they delivered them unto us, which from the beginning were eyewitnesses, and ministers of the word; it seemed good to me also, having had perfect understanding of all things from the very first, to write unto you in order that you might know the certainty of those things wherein you have been instructed.

Birth of John Foretold
Luke 1:5-25

2   There was in the days of Herod, the king of Judea, a certain priest named Zacharias, of the division of Abijah: and his wife was of the daughters of Aaron, and her name was Elizabeth. And they were both righteous before God, walking in all the commandments and ordinances of the Lord blameless. They had no child, because Elizabeth was barren, and they both were now well advanced in years.

3   And it came to pass, that while he executed the priest's office before God in the order of his division, according to the custom of the priest's office, his lot was to burn incense when he went into the temple of the Lord. The whole multitude of the people were praying outside at the time of incense.

4   There appeared unto him an angel of the Lord standing on the right side of the altar of incense. When Zacharias saw him, he was troubled, and fear fell upon him. But the angel said unto him, "Fear not, Zacharias: for your prayer is heard; and your wife Elizabeth shall bear you a son, and you shall call his name John.

"And you shall have joy and gladness; and many shall rejoice at his 5 birth. For he shall be great in the sight of the Lord, and shall drink neither wine nor strong drink; and he shall be filled with the Holy Ghost, even from his mother's womb. Many of the children of Israel shall he turn to the Lord their God. And he shall go before him in the spirit and power of Elijah, '*to turn the hearts of the fathers to the children*,' and the disobedient to the wisdom of the just; to make ready a people prepared for the Lord."

Zacharias said unto the angel, "How shall I know this? for I am an old 6 man, and my wife well advanced in years." The angel answering said unto him, "I am Gabriel, that stands in the presence of God; and am sent to speak unto you, and to show you these glad tidings. And, behold, you shall be mute, and not able to speak, until the day that these things shall be performed, because you believe not my words, which shall be fulfilled in their season."

The people waited for Zacharias, and marveled that he tarried so long 7 in the temple. When he came out, he could not speak unto them: and they perceived that he had seen a vision in the temple: for he beckoned unto them, and remained speechless.

It came to pass, that, as soon as the days of his service were accom- 8 plished, he departed to his own house. And after those days his wife Elizabeth conceived, and hid herself five months, saying, "Thus has the Lord dealt with me in the days wherein he looked on me, to take away my disgrace among men."

Birth of Jesus Foretold
Luke 1:26-38

And in the sixth month the angel Gabriel was sent from God unto a 9 city of Galilee, named Nazareth, to a virgin pledged to be married to a man whose name was Joseph, of the house of David; and the virgin's name was Mary.

The angel came in unto her, and said, "Hail, you that are highly 10 favored, the Lord is with you: blessed are you among women." When she saw him, she was troubled at his saying, and cast in her mind what manner of greeting this should be.

> "FEAR NOT, MARY: FOR YOU HAVE FOUND FAVOR WITH GOD."

The angel said unto her, "Fear not, Mary: for you have found favor 11 with God. And, behold, you shall conceive in your womb, and bring forth a son, and shall call his name Jesus. He shall be great, and shall be called the Son of the Highest: and the Lord God shall give unto him the throne of his father David: and he shall reign over the house of Jacob for ever; and of his kingdom there shall be no end."

Then said Mary unto the angel, "How shall this be, seeing I have no 12 union with a man?" And the angel answered and said unto her, "The Holy

12   Ghost shall come upon you, and the power of the Highest shall overshadow you: therefore also that holy thing which shall be born of you shall be called the Son of God. And, behold, your relative Elizabeth, she has also conceived a son in her old age: and this is the sixth month with her, who was called barren. For with God nothing shall be impossible."

13   Mary said, "Behold the handmaid of the Lord; be it unto me according to your word." And the angel departed from her.

Mary's Visit With Elizabeth
Luke 1:39-45

14   And Mary arose in those days, and went into the hill country with haste, into a city of Judah; and entered into the house of Zacharias, and greeted Elizabeth.

15   And it came to pass, that, when Elizabeth heard the greeting of Mary, the baby leaped in her womb; and Elizabeth was filled with the Holy Ghost: and she spoke out with a loud voice, and said, "Blessed are you among women, and blessed is the fruit of your womb. What is this to me, that the mother of my Lord should come to me? For, lo, as soon as the voice of your greeting sounded in my ears, the baby leaped in my womb for joy. Blessed is she that believed: for there shall be a performance of those things which were told her from the Lord."

Mary's Praise of God
Luke 1:46-56

16   And Mary said, "My soul does magnify the Lord, and my spirit has rejoiced in God my Savior. For he has regarded the low status of his handmaiden: for, behold, from henceforth all generations shall call me blessed. For he that is mighty has done to me great things; and holy is his name. And his mercy is on them that fear him from generation to generation.

17   "He has showed strength with his arm; he has scattered the proud in the imagination of their hearts. He has put down the mighty from their seats, and exalted them of low degree. He has filled the hungry with good things; and the rich he has sent empty away. He has helped his servant Israel, in remembrance of his mercy; as he spoke to our fathers, to Abraham, and to his seed for ever."

18   Mary stayed with her about three months, and returned to her own house.

Birth of John the Baptist
Luke 1:57-66

19   Now Elizabeth's full time came that she should be delivered; and she brought forth a son. And her neighbors and her relatives heard how the Lord had showed great mercy upon her; and they rejoiced with her.

20   It came to pass, that on the eighth day they came to circumcise the child; and they called him Zacharias, after the name of his father. And his

mother answered and said, "Not so; but he shall be called John." And they 20
said unto her, "There is none of your family that is called by this name."

They made signs to his father, how he would have him called. And he 21
asked for a writing tablet, and wrote, saying, "His name is John." And they
all marveled. And his mouth was opened immediately, and his tongue
loosed, and he spoke, and praised God.

Fear came on all that dwelt round about them: and all these sayings 22
were talked about throughout all the hill country of Judea. All they that
heard them laid them up in their hearts, saying, "What manner of child shall
this be!" And the hand of the Lord was with him.

Zacharias Prophesies John's Destiny
Luke 1:67-80

His father Zacharias was filled with the Holy Ghost, and prophesied, 23
saying, "Blessed be the Lord God of Israel; for he has visited and redeemed
his people, and has raised up a horn of salvation for us in the house of his
servant David; as he spoke by the mouth of his holy prophets, which have
been since the world began: that we should be saved from our enemies, and
from the hand of all that hate us; to perform the mercy promised to our
fathers, and to remember his holy covenant; the oath which he swore to our
father Abraham, that he would grant unto us, that we being delivered out of
the hand of our enemies might serve him without fear, in holiness and righteousness before him, all the days of our life.

"And you, child, shall be called the prophet of the Highest: for you 24
shall go before the face of the Lord to prepare his ways; to give knowledge
of salvation unto his people by the remission of their sins, through the tender mercy of our God; by which the dayspring from on high has visited us,
to give light to them that sit in darkness and in the shadow of death, to guide
our feet into the way of peace."

The child grew, and became strong in spirit, and was in the deserts till 25
the day of his showing unto Israel.

CHAPTER 2

THE PROMISE FULFILLED

Birth of Jesus Christ
Matthew 1:18-25; Luke 2:1-7

1   Now the birth of Jesus Christ was in this way: When as his mother Mary was pledged to be married to Joseph, before they came together, she was found with child of the Holy Ghost. Then Joseph her husband, being a just man, and not willing to make her a public example, was minded to put her away secretly.

2   But while he thought on these things, behold, the angel of the Lord appeared unto him in a dream, saying, "Joseph, son of David, fear not to take unto you Mary your wife: for that which is conceived in her is of the Holy Ghost. And she shall bring forth a son, and you shall call his name Jesus: for he shall save his people from their sins."

3   Now all this was done, that it might be fulfilled which was spoken of the Lord by the prophet, saying, *"Behold, a virgin shall be with child, and shall bring forth a son, and they shall call his name Emmanuel,"* which being interpreted is, *"God with us."*

4   Then Joseph being raised from sleep did as the angel of the Lord had commanded him, and took unto him his wife: and had no union with her till she had brought forth her firstborn son: and he called his name Jesus.

5   And it came to pass in those days, that there went out a decree from Caesar Augustus, that all the world should be taxed. (And this taxing was first made when Cyrenius was governor of Syria.)

6   All went to be taxed, everyone into his own city. And Joseph also went up from Galilee, out of the city of Nazareth, into Judea, unto the city of David, which is called Bethlehem; (because he was of the house and lineage of David): to be taxed with Mary his pledged wife, being great with child.

7   And so it was, that, while they were there, the days were accomplished that she should be delivered. She brought forth her firstborn son, and wrapped him in swaddling clothes, and laid him in a manger; because there was no room for them in the inn.

Shepherds Receive Good Tidings
Luke 2:8-20

There were in the same country shepherds abiding in the field, 8 keeping watch over their flock by night.

And, lo, the angel of the Lord came upon them, and the glory of the 9 Lord shone round about them: and they were very afraid. The angel said unto them, "Fear not: for, behold, I bring you good tidings of great joy, which shall be to all people. For unto you is born this day in the city of David a Savior, which is Christ the Lord. And this shall be a sign unto you: You shall find the baby wrapped in swaddling clothes, lying in a manger."

> "FEAR NOT: FOR, BEHOLD, I BRING YOU GOOD TIDINGS OF GREAT JOY."

Suddenly there was with the angel a multitude of the heavenly host 10 praising God, and saying, "Glory to God in the highest, and on earth peace, goodwill toward men."

And it came to pass, as the angels were gone away from them into 11 heaven, the shepherds said one to another, "Let us now go even unto Bethlehem, and see this thing which is come to pass, which the Lord has made known unto us." They came with haste, and found Mary, and Joseph, and the baby lying in a manger.

When they had seen it, they made known abroad the saying which was 12 told them concerning this child. And all they that heard it wondered at those things which were told them by the shepherds.

But Mary kept all these things, and pondered them in her heart. And 13 the shepherds returned, glorifying and praising God for all the things that they had heard and seen, as it was told unto them.

His Name Is Jesus
Luke 2:21

When eight days were accomplished for the circumcision of the child, 14 his name was called Jesus, which was so named of the angel before he was conceived in the womb.

Jesus Is Presented to the Lord
Luke 2:22-24

When the days of her purification according to the law of Moses were 15 accomplished, they brought him to Jerusalem, to present him to the Lord; (as it is written in the law of the Lord, *"Every male that opens the womb shall be called holy to the Lord);"* and to offer a sacrifice according to that which is said in the law of the Lord, *"A pair of turtledoves, or two young pigeons."*

Simeon's Prophecy About Jesus
Luke 2:25-35

Behold, there was a man in Jerusalem, whose name was Simeon; and 16 the same man was just and devout, waiting for the consolation of Israel: and

16 the Holy Ghost was upon him. It was revealed unto him by the Holy Ghost, that he should not see death, before he had seen the Lord's Christ. He came by the Spirit into the temple: and when the parents brought in the child Jesus, to do for him after the custom of the law, then he took him up in his arms, and blessed God, and said, "Lord, now let your servant depart in peace, according to your word: for my eyes have seen your salvation, which you have prepared before the face of all people; a light to enlighten the Gentiles, and the glory of your people Israel."

17   Joseph and his mother marveled at those things which were spoken of him. And Simeon blessed them, and said unto Mary his mother, "Behold, this child is set for the fall and rising again of many in Israel; and for a sign which shall be spoken against; (yes, a sword shall pierce through your own soul also), that the thoughts of many hearts may be revealed."

Anna Testifies of the Savior
Luke 2:36-39

18   And there was one Anna, a prophetess, the daughter of Phanuel, of the tribe of Asher: she was of a great age, and had lived with a husband seven years from her virginity; and she was a widow of about eighty and four years of age, which departed not from the temple, but served God with fastings and prayers night and day. And she coming in that instant gave thanks likewise unto the Lord, and spoke of him to all them that looked for redemption in Jerusalem.

19   When they had performed all things according to the law of the Lord, they returned into Galilee, to their own city Nazareth.

CHAPTER 3

⸱⸱⸱ THE PROTECTED CHILDHOOD ⸱⸱⸱

Wise Men From the East
Matthew 2:1-12

Now when Jesus was born in Bethlehem of Judea in the days of Herod 1
the king, behold, there came wise men from the east to Jerusalem, saying,
"Where is he that is born King of the Jews? for we have seen his star in the
east, and are come to worship him."

When Herod the king had heard these things, he was troubled, and 2
all Jerusalem with him. And when he had gathered all the chief priests
and scribes of the people together, he inquired of them where Christ
should be born. And they said unto him, "In Bethlehem of Judea: for thus
it is written by the prophet, *'And you Bethlehem, in the land of Judah, are
not the least among the princes of Judah: for out of you shall come a Governor, that shall rule my people Israel.'"*

Then Herod, when he had secretly called the wise men, inquired of 3
them diligently what time the star appeared. And he sent them to Bethlehem, and said, "Go and search diligently for the young child; and when you
have found him, bring me word again, that I may come and worship him
also."

When they had heard the king, they departed; and, lo, the star, which 4
they saw in the east, went before them, till it came and stood over where the
young child was. When they saw the star, they rejoiced with exceedingly
great joy.

And when they were come into the house, they saw the young child 5
with Mary his mother, and fell down, and worshiped him: and when they
had opened their treasures, they presented unto him gifts; gold, and frank-
incense, and myrrh.

Being warned of God in a dream that they should not return to Herod, 6
they departed into their own country another way.

Flight Into Egypt With Jesus
Matthew 2:13-18

7   And when they were departed, behold, the angel of the Lord appeared to Joseph in a dream, saying, "Arise, and take the young child and his mother, and flee into Egypt, and be there until I bring you word: for Herod will seek the young child to destroy him." When he arose, he took the young child and his mother by night, and departed into Egypt: and was there until the death of Herod: that it might be fulfilled which was spoken of the Lord by the prophet, saying, *"Out of Egypt have I called my son."*

8   Then Herod, when he saw that he was mocked of the wise men, was exceedingly angry, and sent forth, and slew all the male children that were in Bethlehem, and in all the regions thereof, from two years old and under, according to the time which he had diligently inquired of the wise men. Then was fulfilled that which was spoken by Jeremiah the prophet, saying, *"In Ramah was there a voice heard, lamentation, and weeping, and great mourning, Rachel weeping for her children, and would not be comforted, because they are no more."*

The Family's Return to Nazareth
Matthew 2:19-23; Luke 2:40

9   But when Herod was dead, behold, an angel of the Lord appeared in a dream to Joseph in Egypt, saying, "Arise, and take the young child and his mother, and go into the land of Israel: for they are dead which sought the young child's life."

10   And he arose, and took the young child and his mother, and came into the land of Israel. But when he heard that Archelaus (Herod) did reign in Judea in the succession of his father Herod, he was afraid to go there: nevertheless, being warned of God in a dream, he turned aside into the parts of Galilee: and he came and dwelt in a city called Nazareth: that it might be fulfilled which was spoken by the prophets, "He shall be called a Nazarene."

11   The child grew, and became strong in spirit, filled with wisdom: and the grace of God was upon him.

Young Jesus in the Temple
Luke 2:41-50

12   Now his parents went to Jerusalem every year at the feast of the passover. And when he was twelve years old, they went up to Jerusalem after the custom of the feast. And when they had fulfilled the days, as they returned, the child Jesus tarried behind in Jerusalem; and Joseph and his mother knew not of it. But they, supposing him to have been in the company, went a day's journey; and they sought him among their relatives and acquaintances. And when they did not find him, they turned back again to Jerusalem, seeking him.

13   And it came to pass, that after three days they found him in the temple, sitting in the midst of the teachers, both hearing them, and asking them

questions. And all that heard him were astonished at his understanding and 13 answers.

When they saw him, they were amazed: and his mother said unto him, 14 "Son, why have you thus dealt with us? behold, your father and I have sought you sorrowing." And he said unto them, "How is it that you sought

> "I MUST BE ABOUT MY FATHER'S BUSINESS."

me? knew you not that I must be about my Father's business?" They did not understand the saying which he spoke unto them.

Jesus Increases in Wisdom
Luke 2:51-52

And he went down with them, and came to Nazareth, and was subject 15 unto them: but his mother kept all these sayings in her heart.

And Jesus increased in wisdom and stature, and in favor with God 16 and man.

PART 2

PUBLIC PREPARATION

In conscious awareness of His divine purpose, Jesus accepted baptism by John the Baptist and prepared to fulfill the mission for which He was sent. It was John's hope that this baptism would serve to enforce the conviction that Jesus was indeed the Christ, the Son of God, and that life would come through belief in Him. In patient obedience to a patient God, Jesus affirmed His destiny by His works, purging the temple of moneychangers, turning the wedding water into wine, and rebuking the temptations of the devil. His mission was clear; the Word was with Him.

> THE WORD WAS WITH GOD, AND THE WORD WAS GOD....IN HIM WAS LIFE; AND THE LIFE WAS THE LIGHT OF MEN. AND THE LIGHT SHINES IN DARKNESS. (JOHN 1:1, 4-5)

CHAPTER 4

THE GREAT BEGINNING

Prologue: The Word Made Flesh
John 1:1-5, 10-14, 16-18

In the beginning was the Word, and the Word was with God, and the 1 Word was God. The same was in the beginning with God. All things were made by him; and without him was not anything made that was made. In him was life; and the life was the light of men. And the light shines in darkness; and the darkness comprehended it not.

He was in the world, and the world was made by him, and the world 2 knew him not. He came unto his own, and his own received him not. But as many as received him, to them he gave authority to become the sons of God, even to them that believe on his name: which were born, not of blood, nor of the will of the flesh, nor of the will of man, but of God.

And the Word was made flesh, and dwelt among us, (and we beheld 3 his glory, the glory as of the only begotten of the Father), full of grace and truth. And of his fulness have we all received, and grace for grace. For the law was given by Moses, but grace and truth came by Jesus Christ. No man has seen God at any time; the only begotten Son, which is in the bosom of the Father, he has declared him.

Prologue: The Witness Sent
John 1:6-9

There was a man sent from God, whose name was John. The same came 4 for a witness, to bear witness of the Light, that all men through him might believe. He was not that Light, but was sent to bear witness of that Light. That was the true Light, which lights every man that comes into the world.

John the Baptist Prepares the Way
Matthew 3:1-12; Mark 1:1-8; Luke 3:1-18; John 1:15

Now in the fifteenth year of the reign of Tiberius Caesar, Pontius 5 Pilate being governor of Judea, and Herod (Antipas) being tetrarch (ruler)

5　of Galilee, and his brother Philip tetrarch (ruler) of Iturea and of the region of Trachonitis, and Lysanias the tetrarch (ruler) of Abilene, Annas and Caiaphas being the high priests, the word of God came unto John the son of Zacharias in the wilderness.

6　　　The beginning of the gospel of Jesus Christ, the Son of God; as it is written in the prophets, *"Behold, I send my messenger before your face, which shall prepare your way before you."* In those days came John the Baptist, preaching in the wilderness of Judea, and saying, "Repent: for the kingdom of heaven is at hand."

7　　　And he came into all the country about Jordan, preaching the baptism of repentance for the remission of sins; as it is written in the book of the words of Isaiah the prophet, saying, *"The voice of one crying in the wilderness, 'Prepare the way of the Lord, make his paths straight. Every valley shall be filled, and every mountain and hill shall be brought low; and the crooked shall be made straight, and the rough ways shall be made smooth; and all flesh shall see the salvation of God.'"* John did baptize in the wilderness, and preach the baptism of repentance for the remission of sins.

8　　　And the same John had his clothing of camel's hair, and a leather belt of a skin about his waist; and his food was locusts and wild honey. And there went out unto him all the land of Judea, and all the region round about Jordan, and they of Jerusalem, and were all baptized of him in the river of Jordan, confessing their sins. But when he saw many of the Pharisees and Sadducees come to his baptism, he said unto them, to the multitude that came forth to be baptized of him, "O generation of vipers, who has warned you to flee from the wrath to come?

9　　　"Bring forth therefore fruits worthy of repentance: and begin not to say within yourselves, 'We have Abraham to our father:' for I say unto you that God is able of these stones to raise up children unto Abraham. And now also the ax is laid unto the root of the trees: therefore every tree which brings not forth good fruit is cut down, and cast into the fire."

10　　　And the people asked him, saying, "What shall we do then?" He answered and said unto them, "He that has two coats, let him impart to him that has none; and he that has food, let him do likewise."

11　　　Then came also tax collectors to be baptized, and said unto him, "Teacher, what shall we do?" And he said unto them, "Exact no more than that which is appointed you."

12　　　And the soldiers likewise asked of him, saying, "And what shall we do?" And he said unto them, "Do violence to no man, neither accuse any falsely; and be content with your wages."

13　　　And as the people were in expectation, and all men mused in their hearts of John, whether he were the Christ, or not; John answered, saying unto them all, "I indeed baptize you with water unto repentance; but one mightier than I comes after me, whose shoes I am not worthy to bear, the strap of whose shoes I am not worthy to stoop down and loose: he shall baptize you with the Holy Ghost and with fire: whose fan is in his hand, and he

will thoroughly purge his floor, and will gather the wheat into his store- 14
house; but the chaff he will burn with fire unquenchable."

John bore witness of him, and cried, saying, "This was he of whom I 15
spoke. He that comes after me is preferred before me: for he was before
me." And many other things in his message he preached unto the people.

John Baptizes Jesus
Matthew 3:13-17; Mark 1:9-11; Luke 3:21-22

And Jesus himself began to be about thirty years of age. And it came 16
to pass in those days, that Jesus came from Nazareth of Galilee to Jordan
unto John, to be baptized of him. But John forbade him, saying, "I have
need to be baptized of you, and you come to me?" And Jesus answering said
unto him, "Allow it to be so now: for thus it becomes us to fulfill all righteousness." Then he allowed him.

Now when all the people were baptized, it came to pass, that Jesus also 17
being baptized, and praying, went up straightway out of the water: and, lo,
the heavens were opened unto him, and he saw the Spirit of God descending in a bodily form, like a dove, and lighting upon him: and lo a voice from
heaven, saying, "This is my beloved Son, in whom I am well pleased."

Jesus Tempted of the Devil
Matthew 4:1-11; Mark 1:12-13; Luke 4:1-13

And Jesus being full of the Holy Ghost immediately returned from 18
Jordan, and the Spirit drove him into the wilderness to be tempted of the
devil. In those days he did eat nothing: and when he had fasted forty days
and forty nights, and they were ended, he afterward was hungry.

And when the tempter came to him, the devil said unto him, "If you 19
be the Son of God, command that these stones be made bread." Jesus
answered him saying, "It is written, *'Man shall not live by bread alone, but
by every word that proceeds out of the mouth of God.'*

Then the devil took him up into the holy city, Jerusalem, and set him 20
on a pinnacle of the temple, and said unto him, "If you be the Son of God,
cast yourself down from here: for it is written, *'He shall give his angels
charge over you, to keep you: and in their hands they shall bear you up, lest
at any time you dash your foot against a stone.'*" Jesus answering said unto
him, "It is written again, *'You shall not tempt the Lord your God.'* "

Again, the devil took him up into an exceedingly high mountain, and 21
showed him all the kingdoms of the world in a moment of time, and the glory
of them; and said unto him, "All this authority will I give you, and the glory of
them: for that is delivered unto me; and to whomsoever I will I give it. If you
therefore will fall down and worship me, all these things shall be yours." Jesus
answered and said unto him, "Get you behind me, Satan: for it is written, *'You
shall worship the Lord your God, and him only shall you serve.'* "

And when the devil had ended all the temptation, he departed from 22
him for a season. He was there in the wilderness forty days, tempted of
Satan; and was with the wild beasts; and, behold, the angels came and ministered unto him.

CHAPTER 5

THE FIRST FOLLOWERS

John the Baptist's Testimony
John 1:19-28

1   And this is the testimony of John, when the Jews sent priests and Levites from Jerusalem to ask him, "Who are you?" He confessed, and denied not; but confessed, "I am not the Christ."

2   And they asked him, "What then? Are you Elijah?" He said, "I am not." "Are you that prophet?" And he answered, "No."

3   Then they said unto him, "Who are you that we may give an answer to them that sent us. What do you say of yourself?" He said, "I am *'the voice of one crying in the wilderness, "Make straight the way of the Lord,"* ' as said the prophet Isaiah."

4   And they which were sent were of the Pharisees. They asked him, and said unto him, "Why do you baptize then, if you be not that Christ, nor Elijah, neither that prophet?" John answered them, saying, "I baptize with water: but there stands one among you, whom you know not; he it is, who coming after me is preferred before me, whose shoe's strap I am not worthy to loose."

5   These things were done in Bethany beyond Jordan, where John was baptizing.

"Behold the Lamb of God"
John 1:29-34

6   The next day John saw Jesus coming unto him, and said, "Behold the Lamb of God, which takes away the sin of the world. This is he of whom I said, 'After me comes a man which is preferred before me: for he was before me.' And I knew him not: but that he should be made manifest to Israel, therefore I am come baptizing with water."

7   John bore witness, saying, "I saw the Spirit descending from heaven like a dove, and it rested upon him. And I knew him not: but he that sent me

to baptize with water, the same said unto me, 'Upon whom you shall see the 7
Spirit descending, and remaining on him, the same is he which baptizes
with the Holy Ghost.' And I saw, and bore witness that this is the Son of
God."

First Three Disciples Join Jesus
John 1:35-42

Again the next day after John stood, and two of his disciples; and look- 8
ing upon Jesus as he walked, he said, "Behold the Lamb of God!" And the
two disciples heard him speak, and they followed Jesus.

Then Jesus turned, and saw them following, and said unto them, 9
"What do you seek?" They said unto him, "Rabbi," (which is to say, being
interpreted, Teacher), "where do you dwell?" He said unto them, "Come and
see." They came and saw where he dwelt, and stayed with him that day: for
it was about the tenth hour.

One of the two which heard John speak, and followed him, was 10
Andrew, Simon Peter's brother. He first found his own brother Simon, and
said unto him, "We have found the Messiah," which is, being interpreted,
the Christ.

And he brought him to Jesus. When Jesus beheld him, he said, "You 11
are Simon the son of Jonah: you shall be called Cephas," which is by interpretation, A stone.

Jesus Summons Two More Disciples
John 1:43-51

The following day Jesus went forth into Galilee, and found Philip, and 12
said unto him, "Follow me." Now Philip was of Bethsaida, the city of
Andrew and Peter. Philip found Nathanael, and said unto him, "We have
found him, of whom Moses in the law, and the prophets, did write, Jesus of
Nazareth, the son of Joseph." Nathanael said unto him, "Can there any good
thing come out of Nazareth?" Philip said unto him, "Come and see."

Jesus saw Nathanael coming to him, and said of him, "Behold an 13
Israelite indeed, in whom is no deceit!" Nathanael said unto him, "How do
you know me?" Jesus answered and said unto him, "Before Philip called
you, when you were under the fig tree, I saw you." Nathanael answered and
said unto him, "Rabbi, you are the Son of God; you are the King of Israel."

Jesus answered and said unto him, "Because I said unto you, 'I saw you 14
under the fig tree,' do you believe? you shall see greater things than these." And
he said unto him, "Truly, truly, I say unto you, Hereafter you shall see heaven
open, and the angels of God ascending and descending upon the Son of man."

First Miracle: Water Made Into Wine
John 2:1-12

The third day there was a marriage in Cana of Galilee; and the 15
mother of Jesus was there: and both Jesus was called, and his disciples,
to the marriage.

16   And when they lacked wine, the mother of Jesus said unto him, "They have no wine." Jesus said unto her, "Woman, what have I to do with you? my hour is not yet come." His mother said unto the servants, "Whatsoever he says unto you, do it."

17   There were set there six waterpots of stone, after the manner of the purification of the Jews, containing twenty or thirty gallons apiece. Jesus said unto them, "Fill the waterpots with water." They filled them up to the brim. He said unto them, "Draw out now, and bear unto the steward of the feast." And they bore it.

18   When the steward of the feast had tasted the water that was made wine, and did not know from where it was: (but the servants which drew the water knew); the steward of the feast called the bridegroom, and said unto him, "Every man at the beginning does set forth good wine; and when men have drunk freely, then that which is worse: but you have kept the good wine until now."

19   This beginning of miracles Jesus did in Cana of Galilee, and manifested forth his glory; and his disciples believed on him.

20   After this he went down to Capernaum, he, and his mother, and his brethren, and his disciples: and they continued there not many days.

CHAPTER 6

·:· FIRST MINISTRY AT JERUSALEM ·:·

Jesus Clears the Temple
John 2:13-25

The Jews' passover was at hand, and Jesus went up to Jerusalem, and 1
found in the temple those that sold oxen and sheep and doves, and the
changers of money sitting: and when he had made a scourge of small cords,
he drove them all out of the temple, and the sheep, and the oxen; and poured
out the changers' money, and overturned the tables; and said unto them that
sold doves, "Take these things from here; make not my Father's house a
house of merchandise." And his disciples remembered that it was written,
"The zeal of your house has eaten me up."

Then answered the Jews and said unto him, "What sign do you show 2
unto us, seeing that you do these things?" Jesus answered and said unto
them, "Destroy this temple, and in three days I will raise it up." Then said the
Jews, "Forty and six years was this temple in building, and will you raise it
up in three days?" But he spoke of the temple of his body. When therefore he
was risen from the dead, his disciples remembered that he had said this unto
them; and they believed the scripture, and the word which Jesus had said.

Now when he was in Jerusalem at the passover, in the feast day, many 3
believed in his name, when they saw the miracles which he did. But Jesus
did not commit himself unto them, because he knew all men, and needed
not that any should testify of man: for he knew what was in man.

Jesus Enlightens Nicodemus
John 3:1-21

There was a man of the Pharisees, named Nicodemus, a ruler of the 4
Jews: the same came to Jesus by night, and said unto him, "Rabbi, we know
that you are a teacher come from God: for no man can do these miracles
that you do, except God be with him." Jesus answered and said unto him,

4   "Truly, truly, I say unto you, Except a man be born again, he cannot see the kingdom of God."

5   Nicodemus said unto him, "How can a man be born when he is old? can he enter the second time into his mother's womb, and be born?" Jesus answered, "Truly, truly, I say unto you, Except a man be born of water and of the Spirit, he cannot enter into the kingdom of God. That which is born of the flesh is flesh; and that which is born of the Spirit is spirit. Marvel not that I said unto you, 'You must be born again.' The wind blows where it wishes, and you hear the sound thereof, but cannot tell from where it comes, and where it goes: so is everyone that is born of the Spirit."

> "YOU MUST BE BORN AGAIN."

6   Nicodemus answered and said unto him, "How can these things be?" Jesus answered and said unto him, "Are you a teacher of Israel, and know not these things? Truly, truly, I say unto you, We speak that we do know, and testify that we have seen; and you do not receive our witness. If I have told you earthly things, and you do not believe, how shall you believe, if I tell you of heavenly things?

7   "And no man has ascended up to heaven, but he that came down from heaven, even the Son of man which is in heaven. As Moses lifted up the serpent in the wilderness, even so must the Son of man be lifted up: that whosoever believes in him should not perish, but have eternal life.

8   "For God so loved the world, that he gave his only begotten Son, that whosoever believes in him should not perish, but have everlasting life. For God did not send his Son into the world to condemn the world; but that the world through him might be saved. He that believes on him is not condemned: but he that believes not is condemned already, because he has not believed in the name of the only begotten Son of God.

> "FOR GOD SO LOVED THE WORLD, THAT HE GAVE HIS ONLY BEGOTTEN SON, THAT WHOSOEVER BELIEVES IN HIM SHOULD NOT PERISH, BUT HAVE EVERLASTING LIFE."

9   "And this is the condemnation, that light is come into the world, and men loved darkness rather than light, because their deeds were evil. For everyone that does evil hates the light, neither comes to the light, lest his deeds should be exposed. But he that does truth comes to the light, that his deeds may be made manifest, that they are wrought in God."

John's Final Witness of Christ
John 3:22-36

10   After these things Jesus came and his disciples into the land of Judea; and there he tarried with them, and baptized. John also was baptizing in Aenon near to Salim, because there was much water there: and they came, and were baptized. For John was not yet cast into prison.

Then there arose a question between some of John's disciples and the 11
Jews about purification. They came unto John and said unto him, "Rabbi,
he that was with you beyond Jordan, to whom you bore witness, behold, the
same baptizes, and all men come to him."

John answered and said, "A man can receive nothing, except it be 12
given him from heaven. You your-
selves bear me witness, that I said, 'I
am not the Christ,' but that 'I am sent
before him.' He that has the bride is
the bridegroom: but the friend of the

> "A MAN CAN RECEIVE NOTH-
> ING, EXCEPT IT BE GIVEN HIM
> FROM HEAVEN."

bridegroom, which stands and hears him, rejoices greatly because of the
bridegroom's voice: this my joy therefore is fulfilled. He must increase, but
I must decrease.

"He that comes from above is above all: he that is of the earth is 13
earthly, and speaks of the earth: he that comes from heaven is above all.
And what he has seen and heard, that he testifies; and no man receives his
testimony. He that has received his testimony has certified that God is true.
For he whom God has sent speaks the words of God: for God does not give
the Spirit by measure unto him.

"The Father loves the Son, and has given all things into his hand. He 14
that believes on the Son has everlasting life: and he that does not believe the
Son shall not see life; but the wrath of God remains on him."

CHAPTER 7

THE FIRST BELIEVERS

John's Imprisonment
Luke 3:19-20; John 4:1-4

1   But Herod the tetrarch (ruler), being exposed by him for Herodias his brother Philip's wife, and for all the evils which Herod had done, added yet this above all, that he shut up John in prison.

2   When therefore the Lord knew how the Pharisees had heard that Jesus made and baptized more disciples than John, (though Jesus himself did not baptize, but his disciples), he left Judea, and departed again into Galilee. And he must of necessity go through Samaria.

The Woman at the Well
John 4:5-26

3   Then he came to a city of Samaria, which is called Sychar, near to the parcel of ground that Jacob gave to his son Joseph. Now Jacob's well was there. Jesus therefore, being wearied with his journey, sat thus on the well: and it was about the sixth hour.

4   There came a woman of Samaria to draw water: Jesus said unto her, "Give me to drink." (For his disciples were gone away unto the city to buy food.) Then said the woman of Samaria unto him, "How is it that you, being a Jew, ask drink of me, which am a woman of Samaria? for the Jews have no dealings with the Samaritans."

5   Jesus answered and said unto her, "If you knew the gift of God, and who it is that says to you, 'Give me to drink;' you would have asked of him, and he would have given you living water." The woman said unto him, "Sir, you have nothing to draw with, and the well is deep: from where then have you that living water? Are you greater than our father Jacob, which gave us the well, and drank thereof himself, and his children, and his cattle?"

6   Jesus answered and said unto her, "Whosoever drinks of this water shall thirst again: but whosoever drinks of the water that I shall give him

shall never thirst; but the water that I shall give him shall be in him a well 6
of water springing up into everlasting life." The woman said unto him,
"Sir, give me this water, that I thirst not, neither come here to draw."

Jesus said unto her, "Go, call your husband, and come here." The 7
woman answered and said, "I have no husband." Jesus said unto her, "You
have well said, 'I have no husband:' for you have had five husbands; and he
whom you now have is not your husband: in that said you truly."

The woman said unto him, "Sir, I perceive that you are a prophet. Our 8
fathers worshiped in this mountain; and you say, that in Jerusalem is the
place where men ought to worship."
Jesus said unto her, "Woman, believe
me, the hour comes, when you shall
neither in this mountain, nor at
Jerusalem, worship the Father. You
worship you know not what: we know

> "GOD IS A SPIRIT: AND THEY
> THAT WORSHIP HIM MUST
> WORSHIP HIM IN SPIRIT AND
> IN TRUTH."

what we worship: for salvation is of the Jews. But the hour comes, and now
is, when the true worshipers shall worship the Father in spirit and in truth:
for the Father seeks such to worship him. God is a Spirit: and they that worship him must worship him in spirit and in truth."

The woman said unto him, "I know that Messiah comes, which is 9
called Christ: when he is come, he will tell us all things." Jesus said unto
her, "I that speak unto you am he."

"One Sows and Another Reaps"
John 4:27-38

And upon this came his disciples, and marveled that he talked with the 10
woman: yet no man said, "What do you seek?" or, "Why do you talk with
her?" The woman then left her waterpot, and went her way into the city, and
said to the men, "Come, see a man, which told me all things that ever I did:
is not this the Christ?" Then they went out of the city, and came unto him.

In the meanwhile his disciples asked him, saying, "Rabbi, eat." But he 11
said unto them, "I have food to eat that you know not of." Therefore said the
disciples one to another, "Has any man brought him anything to eat?" Jesus
said unto them, "My food is to do the will of him that sent me, and to finish his work.

"Do you not say, 'There are yet four months, and then comes harvest'? 12
behold, I say unto you, Lift up your eyes, and look on the fields; for they
are white already to harvest. And he
that reaps receives wages, and gathers
fruit unto life eternal: that both he that
sows and he that reaps may rejoice
together. And herein is that saying
true, 'One sows, and another reaps.' I

> "LIFT UP YOUR EYES, AND
> LOOK ON THE FIELDS; FOR
> THEY ARE WHITE ALREADY TO
> HARVEST."

sent you to reap that whereon you bestowed no labor: other men labored,
and you are entered into their labors."

This Is the Savior of the World
John 4:39-42

13   And many of the Samaritans of that city believed on him for the saying of the woman, which testified, "He told me all that ever I did." So when the Samaritans were come unto him, they pleaded with him that he would tarry with them: and he stayed there two days. And many more believed because of his own word; and said unto the woman, "Now we believe, not because of your saying: for we have heard him ourselves, and know that this is indeed the Christ, the Savior of the world."

PART 3

MIRACLES IN GALILEE

With news of His works spreading throughout the region, Jesus set out on His journey to perform the works His Father had sent Him to do. The doctrines He taught and the healings He brought were far removed from those the people were accustomed to accepting. His purpose was to reveal God and to demonstrate the power of His kingdom. In this He had little regard for man-made rules. To this also, the authorities would take great exception.

> JESUS RETURNED IN THE POWER OF THE SPIRIT
> INTO GALILEE, PREACHING THE GOSPEL OF THE
> KINGDOM OF GOD....AND THERE WENT OUT A
> REPORT OF HIM THROUGH ALL THE REGION
> ROUND ABOUT. (LUKE 4:14)

CHAPTER 8

JESUS BEGINS HIS MINISTRY

In the Power of the Spirit
Mark 1:14-15; Luke 4:14-15; John 4:43-45

1 Now after two days he departed from there and went into Galilee. For Jesus himself testified, that a prophet has no honor in his own country. And Jesus returned in the power of the Spirit into Galilee, preaching the gospel of the kingdom of God, and saying, "The time is fulfilled, and the kingdom of God is at hand: repent, and believe the gospel." Then the Galileans received him, having seen all the things that he did at Jerusalem at the feast: for they also went unto the feast. And there went out a report of him through all the region round about. And he taught in their synagogues, being glorified of all.

Jesus Heals a Nobleman's Dying Son
John 4:46-54

2 So Jesus came again into Cana of Galilee, where he made the water wine. And there was a certain nobleman, whose son was sick at Capernaum. When he heard that Jesus was come out of Judea into Galilee, he went unto him, and pleaded with him that he would come down, and heal his son: for he was at the point of death.

3 Then Jesus said unto him, "Except you see signs and wonders, you will not believe." The nobleman said unto him, "Sir, come down before my child dies." Jesus said unto him, "Go your way; your son lives." And the man believed the word that Jesus had spoken unto him, and he went his way.

4 As he was now going down, his servants met him, and told him, saying, "Your son lives." Then he inquired of them the hour when he began to get better. And they said unto him, "Yesterday at the seventh hour the fever left him." So the father knew that it was at the same hour, in which Jesus said unto him, "Your son lives": and he believed, and his whole household.

This is again the second miracle that Jesus did, when he was come out 5 of Judea into Galilee.

"This Scripture Fulfilled"
Luke 4:16-32

And he came to Nazareth, where he had been brought up: and, as his 6 custom was, he went into the synagogue on the sabbath day, and stood up to read. There was delivered unto him the book of the prophet Isaiah. When he had opened the book, he found the place where it was written, *"The Spirit of the Lord is upon me, because he has anointed me to preach the gospel to the poor; he has sent me to heal the brokenhearted, to proclaim deliverance to the captives, and recovery of sight to the blind, to set at liberty them that are oppressed, to proclaim the acceptable year of the Lord."*

He closed the book and he gave it again to the attendant, and sat 7 down. The eyes of all them that were in the synagogue were fastened on him. And he began to say unto them, "This day is this scripture fulfilled in your ears."

And all bore him witness, and wondered at the gracious words which 8 proceeded out of his mouth. They said, "Is not this Joseph's son?" He said unto them, "You will surely say unto me this proverb, 'Physician, heal yourself: whatsoever we have heard done in Capernaum, do also here in your country.'"

He said, "Truly I say unto you, No prophet is accepted in his own 9 country. But I tell you of a truth, many widows were in Israel in the days of Elijah, when the heaven was shut up three years and six months, when great famine was throughout all the land; but unto none of them was Elijah sent, except unto Zarephath, a city of Sidon, unto a woman that was a widow. And many lepers were in Israel in the time of Elisha the prophet; and none of them was cleansed, but only Naaman the Syrian."

All they in the synagogue, when they heard these things, were filled 10 with wrath, and rose up, and thrust him out of the city, and led him unto the brow of the hill whereon their city was built, that they might cast him down headlong. But he passing through the midst of them went his way, and came down to Capernaum, a city of Galilee, and taught them on the sabbath days. They were astonished at his doctrine: for his word was with authority.

His Home Is at Capernaum
Matthew 4:12-17

Now when Jesus had heard that John was cast into prison, he departed 11 into Galilee; and leaving Nazareth, he came and dwelt in Capernaum, which is upon the seacoast, in the borders of Zebulun and Naphtali: that it might be fulfilled which was spoken by Isaiah

> "REPENT: FOR THE KINGDOM OF HEAVEN IS AT HAND."

the prophet, saying, *"The land of Zebulun, and the land of Naphtali, by the way of the sea, beyond Jordan, Galilee of the Gentiles; the people which sat*

11 *in darkness saw great light; and to them which sat in the region and shadow of death light is sprung up.*" From that time Jesus began to preach, and to say, "Repent: for the kingdom of heaven is at hand."

Jesus Calls Four Fishermen
Matthew 4:18-22; Mark 1:16-20; Luke 5:1-11

12 And Jesus, walking by the sea of Galilee, saw two brethren, Simon called Peter, and Andrew his brother, casting a net into the sea: for they were fishers.

13 It came to pass, that, as the people crowded upon him to hear the word of God, he stood by the sea of Galilee, and saw two ships standing by the sea: but the fishermen were gone out of them, and were washing their nets. He entered into one of the ships, which was Simon's, and asked him that he would thrust out a little from the land. And he sat down, and taught the people out of the ship.

14 Now when he had left speaking, he said unto Simon, "Launch out into the deep, and let down your nets for a catch." And Simon answering said unto him, "Master, we have toiled all the night, and have taken nothing: nevertheless at your word I will let down the net." When they had this done, they caught a great multitude of fishes: and their net broke. They beckoned unto their partners, which were in the other ship, that they should come and help them. And they came, and filled both the ships, so that they began to sink.

15 When Simon Peter saw it, he fell down at Jesus' knees, saying, "Depart from me; for I am a sinful man, O Lord." For he was astonished, and all that were with him, at the catch of the fishes which they had taken: and so was also James, and John, the sons of Zebedee, which were partners with Simon. And Jesus said unto

> "FOLLOW ME, AND I WILL MAKE YOU FISHERS OF MEN."

Simon, "Fear not; from henceforth you shall catch men." Jesus said unto them, "Follow me, and I will make you fishers of men." When they had brought their ships to land, they forsook all, and followed him.

16 And going on from there, he saw two other brethren, James the son of Zebedee, and John his brother, in a ship with Zebedee their father, mending their nets. Straightway he called them: and they immediately left their father Zebedee in the ship with the hired servants, and followed him.

Jesus Casts Out Unclean Spirits
Mark 1:21-28; Luke 4:33-37

17 They went into Capernaum; and straightway on the sabbath day he entered into the synagogue, and taught. And they were astonished at his doctrine: for he taught them as one that had authority, and not as the scribes.

18 There was in their synagogue a man with an unclean spirit; and it cried out with a loud voice, saying, "Let us alone; what have we to do with you, Jesus of Nazareth? are you come to destroy us? I know who you are; the Holy

One of God." And Jesus rebuked it, saying, "Hold your peace, and come out 18 of him." When the unclean spirit had convulsed him, and thrown him in the midst, and cried with a loud voice, it came out of him, and did not hurt him.

They were all amazed, insomuch that they questioned among them- 19 selves, saying, "What thing is this? what new doctrine is this?" and spoke among themselves, saying, "What a word is this! for with authority and power he commands even the unclean spirits, and they do obey him, and they come out." Immediately his fame spread abroad throughout all the region round about Galilee.

Healing Peter's Mother-in-Law
Matthew 8:14-15; Mark 1:29-31; Luke 4:38-39

And immediately, when they were come out of the synagogue, they 20 entered into the house of Simon and Andrew, with James and John. But Simon's wife's mother lay sick of a great fever, and at once they told him about her. He came and stood over her, and rebuked the fever; and took her by the hand, and lifted her up; and immediately the fever left her: and immediately she arose and ministered unto them.

Healing All Who Come to Him
Matthew 8:16-17; Mark 1:32-34; Luke 4:40-41

Now when the sun was setting, all they that had any sick with various 21 diseases brought them unto him; and he laid his hands on every one of them, and healed them. All the city was gathered together at the door. They brought unto him many that were possessed with demons: and he cast out the spirits with his word: that it might be fulfilled which was spoken by Isaiah the prophet, saying, "*He took our infirmities, and bore our sicknesses.*" Demons also came out of many, crying out, and saying, "You are Christ the Son of God." He rebuking them did not allow them to speak: for they knew that he was Christ.

CHAPTER 9

MINISTRY IN NEARBY TOWNS

"For This Purpose Am I Sent"
Mark 1:35-39; Luke 4:42-44

1   And in the morning, rising up a great while before daylight, he went out, and departed into a solitary place, and there prayed. Simon and they that were with him followed after him. When they had found him, they said unto him, "All men seek for you." He said unto them, "Let us go into the next towns, that I may preach there also: for this purpose I came forth."

2   When it was day, the people sought him, and came unto him, and detained him, that he should not depart from them. He said unto them, "I must preach the kingdom of God to other cities also: for this purpose am I sent." He preached in their synagogues throughout all Galilee, and cast out demons.

Jesus Cleanses a Man of Leprosy
Matthew 8:2-4; Mark 1:40-45; Luke 5:12-16

3   And it came to pass, when he was in a certain city, behold a man full of leprosy: who seeing Jesus fell on his face and worshiped him, and pleaded with him, saying, "Lord, if you will, you can make me clean." Jesus, moved with compassion, put forth his hand, and touched him, saying, "I will: be clean." As soon as he had spoken, immediately the leprosy departed from him, and he was cleansed.

4   He strictly charged him, and immediately sent him away; and said unto him, "See you say nothing to any man: but go your way, show yourself to the priest, and offer for your cleansing those things which Moses commanded, for a testimony unto them."

5   But he went out, and began to publish it much, and to spread abroad the matter, insomuch that Jesus could no more openly enter into the city, but was outside in desert places: and they came to him from every direction. But so much the more went there a report abroad of him: and great multitudes

came together to hear, and to be healed by him of their infirmities. And he 5
withdrew himself into the wilderness, and prayed.

A Paralytic Man Walks!
Matthew 9:2-8; Mark 2:1-12; Luke 5:17-26

Again he entered into Capernaum after some days; and it was rumored 6
that he was in the house. Straightway many were gathered together, insomuch that there was no room to receive them, no, not so much as about the door: and he preached the word unto them. It came to pass on a certain day, as he was teaching, that there were Pharisees and teachers of the law sitting by, which were come out of every town of Galilee, and Judea, and Jerusalem: and the power of the Lord was present to heal them.

And, behold, men brought in a bed a man which was taken with a 7
paralysis, which was carried by four: and they sought means to bring him in, and to lay him before him. When they could not find by what way they might bring him in because of the multitude, they went upon the housetop, and they uncovered the roof where he was: and when they had broken it up, they let him down through the tiling with his couch into the midst before Jesus. When Jesus saw their faith, he said unto the sick of the paralysis, "Son, be of good cheer; your sins be forgiven you."

But, behold, there were certain of the scribes sitting there, and rea- 8
soning in their hearts, "Why does this man thus speak blasphemies? who can forgive sins but God only?" And immediately when Jesus perceived in his spirit that they so reasoned within themselves, said unto them, "Why do you reason these things in your hearts? Which is it easier to say to the sick of the paralysis, 'Your sins be forgiven you;' or to say, 'Arise, and take up your bed, and walk?' But that you may know that the Son of man has authority on earth to forgive sins, (he said to the sick of the paralysis), I say unto you, Arise, and take up your bed, and go your way into your house."

> "THE SON OF MAN HAS AUTHORITY ON EARTH TO FORGIVE SINS."

Immediately he rose up before them all, and took up the bed whereon 9
he lay, and departed to his own house, glorifying God. But when the multitudes saw it, they marveled, and glorified God, which had given such authority unto men. They were all amazed, and were filled with fear, saying, "We never saw it like this fashion. We have seen strange things today."

Matthew Obeys Jesus' Call
Matthew 9:9; Mark 2:13-14; Luke 5:27-28

And he went forth again by the seaside; and all the multitude came 10
unto him, and he taught them. After these things as Jesus passed forth from there, he saw a tax collector, a man named Matthew, Levi the son of Alphaeus, sitting at the receipt of custom: and said unto him, "Follow me." And he left all, rose up, and followed him.

Eating With Sinners
Matthew 9:10-13; Mark 2:15-17; Luke 5:29-32

11   Levi made him a great feast in his own house: and there was a great company of tax collectors and of others. It came to pass, as Jesus sat at the table in the house, many tax collectors and sinners came and sat together with Jesus and his disciples: for there were many, and they followed him. But when their scribes and Pharisees saw him eat with tax collectors and sinners, they said unto his disciples, "How is it that he eats and drinks with tax collectors and sinners?"

12   When Jesus heard that, he said unto them, "They that are whole have no need of the physician, but they that are sick: I came not to call the righteous, but sinners to repentance. But go and learn what that means, '*I will have mercy, and not sacrifice.*'"

First Parable Concerns Fasting
Matthew 9:14-17; Mark 2:18-22; Luke 5:33-39

13   Then came to him the disciples of John, saying, "Why do we and the Pharisees fast often, but your disciples do not fast?" Likewise the disciples of the Pharisees came and said unto him, "Why do the disciples of John and of the Pharisees fast, and make prayers, but your disciples eat and drink?" Jesus said unto them, "Can the friends of the bridegroom fast, while the bridegroom is with them? as long as they have the bridegroom with them, they cannot fast. But the days will come, when the bridegroom shall be taken away from them, and then shall they fast in those days."

14   And he spoke also a parable unto them; "No man sews a piece of a new cloth on an old garment: else the new piece that filled it up takes away from the old; if otherwise, then both the new makes a tear, and the piece that was taken out of the new does not match with the old, and the tear is made worse.

15   "And no man puts new wine into old wineskins: else the new wine will burst the wineskins, and the wine is spilled, and the wineskins shall perish. But new wine must be put into new wineskins; and both are preserved. No man also having drunk old wine straightway desires new: for he says, 'The old is better.'"

CHAPTER 10

⸪ SECOND MINISTRY AT JERUSALEM ⸪

Sabbath Healing of a Man at the Pool
John 5:1-13

After this there was a feast of the Jews; and Jesus went up to Jerusalem. 1
Now there is at Jerusalem by the sheep gate a pool, which is called in the
Hebrew tongue Bethesda, having five porches. In these lay a great multitude
of paralyzed folks, of blind, lame, withered, waiting for the moving of the
water. For an angel went down at a certain season into the pool, and stirred
the water: whosoever then first after the stirring of the water stepped in was
made whole of whatsoever disease he had.

And a certain man was there, which had an infirmity thirty and eight 2
years. When Jesus saw him lying there, and knew that he had been now a
long time in that condition, he said unto him, "Will you be made whole?"
The paralyzed man answered him, "Sir, I have no man, when the water is
stirred, to put me into the pool: but while I am coming, another steps down
before me." Jesus said unto him, "Rise, take up your bed, and walk." And
immediately the man was made whole, and took up his bed, and walked:
and on the same day was the sabbath.

The Jews therefore said unto him that was cured, "It is the sabbath 3
day: it is not lawful for you to carry your bed." He answered them, "He that
made me whole, the same said unto me, 'Take up your bed, and walk.' "
Then they asked him, "What man is that which said unto you, 'Take up your
bed, and walk?'" And he that was healed knew not who it was: for Jesus had
taken himself away, a multitude being in that place.

Sabbath Healing and the Law
John 5:14-18

Afterward Jesus found him in the temple, and said unto him, "Behold, 4
you are made whole: sin no more, lest a worse thing come unto you." The
man departed, and told the Jews that it was Jesus, which had made him

4   whole. And therefore did the Jews persecute Jesus, and sought to slay him, because he had done these things on the sabbath day.

5   But Jesus answered them, "My Father works until now, and I work." Therefore the Jews sought the more to kill him, because he not only had broken the sabbath, but said also that God was his Father, making himself equal with God.

"The Resurrection of Life"
John 5:19-29

6   Then Jesus answered and said unto them, "Truly, truly, I say unto you, The Son can do nothing of himself, but what he sees the Father do: for whatsoever things he does, these also does the Son likewise. For the Father loves the Son, and shows him all things that he himself does: and he will show him greater works than these, that you may marvel. For as the Father raises up the dead, and quickens them; even so the Son quickens whom he will.

7   "For the Father judges no man, but has committed all judgment unto the Son: that all men should honor the Son, even as they honor the Father. He that does not honor the Son does not honor the Father which has sent him. Truly, truly, I say unto you, He that hears my word, and believes on him that sent me, has everlasting life, and shall not come into condemnation; but is passed from death unto life.

> "HE THAT HEARS MY WORD, AND BELIEVES ON HIM THAT SENT ME, HAS EVERLASTING LIFE."

8   "Truly, truly, I say unto you, The hour is coming, and now is, when the dead shall hear the voice of the Son of God: and they that hear shall live. For as the Father has life in himself; so has he given to the Son to have life in himself; and has given him authority to execute judgment also, because he is the Son of man.

9   "Marvel not at this: for the hour is coming, in which all that are in the graves shall hear his voice, and shall come forth; they that have done good, unto the resurrection of life; and they that have done evil, unto the resurrection of condemnation."

"In My Father's Name"
John 5:30-47

10   "I can of my own self do nothing: as I hear, I judge: and my judgment is just; because I seek not my own will, but the will of the Father which has sent me. If I bear witness of myself, my witness is not true. There is another that bears witness of me; and I know that the witness which he witnesses of me is true.

> "I SEEK NOT MY OWN WILL, BUT THE WILL OF THE FATHER WHICH HAS SENT ME."

11   "You sent unto John, and he bore witness unto the truth. But I do not receive testimony from man: but these things I say, that you might be saved.

He was a burning and a shining light: and you were willing for a season to 11
rejoice in his light. But I have greater witness than that of John: for the
works which the Father has given me to finish, the same works that I do,
bear witness of me, that the Father has sent me.

"And the Father himself, which has sent me, has borne witness of 12
me. You have neither heard his voice
at any time, nor seen his form. You

> "SEARCH THE SCRIPTURES; FOR
> IN THEM YOU THINK YOU HAVE
> ETERNAL LIFE: AND THEY ARE
> THEY WHICH TESTIFY OF ME."

have not his word dwelling in you:
for whom he has sent, him you do not
believe. Search the scriptures; for in
them you think you have eternal life:
and they are they which testify of me. And you will not come to me, that
you might have life.

"I do not receive honor from men. But I know you, that you have not 13
the love of God in you. I am come in my Father's name, and you do not
receive me: if another shall come in his own name, him you will receive.
How can you believe, which receive honor one of another, and seek not the
honor that comes from God only? Do not think that I will accuse you to the
Father: there is one that accuses you, even Moses, in whom you trust. For
had you believed Moses, you would have believed me: for he wrote of me.
But if you do not believe his writings, how shall you believe my words?"

CHAPTER 11

Ministry at Capernaum

Sabbath Harvest and the Law
Matthew 12:1-8; Mark 2:23-28; Luke 6:1-5

1   And it came to pass on the second sabbath after the first, that Jesus went through the grainfields; and his disciples were hungry, and plucked the heads of grain, and did eat, rubbing them in their hands. But when the Pharisees saw it, they said unto him, "Behold, why do your disciples do that which is not lawful to do on the sabbath days?"

2   Jesus answering them said, "Have you never read what David did, when he had need, and was hungry, he, and they that were with him? How he went into the house of God in the days of Abiathar the high priest, and did eat the showbread, which is not lawful to eat but for the priests alone, and gave also to them which were with him? Or have you not read in the law, how that on the sabbath days the priests in the temple profane the sabbath, and are blameless?

3   "But I say unto you, That in this place is one greater than the temple. But if you had known what this means, 'I will have mercy, and not sacrifice,' you would not have condemned the guiltless." And he said unto them, "The sabbath was made for man, and not man for the sabbath: therefore the Son of man is Lord also of the sabbath."

Sabbath Healing of a Withered Hand
Matthew 12:9-14; Mark 3:1-6; Luke 6:6-11

4   And it came to pass also on another sabbath, that he entered into the synagogue and taught: and, behold, there was a man whose right hand was withered. The scribes and Pharisees watched him, whether he would heal on the sabbath day; that they might find an accusation against him. And they asked him, saying, "Is it lawful to heal on the sabbath days?" that they might accuse him.

He said unto them, "What man shall there be among you, that shall 5 have one sheep, and if it falls into a pit on the sabbath day, will he not lay hold on it, and lift it out? How much then is a man better than a sheep? Therefore it is lawful to do well on the sabbath days."

But he knew their thoughts, and said to the man which had the with- 6 ered hand, "Rise up, and stand forth in the midst." And he arose and stood forth. Then said Jesus unto them, "I will ask you one thing; Is it lawful on the sabbath days to do good, or to do evil? to save life, or to destroy it?" But they held their peace. When he had looked round about on them with anger, being grieved for the hardness of their hearts, he said unto the man, "Stretch forth your hand." He did so: and his hand was restored whole as the other.

Then they were filled with fury; and discussed one with another what 7 they might do to Jesus. And straightway the Pharisees went forth, plotted with the Herodians against him, how they might destroy him.

Multitudes Seek Jesus' Healing
Matthew 4:23-25; 12:15-21; Mark 3:7-12

But when Jesus knew it, he withdrew himself with his disciples to the 8 sea: and a great multitude from Galilee followed him, and from Judea, and from Jerusalem, and from Idumaea, and from beyond Jordan; and they about Tyre and Sidon, a great multitude, when they had heard what great things he did, came unto him. He healed them all; and charged them that they should not make him known: that it might be fulfilled which was spoken by Isaiah the prophet, saying, *"Behold my servant, whom I have chosen; my beloved, in whom my soul is well pleased: I will put my spirit upon him, and he shall show judgment to the Gentiles. He shall not quarrel, nor cry; neither shall any man hear his voice in the streets. A bruised reed shall he not break, and smoking wick shall he not quench, till he sends forth judgment unto victory. And in his name shall the Gentiles trust."*

He spoke to his disciples, that a small ship should wait on him 9 because of the multitude, lest they should trample him. For he had healed many; insomuch that they crowded upon him to touch him, as many as had afflictions.

Unclean spirits, when they saw him, fell down before him, and cried, 10 saying, "You are the Son of God." And he strictly charged them that they should not make him known.

Jesus went about all Galilee, teaching in their synagogues, and preach- 11 ing the gospel of the kingdom, and healing all manner of sickness and all manner of disease among the people. And his fame went throughout all Syria: and they brought unto him all sick people that were taken with various diseases and torments, and those which were possessed with demons, and those which were lunatic, and those that had the paralysis; and he healed them. And there followed him great multitudes of people from

11 Galilee, and from Decapolis, and from Jerusalem, and from Judea, and from beyond Jordan.

Twelve Ordained as the Apostles
Mark 3:13-19; Luke 6:12-16

12   And it came to pass in those days, that he went out into a mountain to pray, and continued all night in prayer to God. And when it was day, he called unto him his disciples whom he would: and they came unto him. And of them he ordained twelve, that they should be with him, and that he might send them forth to preach, and to have authority to heal sicknesses, and to cast out demons: whom also he named apostles; Simon, (whom he also named Peter), and Andrew his brother; James the son of Zebedee, and John the brother of James; and he surnamed them Boanerges, which is, "The sons of thunder": Philip and Bartholomew, Matthew and Thomas, James the son of Alphaeus, and Simon the Canaanite called Zelotes, and Judas the brother of James (whose surname was Thaddaeus), and Judas Iscariot, which also was the traitor, which also betrayed him.

To Hear and Be Healed
Luke 6:17-19

13   He came down with them, and stood in the plain, and the company of his disciples, and a great multitude of people out of all Judea and Jerusalem, and from the sea coast of Tyre and Sidon, which came to hear him, and to be healed of their diseases; and they that were tormented with unclean spirits: and they were healed. The whole multitude sought to touch him: for there went power out of him, and healed them all.

PART 4

THE SERMON ON THE MOUNT

Seeking to be understood, Jesus withdrew from the multitudes and, gathering His disciples together, delivered to them one of the purest guides for Christian living found in the Scriptures. The life-giving truths in these Beatitudes were intended not merely as instructions for the disciples, but as enduring guideposts to blessings for all those who seek to build their lives on the firm foundation of Truth.

> "IF YOU FORGIVE MEN THEIR TRESPASSES, YOUR HEAVENLY FATHER WILL ALSO FORGIVE YOU."
>
> (MATTHEW 6:14)

CHAPTER 12

BLESSINGS OF THE NEW LIFE

Blessings
Matthew 5:1-12; Luke 6:22-23

1   And seeing the multitudes, he went up into a mountain: when he was seated, his disciples came unto him: he opened his mouth, and taught them, saying, "Blessed are the poor in spirit: for theirs is the kingdom of heaven. Blessed are they that mourn: for they shall be comforted. Blessed are the meek: for they shall inherit the earth. Blessed are they which do hunger and thirst after righteousness: for they shall be filled. Blessed are the merciful: for they shall obtain mercy. Blessed are the pure in heart: for they shall see God. Blessed are the peacemakers: for they shall be called the children of God. Blessed are they which are persecuted for righteousness' sake: for theirs is the kingdom of heaven.

2   "Blessed are you, when men shall hate you, and when they shall separate you from their company, and shall reproach you, and persecute you, and shall say all manner of evil against you falsely, for the Son of man's sake.

3   "Rejoice in that day, and leap for joy, and be exceedingly glad: for, behold, great is your reward in heaven: for in the like manner they persecuted the prophets which were before you."

Woes
Luke 6:20-21; 24-26

4   And he lifted up his eyes on his disciples, and said, "Blessed be you poor: for yours is the kingdom of God. Blessed are you that hunger now: for you shall be filled. Blessed are you that weep now: for you shall laugh. But woe unto you that are rich! for you have received your consolation. Woe unto you that are full! for you shall hunger. Woe unto you that laugh now! for you shall mourn and weep. Woe unto you, when all men shall speak well of you! for so did their fathers to the false prophets."

The Salt of the Earth
Matthew 5:13

"You are the salt of the earth: but if the salt has lost its savor, with what ⁵ shall it be salted? it is thereafter good for nothing, but to be cast out, and to be trampled underfoot of men."

The Light of the World
Matthew 5:14-16

"You are the light of the world. A city that is set on a hill cannot be ⁶ hidden. Neither do men light a lamp, and put it under a tub, but on a lamp-stand; and it gives light unto all that are in the house. Let your light so shine before men, that they may see your good works, and glorify your Father which is in heaven."

The Law Fulfilled
Matthew 5:17-20

"Think not that I am come to destroy the law, or the prophets: I am not ⁷ come to destroy, but to fulfill. For truly I say unto you, Till heaven and earth pass, one letter or one little stroke shall in no way pass from the law, till all be fulfilled.

"Whosoever therefore shall break one of these least command- ⁸ ments, and shall teach men so, he shall be called the least in the kingdom of heaven: but whosoever shall do and teach them, the same shall be called great in the kingdom of heaven. For I say unto you, That except your righteousness shall exceed the righteousness of the scribes and Pharisees, you shall in no way enter into the kingdom of heaven."

Anger
Matthew 5:21-22

"You have heard that it was said by them of old time, '*You shall not* ⁹ *kill; and whosoever shall kill shall be in danger of the judgment:*' but I say unto you, That whosoever is angry with his brother without a cause shall be in danger of the judgment: and whosoever shall say to his brother, 'Raca' (Fool), shall be in danger of the council: but whosoever shall say, 'You fool,' shall be in danger of hell fire."

Reconciliation
Matthew 5:23-26

"Therefore if you bring your gift to the altar, and there remember ¹⁰ that your brother has anything against you; leave there your gift before the altar, and go your way; first be reconciled to your brother, and then come and offer your gift.

> "FIRST BE RECONCILED TO YOUR BROTHER, AND THEN COME AND OFFER YOUR GIFT."

"Agree with your adversary quickly, while you are on the way with ¹¹ him; lest at any time the adversary deliver you to the judge, and the judge

11 deliver you to the officer, and you be cast into prison. Truly I say unto you, You shall by no means come out from there, till you have paid the uttermost copper coin."

Adultery
Matthew 5:27-30

12 "You have heard that it was said by them of old time, '*You shall not commit adultery*:' but I say unto you, That whosoever looks on a woman to lust after her has committed adultery with her already in his heart.

13 "If your right eye causes you to sin, pluck it out, and cast it from you: for it is profitable for you that one of your members should perish, and not that your whole body should be cast into hell.

14 "If your right hand causes you to sin, cut it off, and cast it from you: for it is profitable for you that one of your members should perish, and not that your whole body should be cast into hell."

Divorce
Matthew 5:31-32

15 "It has been said, '*Whosoever shall put away his wife, let him give her a writing of divorcement*:' but I say unto you, That whosoever shall put away his wife, except for the cause of fornication, causes her to commit adultery: and whosoever shall marry her that is divorced commits adultery."

Oaths
Matthew 5:33-37

16 "Again, you have heard that it has been said by them of old time, '*You shall not falsely swear yourself, but shall perform unto the Lord your oaths*:' but I say unto you, Swear not at all; neither by heaven; for it is God's throne: nor by the earth; for it is his footstool: neither by Jerusalem; for it is the city of the great King. Neither shall you swear by your head, because you cannot make one hair white or black. But let your communication be, Yes, yes; No, no: for whatsoever is more than these comes of evil."

Retaliation
Matthew 5:38-42; Luke 6:29-30

17 "You have heard that it has been said, '*An eye for an eye, and a tooth for a tooth*:' but I say unto you, That you resist not evil: but whosoever shall strike you on your right cheek, turn to him the other also. Unto him that takes away your cloak do not forbid to take your tunic also.

18 "And if any man will sue you at the law, and take away your tunic, let him have your cloak also. And whosoever shall compel you to go a mile, go with him two.

19 "Give to every man that asks you, and from him that would borrow of you do not turn you away; and of him that takes away your goods do not ask for them back."

Enemies
Matthew 5:43-48; Luke 6:27-28; 32-36

"You have heard that it has been said, '*You shall love your neighbor,* 20 and hate your enemy.' But I say unto you which hear, Love your enemies, bless them that curse you, do good to them that hate you, and pray for them which despitefully use you, and persecute you; that you may be the children of your Father which is in heaven: for he makes his sun to rise on the evil and on the good, and sends rain on the just and on the unjust.

> "LOVE YOUR ENEMIES, BLESS THEM THAT CURSE YOU, DO GOOD TO THEM THAT HATE YOU, AND PRAY FOR THEM WHICH DESPITEFULLY USE YOU."

"For if you love them which love you, what reward do you have? do 21 not even the tax collectors the same? for sinners also love those that love them. And if you greet your brethren only, what do you more than others? do not even the tax collectors so? And if you do good to them which do good to you, what thanks do you have? for sinners also do even the same. And if you lend to them of whom you hope to receive, what thanks do you have? for sinners also lend to sinners, to receive as much in return.

"But love your enemies, and do good, and lend, hoping for nothing in 22 return; and your reward shall be great, and you shall be the children of the Highest: for he is kind unto the unthankful and to the evil. Be therefore merciful, as your Father also is merciful.

"Be therefore perfect, even as your Father which is in heaven is perfect." 23

CHAPTER 13

BLESSINGS OF GOD

Charity
Matthew 6:1-4

1   "Take heed that you do not do your righteousness before men, to be seen of them: otherwise you have no reward of your Father which is in heaven.

2   "Therefore when you do your charitable deeds, do not sound a trumpet before you, as the hypocrites do in the synagogues and in the streets, that they may have glory of men. Truly I say unto you, They have their reward.

3   "But when you do charitable deeds, let not your left hand know what your right hand does: that your charitable deeds may be in secret: and your Father which sees in secret himself shall reward you openly."

Prayer
Matthew 6:5-15

4   "And when you pray, you shall not be as the hypocrites are: for they love to pray standing in the synagogues and in the corners of the streets, that they may be seen of men. Truly I say unto you, They have their reward.

5   "But you, when you pray, enter into your inner room, and when you have shut your door, pray to your Father which is in secret; and your Father which sees in secret shall reward you openly. But when you pray, use not vain repetitions, as the heathen do: for they think that they shall be heard for their many words. Be not therefore like them: for your Father knows what things you have need of, before you ask him.

6   "After this manner therefore pray: Our Father which are in heaven, Hallowed be your name. Your kingdom come. Your will be done on earth, as it is in heaven. Give us this day our daily bread. And forgive us our debts, as we forgive our debtors. And lead us not into temptation, but deliver us from evil: For yours is the kingdom, and the power, and the glory, for ever. Amen. For if you forgive men their trespasses, your heavenly Father will

also forgive you: but if you forgive not men their trespasses, neither will 6
your Father forgive your trespasses."

Fasting
Matthew 6:16-18

"Moreover when you fast, be not, as the hypocrites, of a sad counte- 7
nance: for they disfigure their faces, that they may appear unto men to fast.
Truly I say unto you, They have their reward.

"But you, when you fast, anoint your head, and wash your face; that 8
you do not appear unto men to fast, but unto your Father which is in secret:
and your Father, which sees in secret, shall reward you openly."

Treasures
Matthew 6:19-21

"Do not lay up for yourselves treasures upon earth, where moth and 9
rust does corrupt, and where thieves
break in and steal: but lay up for | "LAY UP FOR YOURSELVES
yourselves treasures in heaven, | TREASURES IN HEAVEN."
where neither moth nor rust does
corrupt, and where thieves do not break in nor steal: for where your
treasure is, there will your heart be also."

Light of the Body
Matthew 6:22-23

"The light of the body is the eye: if therefore your eye be single, your 10
whole body shall be full of light. But if your eye be evil, your whole body
shall be full of darkness. If therefore the light that is in you be darkness,
how great is that darkness!"

Consider This
Matthew 6:24-34

"No man can serve two masters: for either he will hate the one, and 11
love the other; or else he will hold to the one, and despise the other. You cannot serve God and money.

"Therefore I say unto you, Be not anxious for your life, what you shall 12
eat, or what you shall drink; nor for your body, what you shall put on. Is not
the life more than food, and the body than clothing? Behold the birds of the
air: for they sow not, neither do they reap, nor gather into barns; yet your
heavenly Father feeds them. Are you not much better than they? Which of
you by worrying can add one cubit unto his stature?

"And why do you worry for clothing? Consider the lilies of the field, 13
how they grow; they toil not, neither
do they spin: and yet I say unto you, | "CONSIDER THE LILIES OF THE
That even Solomon in all his glory | FIELD, HOW THEY GROW."
was not arrayed like one of these. For,
if God so clothe the grass of the field, which today is, and tomorrow is cast
into the oven, shall he not much more clothe you, O you of little faith?

14   "Therefore be not anxious, saying, 'What shall we eat?' or, 'What shall we drink?' or, 'With what shall we be clothed?' (For after all these things do the Gentiles seek): for your heavenly Father knows that you have need of all these things.

15

> "SEEK FIRST THE KINGDOM OF GOD."

"But seek first the kingdom of God, and his righteousness; and all these things shall be added unto you. Therefore be not anxious for tomorrow: for tomorrow shall take care for the things of itself. Sufficient unto the day is the evil thereof."

CHAPTER 14

BLESSINGS OF WISDOM

Judgment
Matthew 7:1-6; Luke 6:37-42

"Judge not, and you shall not be judged: condemn not, and you shall 1
not be condemned: forgive, and you shall be forgiven. Give, and it shall be
given unto you; good measure, pressed down, and shaken together, and running over, shall men give into your bosom. For with what judgment you
judge, you shall be judged: and with what measure you measure, it shall be
measured to you again."

And he spoke a parable unto them, "Can the blind lead the blind? shall 2
they not both fall into the ditch? The disciple is not above his teacher: but
everyone that is perfect shall be as his teacher.

"And why do you behold the speck that is in your brother's eye, but do 3
not consider the log that is in your own eye? Or how can you say to your
brother, 'Brother, let me pull out the speck that is in your eye,' when you
yourself do not behold the log that is in your own eye? You hypocrite, cast
out first the log out of your own eye, and then shall you see clearly to pull
out the speck that is in your brother's eye.

"Give not that which is holy unto the dogs, neither cast your pearls 4
before swine, lest they trample them under their feet, and turn again and
tear you."

The Golden Rule
Matthew 7:7-12; Luke 6:31

"Ask, and it shall be given you; seek, and you shall find; knock, and it 5
shall be opened unto you: for everyone that asks receives; and he that seeks
finds; and to him that knocks it shall be opened.

"Or what man is there of you, whom if his son asks for bread, will he 6
give him a stone? Or if he asks for a fish, will he give him a serpent? If you

6   then, being evil, know how to give good gifts unto your children, how much more shall your Father which is in heaven give good things to them that ask him? Therefore all things whatsoever you would that men should do to you, do you even so to them: for this is the law and the prophets."

Narrow Gate
Matthew 7:13-14

7   "Enter in at the strait gate: for wide is the gate, and broad is the way, that leads to destruction, and many there be which go in thereat: because strait is the gate, and narrow is the way, which leads unto life, and few there be that find it."

False Prophets
Matthew 7:15-20; Luke 6:43-45

8   "Beware of false prophets, which come to you in sheep's clothing, but inwardly they are ravenous wolves. You shall know them by their fruits. Do men gather grapes of bramble bushes, or figs of thornbushes?

9   "Even so every good tree brings forth good fruit; but a corrupt tree brings forth evil fruit. A good tree cannot bring forth evil fruit, neither can a corrupt tree bring forth good fruit. Every tree that does not bring forth good fruit is cut down, and cast into the fire.

10   "For every tree is known by its own fruit. For of thornbushes men do not gather figs, nor of a bramble bush do they gather grapes. A good man out of the good treasure of his heart brings forth that which is good; and an evil man out of the evil treasure of his heart brings forth that which is evil: for of the abundance of the heart his mouth speaks.

> "A GOOD MAN OUT OF THE GOOD TREASURE OF HIS HEART BRINGS FORTH THAT WHICH IS GOOD."

11   "For by their fruits you shall know them."

Kingdom of Heaven
Matthew 7:21-23; Luke 6:46

12   "Not everyone that says unto me, 'Lord, Lord,' shall enter into the kingdom of heaven; but he that does the will of my Father which is in heaven. Many will say to me in that day, 'Lord, Lord, have we not prophesied in your name? and in your name have cast out demons? and in your name done many wonderful works?'

13   "And then will I profess unto them, 'I never knew you: depart from me, you that work iniquity.' And why do you call me, 'Lord, Lord,' and do not the things which I say?"

Wise and Foolish Builders
Matthew 7:24-27; Luke 6:47-49

14   "Therefore whosoever comes to me, and hears these sayings of mine, and does them, I will liken him unto a wise man, which dug deep, and laid

the foundation on a rock: which built his house upon a rock: and the rain 14 descended, and the floods came, and the stream beat violently upon that house, and could not shake it; and the winds blew, and beat upon that house, and it did not fall: for it was founded upon a rock.

"But everyone that hears these sayings of mine, and does not do them, 15 shall be likened unto a foolish man, that without a foundation built his house upon the sand: and the rain descended, and the floods came; against which the stream did beat violently; and the winds blew, and beat upon that house; and immediately it fell: and great was the fall of it; and the ruin of that house was great."

The People's Response
Matthew 7:28-29

And it came to pass, when Jesus had ended these sayings, the people 16 were astonished at his doctrine: for he taught them as one having authority, and not as the scribes.

PART 5

Purpose and Parables

As the fame of Jesus grew and word of His marvelous works became widely known among the people, great multitudes followed Him, seeking healing. Through the many miracles and ministries He performed, the spiritual power of this holy man of God revealed to others who God is and what a right understanding of God can do for man. The grace and wisdom He demonstrated in answering admirers and adversaries alike were lesson to all.

HE WENT THROUGHOUT EVERY CITY AND VIL-
LAGE, PREACHING: AND THE TWELVE WERE WITH
HIM, AND CERTAIN WOMEN, MARY CALLED
MAGDALENE...AND JOANNA...AND SUSANNA,
AND MANY OTHERS, WHICH MINISTERED UNTO
HIM OF THEIR SUBSTANCE.   (LUKE 8:1-3)

CHAPTER 15

JESUS AND JOHN THE BAPTIST

Jesus Heals the Centurion's Servant
Matthew 8:1, 5-13; Luke 7:1-10

Now when he had ended all his sayings in the audience of the people, 1
when he was come down from the mountain, great multitudes followed him
into Capernaum.

And when Jesus was entered into Capernaum, a certain centurion's 2
servant, who was dear unto him, was sick, and about to die. When he heard
of Jesus, he sent unto him the elders of the Jews, pleading with him that he
would come and heal his servant, and saying, "Lord, my servant lies at
home sick of the paralysis, grievously tormented." When they came to
Jesus, they pleaded with him earnestly, saying, "That he was worthy for
whom he should do this: for he loves our nation, and he has built us a synagogue." And Jesus said, "I will come and heal him."

Then Jesus went with them. When he was now not far from the house, 3
the centurion sent friends to him, saying unto him, "Lord, do not trouble
yourself: for I am not worthy that you should enter under my roof: therefore
neither thought I myself worthy to come unto you: but say in a word, and
my servant shall be healed. For I also am a man set under authority, having
under me soldiers, and I say unto one, 'Go,' and he goes; and to another,
'Come,' and he comes; and to my servant, 'Do this,' and he does it."

When Jesus heard these things, he marveled at him, and turned him- 4
self about, and said to them that followed him, "Truly I say unto you, I have
not found so great a faith, no, not in Israel. And I say unto you, That many
shall come from the east and west, and shall sit down with Abraham, and
Isaac, and Jacob, in the kingdom of heaven. But the children of the kingdom shall be cast out into outer darkness: there shall be weeping and gnashing of teeth."

5   Jesus said unto the centurion, "Go your way; and as you have believed, so be it done unto you." His servant was healed in the selfsame hour. They that were sent, returning to the house, found the servant whole that had been sick.

Restoring Life to a Widow's Son
Luke 7:11-17

6   And it came to pass the day after, that he went into a city called Nain; and many of his disciples went with him, and many people. Now when he came near to the gate of the city, behold, there was a dead man carried out, the only son of his mother, and she was a widow: and many people of the city were with her. When the Lord saw her, he had compassion on her, and said unto her, "Weep not."

7   He came and touched the coffin: and they that bore him stood still. And he said, "Young man, I say unto you, Arise." He that was dead sat up, and began to speak. He delivered him to his mother. There came a fear on all: and they glorified God, saying, "That a great prophet is risen up among us;" and, "That God has visited his people." This rumor of him went forth throughout all Judea, and throughout all the region round about.

John the Baptist's Message to Jesus
Matthew 11:2-6; Luke 7:18-23

8   And the disciples of John showed him of all these things. Now when John had heard in the prison the works of Christ, John calling unto him two of his disciples sent them to Jesus, saying, "Are you he that should come? or do we look for another?"

9   When the men were come unto him, they said, "John the Baptist has sent us unto you, saying, 'Are you he that should come? or do we look for another?' " And in that same hour he cured many of their diseases and afflictions, and of evil spirits; and unto many that were blind he gave sight.

10   Then Jesus answering said unto them, "Go your way, and tell John again what things you have seen and heard; how the blind receive their sight, and the lame walk, the lepers are cleansed, and the deaf hear, the dead are raised up, and the poor have the gospel preached to them. And blessed is he, whosoever shall not fall away because of me."

John Is Much More Than a Prophet
Matthew 11:7-19; Luke 7:24-35

11   And as they departed, Jesus began to say unto the multitudes concerning John, "What went you out into the wilderness to see? A reed shaken with the wind? But what went you out to see? A man clothed in soft clothing? Behold, they which are gorgeously appareled, and live in luxury, are in kings' courts. But what went you out to see? A prophet? yes, I say unto you, and much more than a prophet. For this is he, of whom it is written, *'Behold, I send my messenger before your face, which shall prepare your way before you.'*

12   "Truly I say unto you, Among those that are born of women there is not a greater prophet than John the Baptist: but he that is least in the kingdom

of God is greater than he. And from the days of John the Baptist until now 12 the kingdom of heaven suffers violence, and the violent take it by force. For all the prophets and the law prophesied until John. If you will receive it, this is Elijah, which was to come. He that has ears to hear, let him hear."

And all the people that heard him, and the tax collectors, justified God, 13 being baptized with the baptism of John. But the Pharisees and lawyers rejected the purpose of God for themselves, being not baptized of him.

The Lord said, "To what then shall I liken the men of this generation? 14 and to what are they like? They are like children sitting in the marketplace, and calling one to another, and saying, 'We have piped unto you, and you have not danced; we have mourned unto you, and you have not lamented.' For John the Baptist came neither eating bread nor drinking wine; and you say, 'He has a demon.' The Son of man is come eating and drinking; and you say, 'Behold a gluttonous man, and a winebibber, a friend of tax collectors and sinners!' But wisdom is justified of all her children."

A Sinful Woman Is Forgiven
Luke 7:36-50

And one of the Pharisees desired him that he would eat with him. And 15 he went into the Pharisee's house, and sat down to eat. And, behold, a woman in the city, which was a sinner, when she knew that Jesus sat at the table in the Pharisee's house, brought an alabaster jar of ointment, and stood at his feet behind him weeping, and began to wash his feet with tears, and did wipe them with the hairs of her head, and kissed his feet, and anointed them with the ointment.

Now when the Pharisee which had invited him saw it, he spoke within 16 himself, saying, "This man, if he were a prophet, would have known who and what manner of woman this is that touches him: for she is a sinner." Jesus answering said unto him, "Simon, I have something to say unto you." And he said, "Teacher, say on."

"There was a certain creditor which had two debtors: the one owed 17 five hundred silver coins, and the other fifty. And when they had nothing to pay, he freely forgave them both. Tell me therefore, which of them will love him more?" Simon answered and said, "I suppose that he, to whom he forgave more." And he said unto him, "You have rightly judged."

And he turned to the woman, and said unto Simon, "Do you see this 18 woman? I entered into your house, you gave me no water for my feet: but she has washed my feet with tears, and wiped them with the hairs of her head. You gave me no kiss: but this woman since the time I came in has not ceased to kiss my feet. My head with oil you did not anoint: but this woman has anointed my feet with ointment. Therefore I say unto you, Her sins, which are many, are forgiven; for she loved much: but to whom little is forgiven, the same loves little."

He said unto her, "Your sins are forgiven." And they that sat at the table 19 with him began to say within themselves, "Who is this that forgives sins also?" He said to the woman, "Your faith has saved you; go in peace."

CHAPTER 16

Kingdom of God vs. Kingdom of Darkness

Women Minister Unto Jesus
Luke 8:1-3

1   And it came to pass afterward, that he went throughout every city and village, preaching and showing the glad tidings of the kingdom of God: and the twelve were with him, and certain women, which had been healed of evil spirits and infirmities, Mary called Magdalene, out of whom went seven demons, and Joanna the wife of Chuza Herod's steward, and Susanna, and many others, which ministered unto him of their substance.

Jesus Is Not Beelzebub
Matthew 12:22-30; Mark 3:20-27

2   They went into a house and the multitude came together again, so that they could not so much as eat bread. When his friends heard of it, they went out to lay hold on him: for they said, "He is gone mad."

3   Then was brought unto him one possessed with a demon, blind, and mute: and he healed him, insomuch that the blind and mute both spoke and saw. And all the people were amazed, and said, "Is not this the son of David?" But when the Pharisees heard it, said, "This fellow does not cast out demons, but by Beelzebub the prince of the demons." And the scribes which came down from Jerusalem said, "He has Beelzebub, and by the prince of the demons casts he out demons."

4   Jesus knew their thoughts, and he called them unto him, and said unto them in parables, "How can Satan cast out Satan? Every kingdom divided against itself is brought to desolation. And every city divided against itself shall not stand. And if a house be divided against itself, that house cannot stand. And if Satan rises up against himself, and be divided, he cannot stand, but has an end.

5   "And if I by Beelzebub cast out demons, by whom do your children cast them out? therefore they shall be your judges. But if I cast out demons

by the Spirit of God, then the kingdom of God is come unto you. Or else 5
how can one enter into a strong man's house, and steal his goods, except he
first binds the strong man? and then he will rob his house. He that is not
with me is against me; and he that gathers not with me scatters abroad."

The One Unforgiven Sin
Matthew 12:31-32; Mark 3:28-30

"Truly I say unto you, All manner of sin and blasphemy shall be for- 6
given unto men: but the blasphemy against the Holy Ghost shall not be forgiven unto men. And whosoever speaks a word against the Son of man, it
shall be forgiven him: but whosoever speaks against the Holy Ghost, it shall
not be forgiven him, neither in this world, neither in the world to come, but
is in danger of eternal condemnation: because they said, He has an unclean
spirit."

Judged by Your Words
Matthew 12:33-37

"Either make the tree good, and its fruit good; or else make the tree 7
corrupt, and its fruit corrupt: for the
tree is known by its fruit. O generation | "OUT OF THE ABUNDANCE OF
of vipers, how can you, being evil, | THE HEART THE MOUTH
speak good things? for out of the | SPEAKS."
abundance of the heart the mouth
speaks. A good man out of the good treasure of the heart brings forth good
things: and an evil man out of the evil treasure brings forth evil things.

"But I say unto you, That every idle word that men shall speak, they 8
shall give account thereof in the day of judgment. For by your words you
shall be justified, and by your words you shall be condemned."

Seeking a Sign
Matthew 12:38-42

Then certain of the scribes and of the Pharisees answered, saying, 9
"Teacher, we would see a sign from you." But he answered and said unto
them, "An evil and adulterous generation seeks after a sign; and there shall
no sign be given to it, but the sign of the prophet Jonah: for as Jonah was
three days and three nights in the whale's belly; so shall the Son of man be
three days and three nights in the heart of the earth. The men of Nineveh
shall rise in judgment with this generation, and shall condemn it: because
they repented at the preaching of Jonah; and, behold, one greater than Jonah
is here.

"The queen of the south shall rise up in the judgment with this gener- 10
ation, and shall condemn it: for she came from the uttermost parts of the
earth to hear the wisdom of Solomon; and, behold, one greater than
Solomon is here."

Unclean Spirits
Matthew 12:43-45

11   "When the unclean spirit is gone out of a man, it walks through dry places, seeking rest, and finds none. Then it says, 'I will return into my house from which I came out;' and when it is come, it finds it empty, swept, and put in order. Then it goes, and takes with itself seven other spirits more wicked than itself, and they enter in and dwell there: and the last state of that man is worse than the first. Even so shall it be also unto this wicked generation."

Jesus' Mother and Brethren
Matthew 12:46-50; Mark 3:31-35; Luke 8:19-21

12   There came then to him his mother and his brethren, and could not come at him for the crowd, and, standing outside, sent unto him, calling him. While he yet talked to the people, and the multitude sat about him, one said unto him, "Behold, your mother and your brethren stand outside, desiring to speak with you." But he answered and said unto him that told him, "Who is my mother? and who are my brethren?"

13

> "WHOSOEVER SHALL DO THE WILL OF MY FATHER WHICH IS IN HEAVEN, THE SAME IS MY BROTHER, AND SISTER, AND MOTHER."

And he looked round about on them which sat about him, and he stretched forth his hand toward his disciples, and said, "Behold my mother and my brethren! My mother and my brethren are these which hear the word of God, and do it. For whosoever shall do the will of my Father which is in heaven, the same is my brother, and sister, and mother."

CHAPTER 17

PARABLES BY THE SEA

Parable of the Sower
Matthew 13:1-9; Mark 4:1-9; Luke 8:4-8

The same day went Jesus out of the house, and sat by the seaside. And 1
he began again to teach by the seaside: and there was gathered unto him a
great multitude out of every city, so that he entered into a ship, and sat in
the sea; and the whole multitude stood on the shore by the sea. And he
taught them many things by parables, and said unto them in his doctrine, by
a parable: "Hearken; Behold, there went out a sower to sow his seed: and it
came to pass, as he sowed, some fell by the wayside; and was trampled
down, and the birds of the air came and devoured them up.

"And some fell on stony ground, where it had not much earth; and 2
immediately it sprang up, because it had no depth of earth: but when the sun
was up, it was scorched; and because it had no root, it withered away,
because it lacked moisture.

"And some fell among thorns; and the thorns sprang up with it, and 3
the thorns grew up, and choked it, and it yielded no fruit.

"And others fell on good ground, and did yield fruit that sprang up and 4
increased; and brought forth fruit, some a hundredfold, some sixtyfold,
some thirtyfold." When he had said these things, he cried, "He that has ears
to hear, let him hear."

The Divine Purpose of Parables
Matthew 13:10-17; Mark 4:10-12; Luke 8:9-10

The disciples came, and said unto him, "Why do you speak unto them 5
in parables?" He answered and said unto them, "Because it is given unto
you to know the mysteries of the kingdom of heaven, but to them it is not
given. For whosoever has, to him shall be given, and he shall have more
abundance: but whosoever has not, from him shall be taken away even that

5 he has. Therefore I speak to them in parables: because they seeing see not; and hearing they hear not, neither do they understand."

6 And when he was alone, they that were about him with the twelve asked of him the parable, saying, "What might this parable be?" He said unto them, "Unto you it is given to know the mystery of the kingdom of God: but unto them that are outside, all these things are done in parables. In them is fulfilled the prophecy of Isaiah, which says, '*By hearing you shall hear, and shall not understand; and seeing you shall see, and shall not perceive: for this people's heart is grown coarse, and their ears are dull of hearing, and their eyes they have closed; lest at any time they should see with their eyes, and hear with their ears, and should understand with their hearts, and should be converted, and I should heal them,*' and their sins should be forgiven them.

7 "But blessed are your eyes, for they see: and your ears, for they hear. For truly I say unto you, That many prophets and righteous men have desired to see those things which you see, and have not seen them; and to hear those things which you hear, and have not heard them."

Parable of the Sower Explained
Matthew 13:18-23; Mark 4:13-20; Luke 8:11-15

8 And he said unto them, "Do you not know this parable? and how then will you know all parables? Hear therefore the parable of the sower.

9 "Now the parable of the sower is this: The seed is the word of God. The sower sows the word. And these are they by the wayside, where the word of the kingdom is sown. When anyone hears the word of the kingdom, and does not understand it, then comes the wicked one. But when they have heard, Satan comes immediately, and takes away the word that was sown in their hearts, lest they should believe and be saved.

10 "These are they likewise which are sown on stony ground; who, when they have heard the word, immediately receive it with gladness; and these have no root in themselves, which for a while believe, and so endure but for a time: afterward, when affliction or persecution arises for the word's sake, immediately they are fallen away, and in time of temptation fall away.

11 "These are they which are sown among thorns; such as hear the word, which, when they have heard, go forth, and are choked with cares of this world, and the deceitfulness of riches, and pleasures of this life, and the lusts of other things entering in, choke the word, and bring no fruit to maturity.

12 "These are they which are sown on good ground; which in an honest and good heart, having heard the word, receive it, and keep it, and bring forth fruit with patience, some thirtyfold, some sixty, and some a hundred."

Parable of the Lamp
Mark 4:21-25; Luke 8:16-18

13 And he said unto them, "Is a lamp brought to be put under a tub, or under a bed? and not to be set on a lampstand? No man, when he has

lit a lamp, covers it with a vessel, or puts it under a bed; but sets it on 13 a lampstand, that they which enter in may see the light. For nothing is secret, that shall not be made manifest; neither anything hidden, that shall not be known and come to light. If any man has ears to hear, let him hear."

And he said unto them, "Take heed what you hear: with what meas- 14 ure you measure, it shall be measured to you: and unto you that hear shall more be given. Take heed therefore how you hear: for whosoever has, to him shall be given; and whosoever has not, from him shall be taken even that which he seems to have."

> "WITH WHAT MEASURE YOU MEASURE, IT SHALL BE MEASURED TO YOU."

Parable of the Weeds
Matthew 13:24-30

Another parable he put forth unto them, saying, "The kingdom of 15 heaven is likened unto a man which sowed good seed in his field: but while men slept, his enemy came and sowed weeds among the wheat, and went his way. But when the blade was sprung up, and brought forth fruit, then appeared the weeds also.

"So the servants of the landowner came and said unto him, 'Sir, did 16 not you sow good seed in your field? from where then has it weeds?' He said unto them, 'An enemy has done this.' The servants said unto him, 'Will you then that we go and gather them up?' But he said, 'No; lest while you gather up the weeds, you root up also the wheat with them. Let both grow together until the harvest: and in the time of harvest I will say to the reapers, "Gather together first the weeds, and bind them in bundles to burn them: but gather the wheat into my barn." ' "

Parable of the Growth of Seed
Mark 4:26-29

He said, "So is the kingdom of God, as if a man should cast seed into 17 the ground; and should sleep, and rise night and day, and the seed should sprout and grow up, he knows not how. For the earth brings forth fruit of itself; first the blade, then the head, after that the full grain in the head. But when the fruit is brought forth, immediately he puts in the sickle, because the harvest is come."

Parable of the Mustard Seed
Matthew 13:31-32; Mark 4:30-32

Another parable he put forth unto them, saying, "To what shall we 18 liken the kingdom of God? or with what comparison shall we compare it? The kingdom of heaven is like a grain of mustard seed, which a man took, and sowed in his field: which, when it is sown in the earth, is less than all the seeds that be in the earth: but when it is sown, it grows up, and becomes greater than all herbs, and becomes a tree, and shoots out great branches; so

18 that the birds of the air come and lodge in the branches thereof; so may lodge under the shadow of it."

Parable of the Leaven
Matthew 13:33

19 Another parable he spoke unto them; "The kingdom of heaven is like unto leaven, which a woman took, and hid in three measures of meal, till the whole was leavened."

Parables Fulfill Prophecy
Matthew 13:34-35; Mark 4:33-34

20 All these things spoke Jesus unto the multitude in parables: that it might be fulfilled which was spoken by the prophet, saying, *"I will open my mouth in parables; I will utter things which have been kept secret from the foundation of the world."* And with many such parables he spoke the word unto them, as they were able to hear it. But without a parable he spoke not unto them: and when they were alone, he explained all things to his disciples.

Parable of the Weeds Explained
Matthew 13:36-43

21 Then Jesus sent the multitude away, and went into the house: and his disciples came unto him, saying, "Explain unto us the parable of the weeds of the field." He answered and said unto them, "He that sows the good seeds is the Son of man; the field is the world; the good seeds are the children of the kingdom; but the weeds are the children of the wicked one; the enemy that sowed them is the devil; the harvest is the end of the world; and the reapers are the angels.

22 "THEN SHALL THE RIGHTEOUS SHINE FORTH AS THE SUN IN THE KINGDOM OF THEIR FATHER."

"As therefore the weeds are gathered and burned in the fire; so shall it be in the end of this world. The Son of man shall send forth his angels, and they shall gather out of his kingdom all things that cause sin, and them which do iniquity; and shall cast them into a furnace of fire: there shall be wailing and gnashing of teeth. Then shall the righteous shine forth as the sun in the kingdom of their Father. Who has ears to hear, let him hear."

Parable of the Hidden Treasure
Matthew 13:44

23 "Again, the kingdom of heaven is like treasure hidden in a field; which when a man has found, he hides, and for joy thereof goes and sells all that he has, and buys that field."

Parable of the Pearl of Great Price
Matthew 13:45-46

24 "Again, the kingdom of heaven is like a merchant, seeking beautiful pearls: who, when he had found one pearl of great price, went and sold all that he had, and bought it."

Parable of the Net
Matthew 13:47-50

"Again, the kingdom of heaven is like unto a net, that was cast into the 25 sea, and gathered of every kind: which, when it was full, they drew to shore, and sat down, and gathered the good into vessels, but cast the bad away.

"So shall it be at the end of the world: the angels shall come forth, and 26 sever the wicked from among the just, and shall cast them into the furnace of fire: there shall be wailing and gnashing of teeth."

Parable of the Home Owner
Matthew 13:51-53

Jesus said unto them, "Have you understood all these things?" They 27 said unto him, "Yes, Lord."

Then he said unto them, "Therefore every scribe which is instructed 28 unto the kingdom of heaven is like a man that is a home owner, which brings forth out of his treasure things new and old."

And it came to pass, that when Jesus had finished these parables, he 29 departed from there.

CHAPTER 18

MIRACLES BY THE SEA

Jesus Calms the Winds and Sea
Matthew 8:18, 23-27; Mark 4:35-41; Luke 8:22-25

1   Now it came to pass on the same day, when the evening was come, when Jesus saw great multitudes about him, he said unto them, "Let us go over unto the other side of the sea." When he was entered into a ship, his disciples followed him. When they had sent away the multitude, they took him even as he was in the ship. There were also with him other little ships. And they launched forth.

2   But as they sailed he fell asleep: and, behold, there arose a great tempest in the sea, and the waves beat into the ship, insomuch that the ship was covered with the waves; and they were filled with water, and were in jeopardy. He was in the rear part of the ship, asleep on a pillow: and his disciples came to him, and awoke him, saying, "Teacher, teacher, we perish, save us: do you not care that we perish?" He said unto them, "Why are you fearful, O you of little faith?" Then he arose, and rebuked the wind and the raging of the water: and said unto the sea, "Peace, be still." And the wind ceased, and there was a great calm.

3   He said unto them, "Why are you so fearful? how is it that you have no faith? Where is your faith?" And they being afraid wondered, saying one to another, "What manner of man is this! for he commands even the winds and water, and they obey him."

Delivering the Demon-Possessed
Matthew 8:28-34; Mark 5:1-20; Luke 8:26-39

4   And when he was come to the other side of the sea into the country of the Gadarenes, which is opposite Galilee, there met him two possessed with demons, coming out of the tombs, exceedingly fierce, so that no man might pass by that way.

And when he was come out of the ship, immediately there met him out 5
of the city a certain man with an unclean spirit, and wore no clothes, neither lived in any house, who had his dwelling among the tombs. No man
could bind him, no, not with chains: because he had been often bound with
fetters and chains, and the chains had been pulled apart by him, and the fetters broken in pieces: neither could any man tame him. And always, night
and day, he was in the mountains, and in the tombs, crying, and cutting himself with stones.

But when he saw Jesus afar off, he ran and fell down before him and 6
worshiped him, and cried out with a loud voice, and said, "What have I to do
with you, Jesus, Son of the most high God? I beg you, I command you by
God, that you torment me not." For he had commanded the unclean spirit,
"Come out of the man, you unclean spirit." (For many times it had caught
him: and he was kept bound with chains and in fetters; and he broke the
bands, and was driven of the demon into the wilderness.)

And Jesus asked him, saying, "What is your name?" And he answered, 7
saying, "My name is Legion: for we are many:" because many demons were
entered into him. He begged him much that he would not send them away
out of the country. And they begged him that he would not command them
to go out into the deep.

Now there was there a good way off from them near unto the moun- 8
tains a great herd of swine feeding on the mountain. So all the demons
begged him, saying, "If you cast us out, permit us to go away into the herd
of swine." And immediately Jesus gave them permission. He said unto
them, "Go." When they were come out of the man, they went into the herd
of swine: and, behold, the whole herd of swine ran violently down a steep
place into the sea, (they were about two thousand); and perished in the
waters.

When they saw what was done, they that fed the swine fled, and went 9
their ways into the city, and in the country, and told everything, and what
was befallen to the possessed of the demons. Then they went out to see what
was done; and came to Jesus, and found the man, that was possessed with
the demon, and had the legion, out of whom the demons were departed, sitting at the feet of Jesus, clothed, and in his right mind: and they were afraid.
They also which saw it told them by what means he that was possessed of
the demons was healed, and also concerning the swine.

And, behold, the whole city came out to meet Jesus: then the whole 10
multitude of the country of the Gadarenes round about, when they saw him,
asked him to depart from them; for they were taken with great fear: and he
went up into the ship, and returned back again.

When he was come into the ship, the man out of whom the demons 11
were departed begged him that he might be with him: but Jesus sent him
away, saying, "Go home to your friends, and tell them how great things the
Lord has done for you, and has had compassion on you." He went his way,

11 and began to publish in Decapolis, and published throughout the whole city how great things Jesus had done unto him: and all men did marvel.

Restoring Life and Healing a Woman
Matthew 9:1, 18-26; Mark 5:21-43; Luke 8:40-56

12 When Jesus was crossed over again by ship unto the other side, and came into his own city, many people gathered unto him: and he was near unto the sea. And it came to pass, that, the people gladly received him: for they were all waiting for him.

13 And, behold, there came one of the rulers of the synagogue, Jairus by name; and when he saw him, he fell down at Jesus' feet, and pleaded with him greatly that he would come into his house, saying, "My little daughter lies at the point of death: I appeal to you, come and lay your hands on her, that she may be healed; and she shall live." For he had one only daughter, about twelve years of age, and she lay dying. And Jesus arose, and followed him, and so did his disciples. But as he went the people thronged him.

14 And, behold, a woman, which was diseased with a flow of blood twelve years, and had suffered many things of many physicians, and had spent all that she had upon physicians, and was nothing bettered, but rather grew worse, when she had heard of Jesus, came in the crowd behind him, and touched the hem of his garment: for she said within herself, "If I may but touch his garment, I shall be whole." Immediately her flow of blood was dried up; and she felt in her body that she was healed of that affliction. Jesus, immediately knowing in himself that power had gone out of him, turned himself around in the crowd, and said, "Who touched my clothes?" When all denied, Peter and they that were with him said, "Master, the multitudes throng you and crowd you, and you say, 'Who touched me?'" Jesus said, "Somebody has touched me: for I perceive that power is gone out of me." He looked round about to see her that had done this thing.

15 But Jesus turned himself about, and when the woman saw that she was not hidden, she came fearing and trembling, and falling down before him, she told him all the truth, declared unto him before all the people for what cause she had touched him, and how she was healed immediately. He said unto her, "Daughter, be of good cheer: your faith has made you whole; go in peace, and be whole of your affliction." The woman was made whole from that hour.

> "BE OF GOOD CHEER: YOUR FAITH HAS MADE YOU WHOLE."

16 While he yet spoke, there came one from the ruler of the synagogue's house, saying to him, "Your daughter is dead: why do you trouble the Teacher any further?" As soon as Jesus heard the word that was spoken, he said unto the ruler of the synagogue, "Be not afraid, only believe, and she shall be made whole." He allowed no man to follow him, except Peter, and James, and John the brother of James.

He came to the house of the ruler of the synagogue, and saw the 17
tumult and the flute players and the people making a noise, and them
that wept and wailed greatly. When Jesus came into the ruler's house,
he allowed no man to go in, except Peter, and James, and John, and the
father and the mother of the little
girl. And all wept, and bewailed her:
but he said, "Give room: weep not;
she is not dead, but sleeps." And
they laughed him to scorn, knowing that she was dead. But when he had
put them all out, he took the father and the mother of the little girl, and
them that were with him, and entered in where the little girl was lying.

> AND THEY LAUGHED HIM TO
> SCORN.

He took the little girl by the hand, and said unto her, "Talitha cumi;" 18
which is, being interpreted, "Little girl, I say unto you, arise." And her spirit came again, and straightway the little girl arose, and walked; for she was
of the age of twelve years. Her parents were overcome with a great aston-
ishment: but he charged them strictly that they should tell no man what was
done; and commanded that something should be given her to eat. The report
hereof went abroad into all that land.

Jesus Heals Two Blind Men
Matthew 9:27-31

When Jesus departed from there, two blind men followed him, crying, 19
and saying, "Son of David, have mercy on us." When he was come into the
house, the blind men came to him: and Jesus said unto them, "Do you
believe that I am able to do this?" They said unto him, "Yes, Lord."

Then touched he their eyes, saying, "According to your faith be it unto 20
you." And their eyes were opened; and Jesus strictly charged them, saying,
"See that no man knows it." But they, when they were departed, spread
abroad his fame in all that country.

A Mute Man Speaks
Matthew 9:32-34

As they went out, behold, they brought to him a mute man possessed 21
with a demon. When the demon was cast out, the mute spoke: and the multitudes marveled, saying, "It was never so seen in Israel."

But the Pharisees said, "He casts out demons through the prince of the 22
demons."

CHAPTER 19

AUTHORITY GIVEN TO THE APOSTLES

Second Rejection at Nazareth
Matthew 13:54-58; Mark 6:1-6

1   He went out from there, and came into his own country, and his disciples followed him. When the sabbath day was come, he began to teach in their synagogue: and many hearing him were astonished, saying, "From where has this man these things? and what wisdom is this which is given unto him, that even such mighty works are wrought by his hands?

2   "Is not this the carpenter? is not this the carpenter's son? is not his mother called Mary? and his brethren, James, and Joses, and Simon, and Jude? And his sisters, are they not all with us? From where then has this man all these things?" They were offended at him. But Jesus said unto them, "A prophet is not without honor, except in his own country, and among his own relatives, and in his own house."

3   And he could there do no mighty work, except that he laid his hands upon a few sick folks, and healed them. He marveled because of their unbelief. He did not many mighty works there because of their unbelief. He went round about the villages, teaching.

Laborers Are Few
Matthew 9:35-38

4   Jesus went about all the cities and villages, teaching in their synagogues, and preaching the gospel of the kingdom, and healing every sickness and every disease among the people.

5   But when he saw the multitudes, he was moved with compassion on them, because they were discouraged, and were scattered abroad, as sheep having no shepherd. Then he said unto his disciples, "The harvest truly is plentiful, but the laborers are few; pray you therefore the Lord of the harvest, that he will send forth laborers into his harvest."

Authority: Sending Forth Apostles
Matthew 10:1-15; Mark 6:7-11; Luke 9:1-5

And when he had called unto him his twelve disciples, he gave them 6 power and authority over all unclean spirits, to cast them out, and to heal all manner of sickness and all manner of disease. Now the names of the twelve apostles are these; The first, Simon, who is called Peter, and Andrew his brother; James the son of Zebedee, and John his brother; Philip, and Bartholomew; Thomas, and Matthew the tax collector; James the son of Alphaeus, and Lebbaeus, whose surname was Thaddaeus; Simon the Canaanite, and Judas Iscariot, who also betrayed him. These twelve Jesus began to send forth by two and two, and commanded them, saying, "Go not into the land of the Gentiles, and into any city of the Samaritans do not you enter: but go rather to the lost sheep of the house of Israel. And as you go, preach, saying, 'The kingdom of heaven is at hand.' Heal the sick, cleanse the lepers, raise the dead, cast out demons: freely you have received, freely give."

He said unto them, "Take nothing for your journey, neither staves, nor 7 bag, neither bread; neither have two tunics apiece. Provide neither gold, nor silver, nor copper coins in your purses: for the workman is worthy of his food." He commanded them that they should take nothing for their journey, except a staff only; but be shod with sandals.

"And into whatsoever city or town you shall enter, inquire who in it is 8 worthy; and there stay till you go from there. When you come into a house, greet it. If the house be worthy, let your peace come upon it: but if it be not worthy, let your peace return to you. Whatsoever house you enter into, there stay till you depart from that place.

"And whosoever shall not receive you, nor hear your words, when you 9 depart out of that house or when you go out of that city, shake off the very dust from under your feet for a testimony against them. Truly I say unto you, It shall be more tolerable for the land of Sodom and Gomorrah in the day of judgment, than for that city."

Authority: Coming Persecutions
Matthew 10:16-26

"Behold, I send you forth as sheep in the midst of wolves: be therefore 10 wise as serpents, and harmless as doves. But beware of men: for they will deliver you up to the councils, and they will scourge you in their synagogues; and you shall be brought before governors and kings for my sake, for a testimony against them and the Gentiles.

"BE THEREFORE WISE AS SERPENTS, AND HARMLESS AS DOVES."

But when they deliver you up, do not worry how or what you shall speak: for it shall be given you in that same hour what you shall speak. For it is not you that speak, but the Spirit of your Father which speaks in you.

11   "And the brother shall deliver up the brother to death, and the father the child: and the children shall rise up against their parents, and cause them to be put to death. And you shall be hated of all men for my name's sake: but he that endures to the end shall be saved. But when they persecute you in this city, flee into another: for truly I say unto you, You shall not have gone over the cities of Israel, till the Son of man is come.

12   "The disciple is not above his teacher, nor the servant above his mas-

> "THERE IS NOTHING COVERED, THAT SHALL NOT BE REVEALED; AND HIDDEN, THAT SHALL NOT BE KNOWN."

ter. It is enough for the disciple that he be as his teacher, and the servant as his master. If they have called the master of the house Beelzebub, how much more shall they call them of his household? Do not fear them therefore: for there is nothing covered, that shall not be revealed; and hidden, that shall not be known."

Authority: Proclaiming Boldly
Matthew 10:27-31

13   "What I tell you in darkness, that speak in light: and what you hear in the ear, that preach upon the housetops. And fear not them which kill the body, but are not able to kill the soul: but rather fear him which is able to destroy both soul and body in hell. Are not two sparrows sold for a copper coin? and one of them shall not fall on the ground without your Father. But the very hairs of your head are all numbered. Fear not therefore, you are of more value than many sparrows."

Authority: Confessing Christ
Matthew 10:32-39

14   "Whosoever therefore shall confess me before men, him will I confess also before my Father which is in heaven. But whosoever shall deny me before men, him will I also deny before my Father which is in heaven.

15   "Think not that I am come to send peace on earth: I came not to send peace, but a sword. For I am come to '*set a man at variance against his father, and the daughter against her mother, and the daughter-in-law against her mother-in-law.*' And '*a man's foes shall be they of his own household.*'

16   "He that loves father or mother more than me is not worthy of me: and he that loves son or daughter more than me is not worthy of me. He that takes not his cross, and follows after me, is not worthy of me. He that finds his life shall lose it: and he that loses his life for my sake shall find it."

Authority: Receiving Rewards
Matthew 10:40-42

17   "He that receives you receives me, and he that receives me receives him that sent me. He that receives a prophet in the name of a prophet shall receive a prophet's reward; and he that receives a righteous man in the name

of a righteous man shall receive a righteous man's reward. And whosoever 17 shall give to drink unto one of these little ones a cup of cold water only in the name of a disciple, truly I say unto you, he shall in no way lose his reward."

The Twelve Apostles Go Forth
Matthew 11:1; Mark 6:12-13; Luke 9:6

They departed, and went through the towns, preaching the gospel that 18 men should repent. They cast out many demons, and anointed with oil many that were sick, and healed them, and healing everywhere. And it came to pass, when Jesus had made an end of commanding his twelve disciples, he departed from there to teach and to preach in their cities.

John the Baptist Is Beheaded
Matthew 14:1-12; Mark 6:14-29; Luke 9:7-9

Now Herod (Antipas) the tetrarch (ruler) heard of the fame of Jesus, 19 of all that was done by him: and he was perplexed, because it was said of some, that John was risen from the dead; and of some, that Elijah had appeared; and of others, that one of the old prophets was risen again. At that time Herod said unto his servants, "This is John the Baptist; he is risen from the dead; and therefore mighty works do show forth themselves in him." Herod said, "John have I beheaded: but who is this, of whom I hear such things?" And he desired to see him.

For Herod himself had sent forth and laid hold upon John, and bound 20 him in prison for Herodias' sake, his brother Philip's wife: for he had married her. For John had said unto Herod, "It is not lawful for you to have your brother's wife." And when he would have put him to death, he feared the multitude, because they counted him as a prophet. Therefore Herodias had a quarrel against him, and would have killed him; but she could not: for Herod feared John, knowing that he was a just man and holy, and protected him; and when he heard him, he did many things, and heard him gladly.

When the opportune day was come, that Herod on his birthday made 21 a supper to his officials, high captains, and leading men of Galilee; and when the daughter of the said Herodias came in, and danced, and pleased Herod and them that sat with him, the king said unto the girl, "Ask of me whatsoever you will, and I will give it you." He swore unto her, "Whatsoever you shall ask of me, I will give it you, unto the half of my kingdom." She went forth, and said unto her mother, "What shall I ask?" She said, "The head of John the Baptist." She came in straightway with haste unto the king, and asked, saying, "Give me here the head of John the Baptist in a platter."

And the king was exceedingly sorry; yet for his oath's sake, and for 22 their sakes which sat with him at the table, he would not reject her. Immediately the king sent an executioner, and commanded his head to be

22 brought: and he went and beheaded him in the prison, and brought his head in a platter, and gave it to the girl: and the girl gave it to her mother.

23   And when his disciples heard of it, they came and took up the body, and laid it in a tomb, and went and told Jesus.

CHAPTER 20

TRAINING THE APOSTLES

The Twelve Apostles Return
Matthew 14:13-14; Mark 6:30-34; Luke 9:10-11; John 6:1-3

When Jesus heard of it, he departed from there by ship into a deserted 1
place apart: and when the people had heard thereof, they followed him on
foot out of the cities. And the apostles, when they were returned, gathered
themselves together unto Jesus, and told him all things, both what they had
done, and what they had taught. He said unto them, "Come you yourselves
apart into a deserted place, and rest a while:" for there were many coming
and going, and they had no leisure so much as to eat.

And they departed into a deserted place belonging to the city called 2
Bethsaida by ship privately. The people saw them departing, and many
knew him, and ran on foot there out of all cities, and ahead of them, and
came together unto him: and he received them, and spoke unto them of the
kingdom of God, and healed them that had need of healing.

After these things Jesus went over the sea of Galilee, which is the sea 3
of Tiberias. And a great multitude followed him, because they saw his miracles which he did on them that were diseased. And Jesus went up into a
mountain, and there he sat with his disciples. Jesus, when he came out, saw
many people, and was moved with compassion toward them, because they
were as sheep not having a shepherd: and he began to teach them many
things, and he healed their sick.

Feeding the Five Thousand
Matthew 14:15-21; Mark 6:35-44; Luke 9:12-17; John 6:4-13

The passover, a feast of the Jews, was near. When the day began to 4
wear away, the twelve came to him, saying, "This is a deserted place, and
the time is now past; send the multitude away, that they may go into the villages and country round about, and lodge, and buy themselves food: for
they have nothing to eat." But Jesus said unto them, "They need not depart;

4 give them to eat." And they said unto him, "Shall we go and buy two hundred silver coins worth of bread, and give them to eat?"

5   When Jesus then lifted up his eyes, and saw a great company come unto him, he said unto Philip, "Where shall we buy bread, that these may eat?" And this he said to test him: for he himself knew what he would do. Philip answered him, "Two hundred silver coins worth of bread is not sufficient for them, that every one of them may take a little."

6   He said unto them, "How many loaves do you have? go and see." One of his disciples, Andrew, Simon Peter's brother, said unto him, "There is a lad here, which has five barley loaves, and two small fishes: but what are they among so many?" And when they knew, they said unto him, "We have here but five loaves, and two fishes." But he said unto them, "Give them to eat." They said, "We have no more but five loaves and two fishes; except we should go and buy food for all these people." Jesus said, "Bring them here to me."

7   Now there was much grass in the place. Jesus said, to his disciples, "Make them sit down by fifties in a company." They did so, and made them all sit down upon the green grass in ranks, by hundreds, and by fifties. So the men sat down, in number about five thousand. Then he took the five loaves and the two fishes, and looking up to heaven, he blessed them, and broke the loaves, and gave to the disciples to set before the multitude that were seated; and the two fishes he divided among them all.

8   And they did all eat, and were filled. When they were filled, he said unto his disciples, "Gather up the fragments that remain, that nothing be lost." Therefore they gathered them together, and filled twelve baskets with the fragments of the five barley loaves, which remained over and above unto them that had eaten. They that had eaten were about five thousand men, besides women and children.

Jesus Goes Apart to Pray Alone
Matthew 14:22-23; Mark 6:45-46; John 6:14-15

9   Straightway Jesus persuaded his disciples to get into a ship, and to go before him unto the other side unto Bethsaida, while he sent the multitudes away.

10   Then those men, when they had seen the miracle that Jesus did, said, "This is of a truth that prophet that should come into the world." When Jesus therefore perceived that they would come and take him by force, to make him a king, he sent them away, and he went up again into a mountain apart to pray: and when the evening was come, he was there alone.

> "THIS IS OF A TRUTH THAT PROPHET THAT SHOULD COME INTO THE WORLD."

Jesus Walks on the Water
Matthew 14:24-33; Mark 6:47-52; John 6:16-21

11   And when evening was now come, his disciples went down unto the sea, and entered into a ship, and went over the sea toward Capernaum. It

was now dark, and Jesus was not come to them, and he alone on the land. 11
The sea arose by reason of a great wind that blew. But the ship was now in
the midst of the sea, tossed with waves: for the wind was contrary.

He saw them toiling in rowing; for the wind was contrary unto them: 12
and about the fourth watch of the night he came unto them, walking upon
the sea, and would have passed by them. So when they had rowed about
three or four miles, they saw Jesus walking on the sea, and drawing near
unto the ship: and the disciples were troubled, saying, "It is a spirit;" and
they cried out for fear. But immediately Jesus talked with them, and said
unto them, "Be of good cheer: it is I; be not afraid."

Peter answered him and said, "Lord, if it be you, tell me come unto you 13
on the water." And he said, "Come." When Peter was come down out of the
ship, he walked on the water, to go to Jesus. But when he saw the wind bois-
terous, he was afraid; and beginning to sink, he cried, saying, "Lord, save
me." Immediately Jesus stretched forth his hand, and caught him, and said
unto him, "O you of little faith, why did you doubt?"

When they were come into the ship, the wind ceased: and they were 14
very amazed in themselves beyond measure, and wondered. For they had
not understood the miracle of the
loaves: for their heart was hardened.   "OF A TRUTH YOU ARE THE
Then they willingly received him into   SON OF GOD."
the ship: and immediately the ship was
at the land where they were heading. Then they that were in the ship came
and worshiped him, saying, "Of a truth you are the Son of God."

Healed by Touching Jesus' Garment
Matthew 14:34-36; Mark 6:53-56

When they had crossed over, they came into the land of Gennesaret, and 15
drew to the shore.

And when they were come out of the ship, straightway the men of that 16
place had knowledge of him, they sent out into all that country round about,
and ran through that whole region round about, and began to carry about in
beds those that were sick, where they heard he was, and brought unto him
all that were diseased; and begged him that they might only touch the hem
of his garment: and as many as touched were made perfectly whole.

Wherever he entered, into villages, or cities, or country, they laid the 17
sick in the marketplaces, and begged him that they might touch if it were but
the border of his garment: and as many as touched him were made whole.

CHAPTER 21

TEACHING THE APOSTLES

"True Bread From Heaven"
John 6:22-40

1   The following day, when the people which stood on the other side of the sea saw that there was no other boat there, except that one whereinto his disciples were entered, and that Jesus went not with his disciples into the boat, but that his disciples were gone away alone; (howbeit there came other boats from Tiberias near unto the place where they did eat bread, after that the Lord had given thanks): when the people therefore saw that Jesus was not there, neither his disciples, they also took boats, and came to Capernaum, seeking for Jesus.

2   And when they had found him on the other side of the sea, they said unto him, "Rabbi, when did you come here?" Jesus answered them and said, "Truly, truly, I say unto you, You seek me, not because you saw the miracles, but because you did eat of the loaves, and were filled. Labor not for the food which perishes, but for that food which endures unto everlasting life, which the Son of man shall give unto you: for him has God the Father sealed."

3   Then they said unto him, "What shall we do, that we might work the works of God?" Jesus answered and said unto them, "This is the work of God, that you believe on him whom he has sent."

4   They said therefore unto him, "What sign do you show then, that we may see, and believe you? what do you work? Our fathers did eat manna in the desert; as it is written, *'He gave them bread from heaven to eat.'"* Then Jesus said unto them, "Truly, truly, I say unto you, Moses did not give you that bread from heaven; but my Father gives you the true bread from heaven. For the bread of God is he which comes down from heaven, and gives life unto the world."

Then they said unto him, "Lord, evermore give us this bread." And 5 Jesus said unto them, "I am the bread of life: he that comes to me shall never hunger; and he that believes on me shall never thirst. But I said unto you, That you also have seen me, and do not believe. All that the Father gives me shall come to me; and him

> "I AM THE BREAD OF LIFE: HE THAT COMES TO ME SHALL NEVER HUNGER."

that comes to me I will in no way cast out. For I came down from heaven, not to do my own will, but the will of him that sent me.

"And this is the Father's will which has sent me, that of all which he 6 has given me I should lose nothing, but should raise it up again at the last day. This is the will of him that sent me, that everyone which sees the Son, and believes on him, may have everlasting life: and I will raise him up at the last day."

"I Am That Bread of Life"
John 6:41-59

The Jews then murmured at him, because he said, "I am the bread 7 which came down from heaven." And they said, "Is not this Jesus, the son of Joseph, whose father and mother we know? how is it then that he says, 'I came down from heaven?'" Jesus therefore answered and said unto

> "NO MAN CAN COME TO ME, EXCEPT THE FATHER WHICH HAS SENT ME DRAWS HIM."

them, "Murmur not among yourselves. No man can come to me, except the Father which has sent me draws him: and I will raise him up at the last day.

"It is written in the prophets, *'And they shall be all taught of God.'* 8 Every man therefore that has heard, and has learned of the Father, comes unto me. Not that any man has seen the Father, except he which is of God, he has seen the Father. Truly, truly, I say unto you, He that believes on me has everlasting life. I am that bread of life.

"Your fathers did eat manna in the wilderness, and are dead. This is 9 the bread which comes down from heaven, that a man may eat thereof, and not die. I am the living bread which came down from heaven: if any man eats of this bread, he shall live for ever: and the bread that I will give is my flesh, which I will give for the life of the world."

The Jews therefore quarreled among themselves, saying, "How can 10 this man give us his flesh to eat?" Then Jesus said unto them, "Truly, truly, I say unto you, Except you eat the flesh of the Son of man, and drink his blood, you have no life in you. Whoever eats my flesh, and drinks my blood, has eternal life; and I will raise him up at the last day. For my flesh is food indeed, and my blood is drink indeed. He that eats my flesh, and drinks my blood, dwells in me, and I in him.

"As the living Father has sent me, and I live by the Father: so he that 11 eats me, even he shall live by me. This is that bread which came down from

11 heaven: not as your fathers did eat manna, and are dead: he that eats of this bread shall live for ever."

12 These things he said in the synagogue, as he taught in Capernaum.

"It Is the Spirit That Quickens"
John 6:60-65

13 Many therefore of his disciples, when they had heard this, said, "This is a hard saying; who can hear it?" When Jesus knew in himself that his disciples murmured at it, he said unto them, "Does this offend you?

> "THE WORDS THAT I SPEAK UNTO YOU, THEY ARE SPIRIT, AND THEY ARE LIFE."

What and if you shall see the Son of man ascend up where he was before? It is the spirit that quickens; the flesh profits nothing: the words that I speak unto you, they are spirit, and they are life. But there are some of you that do not believe." For Jesus knew from the beginning who they were that believed not, and who should betray him. And he said, "Therefore I said unto you, that no man can come unto me, except it were given unto him of my Father."

Peter's First Confession
John 6:66-71

14 From that time many of his disciples went back, and walked no more with him. Then said Jesus unto the twelve, "Will you also go away?" Then Simon Peter answered him, "Lord, to whom shall we go? you have the words of eternal life. And we believe and are sure that you are that Christ, the Son of the living God." Jesus answered them, "Have not I chosen you twelve, and one of you is a devil?" He spoke of Judas Iscariot the son of Simon: for he it was that should betray him, being one of the twelve.

Defilement: Teaching Man's Tradition
Matthew 15:1-9; Mark 7:1-13

15 Then came together unto him the Pharisees, and certain of the scribes, which came from Jerusalem. And when they saw some of his disciples eat bread with defiled, that is to say, with unwashed, hands, they found fault. For the Pharisees, and all the Jews, unless they wash their hands often, do not eat, holding the tradition of the elders. And when they come from the marketplace, unless they wash, they do not eat. And many other things there be, which they have received to hold, as the washing of cups, and pots, copper vessels, and of tables. Then the Pharisees and scribes asked him, "Why do your disciples transgress the tradition of the elders? for they do not wash their hands when they eat bread."

16 He answered and said unto them, "Well has Isaiah prophesied of you hypocrites, as it is written, '*This people draws near unto me with their mouth, and honors me with their lips; but their heart is far from me. Howbeit in vain do they worship me, teaching for doctrines the commandments of men.*' For laying aside the commandment of God, you hold the tradition

of men, as the washing of pots and cups: and many other such like things 16
you do."

And he said unto them, "Full well you reject the commandment of 17
God, that you may keep your own tradition. For Moses said, *'Honor your
father and your mother;'* and, *'Whoever curses father or mother, let him die
the death.'* But you say, 'If a man shall say to his father or his mother, "It is
Corban," that is to say, a gift, by whatsoever you might be profited from me;
and honors not his father or his mother, he shall be free.' And you permit
him no longer to do anything for his father or his mother; making the word
of God of no effect through your tradition, which you have delivered: and
many such like things do you."

Defilement: Evil Comes From Within
Matthew 15:10-20; Mark 7:14-23

And when he had called all the people unto him, he said unto them, 18
"Hearken unto me every one of you, and understand: there is nothing from
outside a man, that entering into the mouth can defile him: but the things
which come out of the mouth, those are they that defile a man. If any man
has ears to hear, let him hear."

Then came his disciples, and said unto him, "Do you know that the 19
Pharisees were offended, after they
heard this saying?" But he answered
and said, "Every plant, which my
heavenly Father has not planted, shall
be rooted up. Let them alone: they be

> "IF THE BLIND LEADS THE
> BLIND, BOTH SHALL FALL INTO
> THE DITCH."

blind leaders of the blind. And if the blind leads the blind, both shall fall into
the ditch."

And when he was entered into the house from the people, his disciples 20
asked him concerning the parable. Then Peter answered and said unto him,
"Explain unto us this parable." And
Jesus said unto them, "Are you so
without understanding also? Do you
not perceive, that whatsoever thing
from outside enters into the man, it
cannot defile him; because it enters

> "THOSE THINGS WHICH PRO-
> CEED OUT OF THE MOUTH
> COME FORTH FROM THE
> HEART."

not into his heart, but into the belly, and goes out into the elimination, purging all foods? But those things which proceed out of the mouth come forth
from the heart; and they defile the man.

"For from within, out of the heart of men, proceed evil thoughts, mur- 21
ders, adulteries, fornications, thefts, false witness, covetousness, wickedness, deceit, lewdness, an evil eye, blasphemy, conceit, foolishness: all these
evil things come from within, and defile a man: but to eat with unwashed
hands does not defile a man."

PART 6

EARLY REVELATIONS

Jesus was aware of His ultimate fate. Admonishing His disciples continually to turn from the limited laws of man to the infinite laws of God, He offered strict spiritual guidance to those who would follow in His ways, and revealed through His own testimony and transfiguration that He was indeed the Son of the living God. Jesus knew the manner of His impending death, but more importantly, He knew the manner of His resurrection that would inevitably follow.

"THE SON OF MAN SHALL COME IN THE GLORY OF HIS FATHER WITH HIS ANGELS; AND THEN HE SHALL REWARD EVERY MAN ACCORDING TO HIS WORKS." (MATTHEW 16:27)

CHAPTER 22

WIDENING THE MINISTRY

Healing a Gentile Woman's Daughter
Matthew 15:21-28; Mark 7:24-30

And from there he arose, and went into the borders of Tyre and Sidon, and 1 entered into a house, and would have no man know it: but he could not be hidden. For behold, a woman of Canaan, whose young daughter had an unclean spirit, heard of him, came out of the same region, and cried unto him, saying, "Have mercy on me, O Lord, Son of David; my daughter is grievously possessed with a demon." But he answered her not a word. And his disciples came and urged him, saying, "Send her away; for she cries after us."

But he answered and said, "I am not sent except unto the lost sheep of 2 the house of Israel." Then came she and fell at his feet and worshiped him, saying, "Lord, help me." The woman was a Greek, a Syrophoenician by nation; and she pleaded with him that he would cast forth the demon out of her daughter.

But Jesus said unto her, "Let the children first be filled: for it is not 3 right to take the children's bread, and to cast it unto the little dogs." And she answered and said unto him, "Yes, Lord: yet the little dogs under the table eat of the children's crumbs which fall from their masters' table." Then Jesus answered and said unto her, "O woman, great is your faith: be it unto you even as you will." And her daughter was made whole from that very hour.

And he said unto her, "For this saying go your way; the demon is gone 4 out of your daughter." When she was come to her house, she found the demon gone out, and her daughter lying upon the bed.

Healing a Deaf-Mute
Mark 7:31-37

And again, departing from the region of Tyre and Sidon, he came unto 5 the sea of Galilee, through the midst of the region of Decapolis.

6   And they brought unto him one that was deaf, and had an impediment in his speech; and they begged him to put his hand upon him. He took him aside from the multitude, and put his fingers into his ears, and he spit, and touched his tongue; and looking up to heaven, he sighed, and said unto him, "Ephphatha," that is, "Be opened." Straightway his ears were opened, and the binding of his tongue was loosed, and he spoke plainly.

7   And he charged them that they should tell no man: but the more he charged them, so much the more a great deal they published it; and were beyond measure astonished, saying, "He has done all things well: he makes both the deaf to hear, and the mute to speak."

Healed to the Glory of God
Matthew 15:29-31

8   Jesus departed from there, and came near unto the sea of Galilee; and went up into a mountain, and sat down there. Great multitudes came unto him, having with them those that were lame, blind, mute, maimed, and many others, and cast them down at Jesus' feet; and he healed them: insomuch that the multitude wondered, when they saw the mute to speak, the maimed to be whole, the lame to walk, and the blind to see: and they glorified the God of Israel.

Feeding the Four Thousand
Matthew 15:32-39; Mark 8:1-10

9   In those days the multitude being very great, and having nothing to eat, Jesus called his disciples unto him, and said unto them, "I have compassion on the multitude, because they have now been with me now three days, and have nothing to eat: and if I send them away fasting to their own houses, they will faint on the way: for many of them came from far away." And his disciples answered him, "From where should we have so much bread here in the wilderness, as to fill so great a multitude?" Jesus asked them, "How many loaves have you?" And they said, "Seven, and a few little fishes."

10   He commanded the multitude to sit down on the ground. And he took the seven loaves and the few small fishes, and gave thanks, and broke them, and gave to his disciples, and the disciples to the multitude.

11   They did all eat, and were filled: and they took up of the broken food that was left seven baskets full. They that had eaten were about four thousand men, besides women and children: and he sent the multitude away.

12   Straightway he entered into a ship with his disciples, and came into the region of Magdala and Dalmanutha.

"Discern the Signs of the Times"
Matthew 16:1-4; Mark 8:11-13

13   The Pharisees also with the Sadducees came forth, and began to question with him, seeking of him that he would show them a sign from heaven,

tempting him. He answered and said unto them, "When it is evening, you 13
say, 'It will be fair weather: for the sky is red.' And in the morning, 'It will
be foul weather today: for the sky is red and threatening.' O you hypocrites,
you can discern the face of the sky; but can you not discern the signs of the
times?"

He sighed deeply in his spirit, and said, "Why does this wicked and 14
adulterous generation seek after a sign? truly I say unto you, There shall no
sign be given unto this generation, but the sign of the prophet Jonah." He
left them, and entering into the ship again departed to the other side.

Beware of the Leaven of Man's Doctrine
Matthew 16:5-12; Mark 8:14-21

And when his disciples were come to the other side, they had forgot- 15
ten to take bread, neither had they in the ship with them more than one loaf.
He charged them, saying, "Take heed, beware of the leaven of the Pharisees,
and of the leaven of Herod." And they reasoned among themselves, saying,
"It is because we have taken no bread."

When Jesus perceived it, he said unto them, "O you of little faith, why 16
do you reason among yourselves, because you have brought no bread? Do
you not yet understand, neither remember the five loaves of the five thousand, and how many baskets you took up? Neither the seven loaves of the
four thousand, and how many baskets you took up? have you your heart yet
hardened?

"Having eyes, do you not see? and having ears, do you not hear? and 17
do you not remember? When I broke the five loaves among five thousand,
how many baskets full of fragments did you take up?" They said unto him,
"Twelve." "And when the seven among four thousand, how many baskets
full of fragments did you take up?" They said, "Seven."

He said unto them, "How is it that you do not understand that I spoke 18
it not to you concerning bread, that you should beware of the leaven of the
Pharisees and of the Sadducees?" Then they understood how that he told
them not beware of the leaven of bread, but of the doctrine of the Pharisees
and of the Sadducees.

A Blind Man's Eyes Restored
Mark 8:22-26

He came to Bethsaida; and they brought a blind man unto him, and 19
begged him to touch him. He took the blind man by the hand, and led him
out of the town; and when he had spit on his eyes, and put his hands upon
him, he asked him if he saw anything. He looked up, and said, "I see men
as trees, walking."

After that he put his hands again upon his eyes, and made him look up: 20
and he was restored, and saw every man clearly. And he sent him away to his
house, saying, "Neither go into the town, nor tell it to any in the town."

Peter's Second Confession
Matthew 16:13-20; Mark 8:27-30; Luke 9:18-22

21   And Jesus went out, and his disciples, into the towns of Caesarea Philippi: and on the road, it came to pass, as he was alone praying, his disciples were with him: and he asked them, saying, "Whom say the people that I the Son of man am?" And they answered, "Some say that you are John the Baptist: but some say, Elijah; and others, Jeremiah, or one of the prophets; and others say, that one of the old prophets is risen again." And he said unto them, "But whom do you say that I am?" Simon Peter answered and said, "You are the Christ, the Son of the living God."

> "YOU ARE THE CHRIST, THE SON OF THE LIVING GOD."

22   Jesus answered and said unto him, "Blessed are you, Simon Bar-Jonah: for flesh and blood has not revealed it unto you, but my Father which is in heaven. I say also unto you, That you are Peter, and upon this rock I will build my church; and the gates of Hades shall not prevail against it. I will give unto you the keys of the kingdom of heaven: and whatsoever you shall bind on earth shall be bound in heaven: and whatsoever you shall loose on earth shall be loosed in heaven."

> "I WILL GIVE UNTO YOU THE KEYS OF THE KINGDOM OF HEAVEN."

23   And he strictly charged and commanded his disciples that they should tell no man that he was Jesus the Christ; saying, "The Son of man must suffer many things, and be rejected of the elders and chief priests and scribes, and be slain, and be raised the third day."

CHAPTER 23

MYSTERIES OF THE MINISTRY

God's Plan for Redemption
Matthew 16:21-23; Mark 8:31-33

From that time forth Jesus began to show unto his disciples, how that 1 he must go unto Jerusalem, and the Son of man must suffer many things, and be rejected of the elders, and of the chief priests, and scribes, and be killed, and be raised again the third day.

And he spoke that saying openly. Then Peter took him, and began to 2 rebuke him, saying, "Far be it from you, Lord: this shall not be unto you." But when he had turned about and looked on his disciples, he rebuked Peter, saying, "Get you behind me, Satan: you are an offense unto me: for you set your mind not the things that be of God, but the things that be of men."

Taking Up Our Own Crosses Daily
Matthew 16:24-28; Mark 8:34-38; 9:1; Luke 9:23-27

And when he had called the people unto him with his disciples also, 3 he said unto them all, "Whosoever will come after me, let him deny himself, and take up his cross daily, and follow me. For whosoever will save his life shall lose it; but whosoever shall lose his life for my sake and the gospel's, the same shall save it.

"For what shall it profit a man, if he shall gain the whole world, and 4 lose his own soul? Or what shall a man give in exchange for his soul? For what is a man advantaged, if he gains the whole world, and loses himself, or be cast away?

"Whosoever therefore shall be ashamed of me and of my words in this 5 adulterous and sinful generation; of him also shall the Son of man be ashamed, when he shall come in his own glory, and in his Father's, and of the holy angels. For the Son of man shall come in the glory of his Father with his angels; and then he shall reward every man according to his works."

6 And he said unto them, "I tell you of a truth, there be some standing here, which shall not taste of death, till they see the kingdom of God come with power, till they see the Son of man coming in his kingdom."

The Transfiguration
Matthew 17:1-13; Mark 9:2-13; Luke 9:28-36

7 And it came to pass about eight days after these sayings, Jesus took with him Peter, James, and John his brother, and led them up into a high mountain apart by themselves to pray: and he was transfigured before them. As he prayed, the fashion of his countenance was altered, and his face did shine as the sun, and his clothing was white as the light. His clothing became shining, exceedingly white as snow and glistening; so as no bleacher on earth can whiten them.

8 And, behold, there appeared unto them two men talking with Jesus, which were Moses and Elijah: who appeared in glory, and spoke of his decease which he should accomplish at Jerusalem. But Peter and they that were with him were heavy with sleep: and when they were awake, they saw his glory, and the two men that stood with him.

9 And it came to pass, as they departed from him, Peter said unto Jesus, "Rabbi, it is good for us to be here: and let us make three tabernacles; one for you, and one for Moses, and one for Elijah:" not knowing what he said. For he knew not what to say; for they were very afraid.

10 While he yet spoke, behold, there came a bright cloud, and overshadowed them: and they feared as they entered into the cloud. There came a voice out of the cloud, saying, "This is my beloved Son, in whom I am well pleased; hear him." When the disciples heard it, they fell on their faces, and were very afraid. When the voice was past, Jesus was found alone. Jesus came and touched them, and said, "Arise, and be not afraid." Suddenly, when they had lifted up their eyes, and looked round about, they saw no man anymore, except Jesus only with themselves. They kept it close, and told no man in those days any of those things which they had seen.

> THERE CAME A VOICE OUT OF THE CLOUD, SAYING, "THIS IS MY BELOVED SON."

11 As they came down from the mountain, Jesus charged them, saying, "Tell the vision to no man, until the Son of man be risen again from the dead." And they kept that saying with themselves, questioning one with another what the rising from the dead should mean.

12 His disciples asked him, saying, "Why then say the scribes that Elijah must first come?" Jesus answered and said unto them, "Elijah truly shall first come, and restore all things. But I say unto you, That Elijah is come already, and they knew him not, but have done unto him whatsoever they wished, as it is written of him. Likewise it is written of the Son of man, that he must suffer many things, and be rejected." Then the disciples understood that he spoke unto them of John the Baptist.

Jesus Heals a Lunatic Son
Matthew 17:14-21; Mark 9:14-29; Luke 9:37-42

And it came to pass, that on the next day, when they were come down 13 from the mountain, many people met him. When he came to his disciples, he saw a great multitude about them, and the scribes questioning with them. Straightway all the people, when they beheld him, were greatly amazed, and running to him greeted him. He asked the scribes, "What do you question with them?"

And, behold, a man of the company cried out, saying, "Teacher, I beg 14 you, look upon my son: for he is my only child." And came to him, kneeling down to him, saying, "Lord, have mercy on my son: for he is lunatic, and very possessed. I have brought unto you my son, which has a mute spirit; and wheresoever it takes him, it convulses him: and he foams, and gnashes with his teeth, and withers away: and he suddenly cries out; and it convulses him that he foams again, and bruising him with difficulty departs from him. And I begged your disciples to cast it out; and they could not."

Then Jesus answered and said, "O faithless and perverse generation, 15 how long shall I be with you? how long shall I be patient with you? Bring your son here to me." They brought him unto him: and when he saw him, straightway the spirit convulsed him; and he fell on the ground, and wallowed foaming. He asked his father, "How long is it ago since this came unto him?" He said, "Of a child. And many times it has cast him into the fire, and into the waters, to destroy him: but if you can do anything, have compassion on us, and help us."

Jesus said unto him, "If you can believe, all things are possible to him that believes." Straightway the | "ALL THINGS ARE POSSIBLE TO HIM THAT BELIEVES." | 16

father of the child cried out, and said with tears, "Lord, I believe; help my unbelief."

And as he was yet coming, the demon threw him down, and convulsed 17 him. When Jesus saw that the people came running together, he rebuked the unclean spirit, saying unto it, "You mute and deaf spirit, I command you, come out of him, and enter no more into him." The spirit cried, and convulsed him greatly, and came out of him: and he was as one dead; insomuch that many said, "He is dead." But Jesus took him by the hand, and lifted him up; and he arose. Jesus delivered him again to his father: and the child was cured from that very hour.

When he was come into the house, his disciples asked him privately, 18 "Why could not we cast it out?" Jesus said unto them, "Because of your unbelief: for truly I say unto you, If you have faith as a grain of mustard seed, you shall say unto this mountain, 'Move from here to yonder place;' and it shall move; and nothing shall be impossible unto you. Howbeit this kind does not go out except by prayer and fasting."

CHAPTER 24

⊷ CHILDREN IN GOD'S KINGDOM ⊷

Jesus Again Predicts His Death
Matthew 17:22-23; Mark 9:30-32; Luke 9:43-45

1   They were all amazed at the mighty power of God. But while they wondered every one at all things which Jesus did, he said unto his disciples, "Let these sayings sink down into your ears: for the Son of man shall be delivered into the hands of men."

2   They departed from there, and passed through Galilee; and he would not that any man should know it. For while they stayed in Galilee, he taught his disciples, and said unto them, "The Son of man shall be betrayed into the hands of men: and they shall kill him, and the third day he shall be raised again." And they were exceedingly sorry.

3   But they did not understand this saying, and it was hidden from them, that they did not perceive it: and they feared to ask him of that saying.

Peter and Jesus Pay Taxes
Matthew 17:24-27

4   When they were come to Capernaum, they that received tribute money came to Peter, and said, "Does not your Teacher pay tribute?" He said, "Yes." When he was come into the house, Jesus preceded him, saying, "What do you think, Simon? of whom do the kings of the earth take custom or tribute? of their own children, or of strangers?" Peter said unto him, "Of strangers." Jesus said unto him, "Then are the children free.

5   "Notwithstanding, lest we should offend them, go to the sea, and cast a hook, and take up the fish that first comes up; and when you have opened its mouth, you shall find a piece of money: that take, and give unto them for me and you."

Children: Greatest in God's Kingdom
Matthew 18:1-5; Mark 9:33-37; Luke 9:46-48

6   He came to Capernaum: and at the same time the disciples came unto Jesus, saying, "Who is the greatest in the kingdom of heaven?" Being in the

house he asked them, "What was it that you disputed among yourselves on 6 the road?" But they held their peace: for on the road they had disputed among themselves, who should be the greatest.

He sat down, and called the twelve, and said unto them, "If any man 7 desires to be first, the same shall be last of all, and servant of all."

Jesus, perceiving the thought of their heart, called a little child unto 8 him, and set him in the midst of them, and said, "Truly I say unto you, Except you be converted, and become as little children, you shall not enter into the kingdom of heaven. Whosoever therefore shall humble himself as this little child, the same is greatest in the kingdom of heaven."

> "EXCEPT YOU BE CONVERTED, AND BECOME AS LITTLE CHILDREN, YOU SHALL NOT ENTER INTO THE KINGDOM OF HEAVEN."

When he had taken him in his arms, he said unto them, "Whosoever 9 shall receive one of such children in my name, receives me: and whosoever shall receive me, receives not me, but him that sent me: for he that is least among you all, the same shall be great."

Doing Good Is Rewarded
Mark 9:38-41; Luke 9:49-50

And John answered him, saying, "Teacher, we saw one casting out 10 demons in your name, and he does not follow us: and we forbade him, because he does not follow with us."

And Jesus said unto him, "Do not forbid him: for there is no man 11 which shall do a miracle in my name, that can lightly speak evil of me. For he that is not against us is for us. For whosoever shall give you a cup of water to drink in my name, because you belong to Christ, truly I say unto you, he shall not lose his reward."

Causing Sin Is Punished
Matthew 18:6-7; Mark 9:42

"But whosoever shall cause sin to one of these little ones that believe 12 in me, it is better for him that a millstone were hung about his neck, and he were cast into the sea, and that he were drowned in the depth of the sea.

"Woe unto the world because of causes to sin! for it must of neces- 13 sity be that causes to sin come; but woe to that man by whom the cause to sin comes!"

Keeping Yourself From Sin
Matthew 18:8-9; Mark 9:43-50

"And if your hand causes you to sin, cut it off: it is better for you to 14 enter into life maimed, than having two hands to go into hell, into the fire that never shall be quench: where *their worm dies not, and the fire is not quenched.* And if your foot causes you to sin, cut it off: it is better for you to enter lame into life, than having two feet to be cast into hell, into the fire that never shall be quenched: *where their worm dies not, and the fire is not quenched.*

15   "And if your eye causes sin of you, pluck it out: it is better for you to enter into life with one eye, into the kingdom of God with one eye, than having two eyes to be cast into hell fire: where '*their worm dies not, and the fire is not quenched.*' For everyone shall be salted with fire, and every sacrifice shall be salted with salt.

16   "Salt is good: but if the salt has lost its flavor, with what will you season it? Have salt in yourselves, and have peace one with another."

Parable of the Lost Sheep
Matthew 18:10-14

17   "Take heed that you do not despise one of these little ones; for I say unto you, That in heaven their angels do always behold the face of my Father which is in heaven. For the Son of man is come to save that which was lost.

18   "How do you think? if a man has a hundred sheep, and one of them be gone astray, does he not leave the ninety and nine, and go into the mountains, and seek that which is gone astray? And if so be that he finds it, truly I say unto you, he rejoices more of that sheep, than of the ninety and nine which went not astray.

> "THE SON OF MAN IS COME TO SAVE THAT WHICH WAS LOST."

19   "Even so it is not the will of your Father which is in heaven, that one of these little ones should perish."

CHAPTER 25

COMING TOGETHER IN JESUS' NAME

Brotherly Correction and Unity
Matthew 18:15-20

"Moreover if your brother shall trespass against you, go and tell him 1
his fault between you and him alone: if he shall hear you, you have gained
your brother. But if he will not hear you, then take with you one or two
more, that '*in the mouth of two or three witnesses every word may be estab-
lished.*' And if he shall neglect to hear them, tell it unto the church: but if
he neglects to hear the church, let him be unto you as a heathen man and a
tax collector.

"Truly I say unto you, Whatsoever you shall bind on earth shall be 2
bound in heaven: and whatsoever you shall loose on earth shall be loosed in
heaven.

"Again I say unto you, That if two of you shall agree on earth as con- 3
cerning anything that they shall ask, it shall be done for them of my Father
which is in heaven. For where two or three are gathered together in my
name, there am I in the midst of them."

Parable of the Wicked Servant
Matthew 18:21-35

Then Peter came to him, and said, "Lord, how often shall my brother 4
sin against me, and I forgive him? until seven times?" Jesus said unto him,
"I say not unto you, Until seven times: but, Until seventy times seven.

"Therefore is the kingdom of heaven likened unto a certain king, 5
which would take account of his servants. And when he had begun to take
account, one was brought unto him, which owed him ten thousand talents. But inasmuch as he had nothing to pay, his master commanded him
to be sold, and his wife, and children, and all that he had, and payment to
be made.

6   "The servant therefore fell down, and worshiped him, saying, 'Master, have patience with me, and I will pay you all.' Then the master of that servant was moved with compassion, and loosed him, and forgave him the debt.

7   "But the same servant went out, and found one of his fellow servants, which owed him a hundred silver coins: and he laid hands on him, and took him by the throat, saying, 'Pay me that you owe.'

8   "And his fellow servant fell down at his feet, and begged him, saying, 'Have patience with me, and I will pay you all.' And he would not: but went and cast him into prison, till he should pay the debt.

9   "So when his fellow servants saw what was done, they were very sorry, and came and told unto their master all that was done. Then his master, after he had called him, said unto him, 'O you wicked servant, I forgave you all that debt, because you appealed to me: should not you also have had compassion on your fellow servant, even as I had pity on you?' And his master was angry, and delivered him to the jailers, till he should pay all that was due unto him.

10   "So likewise shall my heavenly Father do also unto you, if you from your hearts do not forgive every one of you his brother their trespasses."

Jesus' Brethren Do Not Believe
John 7:1-9

11   After these things Jesus walked in Galilee: for he would not walk in Judea, because the Jews sought to kill him. Now the Jews' feast of tabernacles was at hand. His brethren therefore said unto him, "Depart from here, and go into Judea, that your disciples also may see the works that you do. For there is no man that does anything in secret, and he himself seeks to be known openly. If you do these things, show yourself to the world." For neither did his brethren believe in him.

12   Then Jesus said unto them, "My time is not yet come: but your time is always ready. The world cannot hate you; but me it hates, because I testify of it, that the works thereof are evil. You go up unto this feast: I do not go up yet unto this feast; for my time is not yet fully come." When he had said these words unto them, he stayed on in Galilee.

Samaritans Refuse Jesus' Messengers
Luke 9:51-56

13   And it came to pass, when the time was come that he should be received up, he steadfastly set his face to go to Jerusalem, and sent messengers before his face: and they went, and entered into a village of the Samaritans, to make ready for him. And they did not receive him, because his face was as though he would go to Jerusalem.

14   And when his disciples James and John saw this, they said, "Lord, will you that we command fire to come down from heaven, and consume them,

even as Elijah did?" But he turned, and rebuked them, and said, "You know 14
not what manner of spirit you are of. For the Son of man is not come to
destroy men's lives, but to save them." And they went to another village.

The Cost of Following Jesus
Matthew 8:19-22; Luke 9:57-62

And it came to pass, that, as they went on the road, a certain scribe 15
came, and said unto him, "Teacher, I will follow you wherever you go." And
Jesus said unto him, "The foxes have holes, and the birds of the air have
nests; but the Son of man has nowhere to lay his head."

He said unto another of his disciples, "Follow me." But he said, "Lord, 16
let me first to go and bury my father." But Jesus said unto him, "Let the
dead bury their dead: but go you and preach the kingdom of God."

And another also said, "Lord, I will follow you; but let me first go bid 17
them farewell, which are at home at my house." Jesus said unto him, "No
man, having put his hand to the plow, and looking back, is fit for the kingdom of God."

PART 7

Doctrines of Truth

Jesus spoke as one having authority. The doctrines He taught were from above, not from this world. His adversaries accused Him of transgressing the written Law of Moses and plotted to find fault with Him so that they could arrest Him. Yet Jesus confounded His opponents with answers of divine wisdom and moved through their company unseen. They ruled in darkness. He brought the Light.

> "BLESSED ARE THE EYES WHICH SEE THE THINGS THAT YOU SEE: FOR I TELL YOU, THAT MANY PROPHETS AND KINGS HAVE DESIRED TO SEE THOSE THINGS WHICH YOU SEE, AND HAVE NOT SEEN THEM; AND TO HEAR THOSE THINGS WHICH YOU HEAR, AND HAVE NOT HEARD THEM." (LUKE 10:23-24)

CHAPTER 26

THIRD MINISTRY AT JERUSALEM

"My Doctrine Is Not Mine"
John 7:10-24

But when his brethren were gone up, then went he also up unto the feast, not openly, but as it were in secret. Then the Jews sought him at the feast, and said, "Where is he?" And there was much murmuring among the people concerning him: for some said, "He is a good man:" others said, "No; but he deceives the people." Howbeit no man spoke openly of him for fear of the Jews. 1

Now about the middle of the feast Jesus went up into the temple, and taught. And the Jews marveled, saying, "How does this man know letters, having never studied?" Jesus answered them, and said, "My doctrine is not mine, but his that sent me. If any man will do his will, he shall know of the doctrine, whether it be of God, or whether I speak of myself. He that speaks of himself seeks his own glory: but he that seeks his glory that sent him, the same is true, and no unrighteousness is in him. 2

"Did not Moses give you the law, and yet none of you keeps the law? Why do you go about to kill me?" The people answered and said, "You have a demon: who goes about to kill you?" Jesus answered and said unto them, "I have done one work, and you all marvel. Moses therefore gave unto you circumcision; (not because it is of Moses, but of the fathers); and you on the sabbath day circumcise a man. If a man on the sabbath day receives circumcision, that the law of Moses should not be broken; are you angry at me, because I have made a man every bit whole on the sabbath day? Judge not according to the appearance, but judge righteous judgment." 3

"He That Sent Me Is True"
John 7:25-36

Then said some of them of Jerusalem, "Is not this he, whom they seek to kill? But, lo, he speaks boldly, and they say nothing unto him. Do 4

4 the rulers know indeed that this is the very Christ? Howbeit we know this man from where he is: but when Christ comes, no man knows from where he is."

5 Then cried Jesus in the temple as he taught, saying, "You both know me, and you know from where I am: and I am not come of myself, but he that sent me is true, whom you know not. But I know him: for I am from him, and he has sent me."

6 Then they sought to take him: but no man laid hands on him, because his hour was not yet come. And many of the people believed on him, and said, "When Christ comes, will he do more miracles than these which this man has done?"

7 The Pharisees heard that the people murmured such things concerning him; and the Pharisees and the chief priests sent officers to take him. Then Jesus said unto them, "Yet a little while am I with you, and then I go unto him that sent me. You shall seek me, and shall not find me: and where I am, there you cannot come."

8 Then the Jews said among themselves, "Where will he go, that we shall not find him? will he go unto the dispersed among the Gentiles, and teach the Gentiles? What manner of saying is this that he said, 'You shall seek me, and shall not find me: and where I am, there you cannot come?'"

"Rivers of Living Water"
John 7:37-44

9 In the last day, that great day of the feast, Jesus stood and cried, saying, "If any man thirsts, let him come unto me, and drink. He that believes on me, as the scripture has said, out of his heart shall flow rivers of living water." (But this spoke he of the Spirit, which they that believe on him should receive: for the Holy Ghost was not yet given; because Jesus was not yet glorified.)

10 Many of the people therefore, when they heard this saying, said, "Of a truth this is the Prophet." Others said, "This is the Christ." But some said, "Shall Christ come out of Galilee? Has not the scripture said, That Christ comes of the seed of David, and out of the town of Bethlehem, where David was?" So there was a division among the people because of him. And some of them would have taken him; but no man laid hands on him.

Leaders Dispute Over Jesus
John 7:45-53

11 Then came the officers to the chief priests and Pharisees; and they said

"NEVER MAN SPOKE LIKE THIS MAN."

unto them, "Why have you not brought him?" The officers answered, "Never man spoke like this man." Then the Pharisees answered them, "Are you also deceived? Have any of the rulers or of the Pharisees believed on him? But these people who do not know the law are accursed."

Nicodemus said unto them, (he that came to Jesus by night, being one 12 of them), "Does our law judge any man, before it hears him, and knows what he does?" They answered and said unto him, "Are you also of Galilee? Search, and look: for out of Galilee arises no prophet." And every man went unto his own house.

An Adulterous Woman Is Forgiven
John 8:1-11

Jesus went unto the Mount of Olives. And early in the morning he 13 came again into the temple, and all the people came unto him; and he sat down, and taught them. The scribes and Pharisees brought unto him a woman taken in adultery; and when they had set her in the midst, they said unto him, "Teacher, this woman was taken in adultery, in the very act."

"Now Moses in the law commanded us, that such should be stoned: 14 but what do you say?" This they said, tempting him, that they might have to accuse him. But Jesus stooped down, and with his finger wrote on the ground, as though he did not hear them.

So when they continued asking him, he lifted up himself, and said 15 unto them, "He that is without sin among you, let him first cast a stone at her." And again he stooped down, and wrote on the ground. They which heard it, being convicted by their own

> "HE THAT IS WITHOUT SIN AMONG YOU, LET HIM FIRST CAST A STONE."

conscience, went out one by one, beginning at the eldest, even unto the last: and Jesus was left alone, and the woman standing in the midst.

When Jesus had lifted up himself, and saw none but the woman, he 16 said unto her, "Woman, where are those your accusers? has no man condemned you?" She said, "No man, Lord." And Jesus said unto her, "Neither do I condemn you: go, and sin no more."

"I Am the Light of the World"
John 8:12-30

Then spoke Jesus again unto them, saying, "I am the light of the 17 world: he that follows me shall not walk in darkness, but shall have the light of life." The Pharisees therefore said unto him, "You bear witness of yourself; your witness is not true." Jesus answered and said unto them, "Though I bear witness of myself, yet my witness is true: for I know from where I came, and where I go; but you

> "I AM THE LIGHT OF THE WORLD: HE THAT FOLLOWS ME SHALL NOT WALK IN DARKNESS, BUT SHALL HAVE THE LIGHT OF LIFE."

cannot know from where I come, and where I go. You judge after the flesh; I judge no man. And yet if I judge, my judgment is true: for I am not alone, but I and the Father that sent me. It is also written in your law,

17 that the testimony of two men is true. I am one that bears witness of myself, and the Father that sent me bears witness of me."

18   Then they said unto him, "Where is your Father?" Jesus answered, "You neither know me, nor my Father: if you had known me, you should have known my Father also." These words Jesus spoke in the treasury, as he taught in the temple: and no man laid hands on him; for his hour was not yet come.

19   Then said Jesus again unto them, "I go my way, and you shall seek me, and shall die in your sins: where I go, you cannot come." Then the Jews said, "Will he kill himself? because he says, 'Where I go, you cannot come.'" And he said unto them, "You are from beneath; I am from above: you are of this world; I am not of this world. I said therefore unto you, that you shall die in your sins: for if you do not believe that I am he, you shall die in your sins."

20   Then they said unto him, "Who are you?" And Jesus said unto them, "Even the same that I said unto you from the beginning. I have many things to say and to judge of you: but he that sent me is true; and I speak to the world those things which I have heard of him." They did not understand that he spoke to them of the Father.

21   Then Jesus said unto them, "When you have lifted up the Son of man, then shall you know that I am he, and that I do nothing of myself; but as my Father has taught me, I speak these things. And he that sent me is with me: the Father has not left me alone; for I do always those things that please him." As he spoke these words, many believed on him.

"You Shall Know the Truth"
John 8:31-41

22   Then said Jesus to those Jews which believed on him, "If you continue in my word, then are you my disciples indeed; and you shall know the truth, and the truth shall make you free." They answered him, "We be Abraham's seed, and were never in bondage to any man: how do you say, 'You shall be made free?'"

> "YOU SHALL KNOW THE TRUTH, AND THE TRUTH SHALL MAKE YOU FREE."

23   Jesus answered them, "Truly, truly, I say unto you, Whosoever commits sin is the servant of sin. And the servant does not abide in the house for ever: but the Son abides ever. If the Son therefore shall make you free, you shall be free indeed. I know that you are Abraham's seed; but you seek to kill me, because my word has no place in you. I speak that which I have seen with my Father: and you do that which you have seen with your father."

> "WHOSOEVER COMMITS SIN IS THE SERVANT OF SIN."

24   They answered and said unto him, "Abraham is our father." Jesus said unto them, "If you were Abraham's children, you would do the works of Abraham. But now you seek to kill me, a man that has told you the truth,

which I have heard of God: this did not Abraham. You do the deeds of your 24
father." Then they said to him, "We be not born of fornication; we have one
Father, even God."

"I Tell You the Truth"
John 8:42-47

Jesus said unto them, "If God were your Father, you would love me: 25
for I proceeded forth and came from God; neither came I of myself, but he
sent me. Why do you not understand my speech? even because you cannot
hear my word. You are of your father the devil, and the lusts of your father
you will do. He was a murderer from the beginning, and dwelt not in the
truth, because there is no truth in him. When he speaks a lie, he speaks of
his own: for he is a liar, and the father of it. And because I tell you the truth,
you do not believe me.

"Which of you convicts me of sin? And if I say the truth, why do you 26
not believe me? He that is of God hears God's words: you therefore do not
hear them, because you are not of God."

"I Honor My Father"
John 8:48-59

Then answered the Jews, and said unto him, "Say we not rightly that 27
you are a Samaritan, and have a demon?" Jesus answered, "I have not a
demon; but I honor my Father, and you do dishonor me. And I seek not my
own glory: there is one that seeks and judges.

"Truly, truly, I say unto you, If a man keeps my saying, he shall 28
never see death." Then the Jews said unto him, "Now we know that you
have a demon. Abraham is dead, and
the prophets; and you say, 'If a man
keeps my saying, he shall never taste
of death.' Are you greater than our

> "IF A MAN KEEPS MY SAYING, HE SHALL NEVER SEE DEATH."

father Abraham, which is dead? and the prophets are dead: whom do you
make yourself?"

Jesus answered, "If I honor myself, my honor is nothing: it is my 29
Father that honors me; of whom you say, that he is your God: yet you have
not known him; but I know him: and if I should say, I do not know him, I
shall be a liar like you: but I know him, and keep his saying. Your father
Abraham rejoiced to see my day: and he saw it, and was glad."

Then the Jews said unto him, "You are not yet fifty years old, and have 30
you seen Abraham?" Jesus said unto
them, "Truly, truly, I say unto you,
Before Abraham was, I am." Then they
took up stones to cast at him: but Jesus

> "BEFORE ABRAHAM WAS, I AM."

hid himself, and went out of the temple, going through the midst of them,
and so passed by.

CHAPTER 27

MINISTERING IN JERUSALEM

Healing a Man Born Blind
John 9:1-12

1   And as Jesus passed by, he saw a man which was blind from his birth. And his disciples asked him, saying, "Rabbi, who did sin, this man, or his parents, that he was born blind?" Jesus answered, "Neither has this man sinned, nor his parents: but that the works of God should be made manifest in him. I must work the works of him that sent me, while it is day: the night comes, when no man can work. As long as I am in the world, I am the light of the world."

2   When he had thus spoken, he spit on the ground, and made clay of the saliva, and he anointed the eyes of the blind man with the clay, and said unto him, "Go, wash in the pool of Siloam," (which is by interpretation, Sent). He went his way therefore, and washed, and came seeing.

3   The neighbors therefore, and they which before had seen him that he was blind, said, "Is not this he that sat and begged?" Some said, "This is he:" others said, "He is like him:" but he said, "I am he."

4   Therefore they said unto him, "How were your eyes opened?" He answered and said, "A man that is called Jesus made clay, and anointed my eyes, and said unto me, 'Go to the pool of Siloam, and wash:' and I went and washed, and I received sight." Then they said unto him, "Where is he?" He said, "I know not."

Pharisees Reject Healed Man
John 9:13-34

5   They brought to the Pharisees him that before was blind. And it was the sabbath day when Jesus made the clay, and opened his eyes. Then again the Pharisees also asked him how he had received his sight. He said unto them, "He put clay upon my eyes, and I washed, and do see." Therefore said

some of the Pharisees, "This man is not of God, because he does not keep 5
the sabbath day." Others said, "How can a man that is a sinner do such miracles?" And there was a division among them. They said unto the blind man
again, "What do you say of him, that he has opened your eyes?" He said,
"He is a prophet."

But the Jews did not believe concerning him, that he had been blind, 6
and received his sight, until they called the parents of him that had received
his sight. And they asked them, saying, "Is this your son, who you say was
born blind? how then does he now see?"

His parents answered them and said, "We know that this is our son, 7
and that he was born blind: but by what means he now sees, we know not;
or who has opened his eyes, we know not: he is of age; ask him: he shall
speak for himself." These words spoke his parents, because they feared the
Jews: for the Jews had agreed already, that if any man did confess that he
was Christ, he should be put out of the synagogue. Therefore his parents
said, "He is of age; ask him."

Then again called they the man that was blind, and said unto him, 8
"Give God the praise: we know that this man is a sinner." He answered and
said, "Whether he be a sinner or not, I know not: one thing I know, that,
whereas I was blind, now I see."

Then they said to him again, "What did he to you? how opened he 9
your eyes?" He answered them, "I have told you already, and you did not
hear: why would you hear it again? will you also be his disciples?"

Then they insulted him, and said, "You are his disciple; but we are 10
Moses' disciples. We know that God spoke unto Moses: as for this fellow,
we know not from where he is."

The man answered and said unto them, "Why herein is a marvelous 11
thing, that you know not from where he is, and yet he has opened my eyes.
Now we know that God hears not sinners: but if any man be a worshiper of
God, and does his will, him he hears. Since the world began it was not heard
that any man opened the eyes of one that was born blind. If this man were
not of God, he could do nothing."

They answered and said unto him, "You were altogether born in sins, 12
and do you teach us?" And they cast him out.

Spiritual Blindness
John 9:35-41

Jesus heard that they had cast him out; and when he had found him, 13
he said unto him, "Do you believe on the Son of God?" He answered and
said, "Who is he, Lord, that I might believe on him?" And Jesus said unto
him, "You have both seen him, and it is he that talks with you." And he said,
"Lord, I believe." And he worshiped him. And Jesus said, "For judgment I
am come into this world, that they which see not might see; and that they
which see might be made blind."

14   And some of the Pharisees which were with him heard these words, and said unto him, "Are we blind also?" Jesus said unto them, "If you were blind, you should have no sin: but now you say, 'We see;' therefore your sin remains."

"I Am the Good Shepherd"
John 10:1-21

15   "Truly, truly, I say unto you, He that enters not by the door into the sheepfold, but climbs up some other way, the same is a thief and a robber. But he that enters in by the door is the shepherd of the sheep. To him the doorkeeper opens; and the sheep hear his voice: and he calls his own sheep by name, and leads them out. And when he puts forth his own sheep, he goes before them, and the sheep follow him: for they know his voice. And a stranger will they not follow, but will flee from him: for they do not know the voice of strangers." This illustration Jesus spoke unto them: but they did not understand what things they were which he spoke unto them.

16   Then said Jesus unto them again, "Truly, truly, I say unto you, I am the door of the sheep. All that ever came before me are thieves and robbers: but the sheep did not hear them. I am the door: by me if any man enters in, he shall be saved, and shall go in and out, and find pasture. The thief does not

> "I AM COME THAT THEY MIGHT HAVE LIFE, AND THAT THEY MIGHT HAVE IT MORE ABUNDANTLY."

come, except to steal, and to kill, and to destroy: I am come that they might have life, and that they might have it more abundantly.

17   "I am the good shepherd: the good shepherd gives his life for the sheep. But he that is a hireling, and not the shepherd, whose own the sheep are not, sees the wolf coming, and leaves the sheep, and flees: and the wolf catches them, and scatters the sheep. The hireling flees, because he is a hireling, and cares not for the sheep.

18   "I am the good shepherd, and know my sheep, and am known of mine. As the Father knows me, even so I know the Father: and I lay down my life for the sheep. And other sheep I have, which are not of this fold: them also I must bring, and they shall hear my voice; and there shall be one flock, and one shepherd. Therefore does my Father love me, because I lay down my life, that I might take it again. No man takes it from me, but I lay it down of myself. I have power to lay it down, and I have power to take it again. This commandment have I received of my Father."

19   There was a division therefore again among the Jews for these sayings. And many of them said, "He has a demon, and is gone mad; why do you hear him?" Others said, "These are not the words of him that has a demon. Can a demon open the eyes of the blind?"

CHAPTER 28

JESUS' MINISTRY MULTIPLIES

Seventy Sent Forth to Minister
Luke 10:1-12

1 After these things the Lord appointed seventy others also, and sent them two and two before his face into every city and place, where he himself would come. Therefore he said unto them, "The harvest truly is great, but the laborers are few: pray therefore the Lord of the harvest, that he would send forth laborers into his harvest. Go your ways: behold, I send you forth as lambs among wolves. Carry neither purse, nor bag, nor shoes: and greet no man on the road.

2 "And into whatsoever house you enter, first say, 'Peace be to this house.' And if the son of peace be there, your peace shall rest upon it: if not, it shall turn to you again. And in the same house remain, eating and drinking such things as they give: for the laborer is worthy of his wages. Go not from house to house.

3 "And into whatsoever city you enter, and they receive you, eat such things as are set before you: and heal the sick that are therein, and say unto them, 'The kingdom of God is come near unto you.'

4 "But into whatsoever city you enter, and they do not receive you, go your ways out into the streets of the same, and say, 'Even the very dust of your city, which cleaves on us, we do wipe off against you: nevertheless be sure of this, that the kingdom of God is come near unto you.' But I say unto you, that it shall be more tolerable in that day for Sodom, than for that city."

Jesus Laments for Four Cities
Matthew 11:20-24; Luke 10:13-16

5 Then he began to denounce the cities wherein most of his mighty works were done, because they had not repented: "Woe unto you, Chorazin! woe unto you, Bethsaida! for if the mighty works, which were done in you, had been done in Tyre and Sidon, they would have repented long ago, sitting

5 in sackcloth and ashes. But I say unto you, It shall be more tolerable for Tyre and Sidon at the day of judgment, than for you.

6   "And you, Capernaum, which are exalted unto heaven, shall be brought down to Hades: for if the mighty works, which have been done in you, had been done in Sodom, it would have remained until this day. But I say unto you, That it shall be more tolerable for the land of Sodom in the day of judgment, than for you.

7   "He that hears you hears me; and he that rejects you rejects me; and he that rejects me rejects him that sent me."

Seventy Return and Are Given Authority
Luke 10:17-20

8   And the seventy returned again with joy, saying, "Lord, even the demons are subject unto us through your name." And he said unto them,

> "REJOICE, BECAUSE YOUR NAMES ARE WRITTEN IN HEAVEN."

"I saw Satan fall as lightning from heaven. Behold, I give unto you authority to trample on serpents and scorpions, and over all the power of the enemy: and nothing shall by any means hurt you. Nevertheless in this rejoice not, that the spirits are subject unto you; but rather rejoice, because your names are written in heaven."

Jesus Rejoices in Spirit and Prayer
Matthew 11:25-30; Luke 10:21-24

9   In that hour Jesus rejoiced in spirit, and said, "I thank you, O Father, Lord of heaven and earth, that you have hidden these things from the wise and prudent, and have revealed them unto babies: even so, Father; for so it seemed good in your sight. All things are delivered to me of my Father: and no man knows who the Son is, but the Father; and who the Father is, but the Son, and he to whom the Son chooses to reveal him.

10   "Come unto me, all you that labor and are heavy laden, and I will give

> "COME UNTO ME, ALL YOU THAT LABOR AND ARE HEAVY LADEN, AND I WILL GIVE YOU REST."

you rest. Take my yoke upon you, and learn of me; for I am meek and lowly in heart: and you shall find rest unto your souls. For my yoke is easy, and my burden is light."

11   And he turned himself unto his disciples, and said privately, "Blessed are the eyes which see the things that you see: for I tell you, that many prophets and kings have desired to see those things which you see, and have not seen them; and to hear those things which you hear, and have not heard them."

Parable of the Good Samaritan
Luke 10:25-37

12   And, behold, a certain lawyer stood up, and tempted him, saying, "Teacher, what shall I do to inherit eternal life?" He said unto him, "What

is written in the law? how do you read?" And he answering said, *"You shall* 12
love the Lord your God with all your heart, and with all your soul, and with
all your strength, and with all your mind; and your neighbor as yourself."
And he said unto him, "You have answered rightly: this do, and you shall
live."

But he, willing to justify himself, said unto Jesus, "And who is my 13
neighbor?" And Jesus answering said, "A certain man went down from
Jerusalem to Jericho, and fell among thieves, which stripped him of his
clothing, and wounded him, and departed, leaving him half dead.

"And by chance there came down a certain priest that way: and when 14
he saw him, he passed by on the other side. And likewise a Levite, when he
was at the place, came and looked on him, and passed by on the other side.

"But a certain Samaritan, as he journeyed, came where he was: and 15
when he saw him, he had compassion on him, and went to him, and bound
up his wounds, pouring in oil and wine, and set him on his own animal, and
brought him to an inn, and took care of him. And the next day when he
departed, he took out two silver coins, and gave them to the host, and said
unto him, 'Take care of him; and whatsoever you spend more, when I come
again, I will repay you.'

"Which now of these three, do you think, was neighbor unto him that 16
fell among the thieves?" And he said, "He that showed mercy on him." Then
said Jesus unto him, "Go, and do likewise."

Jesus Visits Martha and Mary
Luke 10:38-42

Now it came to pass, as they went, that he entered into a certain vil- 17
lage: and a certain woman named Martha received him into her house. And
she had a sister called Mary, which also sat at Jesus' feet, and heard his
word. But Martha was distracted about much serving, and came to him, and
said, "Lord, do you not care that my sister has left me to serve alone? tell
her therefore that she help me." And Jesus answered and said unto her,
"Martha, Martha, you are anxious and troubled about many things: but one
thing is needful: and Mary has chosen that good part, which shall not be
taken away from her."

CHAPTER 29

Words of Truth to the Pharisees

Again: Prayer
Luke 11:1-4

1   And it came to pass, that, as he was praying in a certain place, when he ceased, one of his disciples said unto him, "Lord, teach us to pray, as John also taught his disciples." And he said unto them, "When you pray, say, Our Father which are in heaven, Hallowed be your name. Your kingdom come. Your will be done, as in heaven, so on earth. Give us day by day our daily bread. And forgive us our sins; for we also forgive everyone that is indebted to us. And lead us not into temptation; but deliver us from evil."

Parable of the Persistent Friend
Luke 11:5-13

2   He said unto them, "Which of you shall have a friend, and shall go unto him at midnight, and say unto him, 'Friend, lend me three loaves; for a friend of mine in his journey is come to me, and I have nothing to set before him'? He from within shall answer and say, 'Do not trouble me: the door is now shut, and my children are with me in bed; I cannot rise and give you.' I say unto you, Though he will not rise and give him, because he is his friend, yet because of his persistence he will rise and give him as many as he needs.

3   "And I say unto you, Ask, and it shall be given you; seek, and you shall find; knock, and it shall be opened unto you. For everyone that asks receives; and he that seeks finds; and to him that knocks it shall be opened.

4   "If a son shall ask for bread of any of you that is a father, will he give him a stone? or if he asks for a fish, will he for a fish give him a serpent? Or if he shall ask for an egg, will he offer him a scorpion? If you then, being evil, know how to give good gifts unto your children: how much more shall your heavenly Father give the Holy Spirit to them that ask him?"

Again: Jesus Is Not Beelzebub
Luke 11:14-23

5   He was casting out a demon, and it was mute. And it came to pass, when the demon was gone out, the mute spoke; and the people wondered.

But some of them said, "He casts out demons through Beelzebub the prince 5 of the demons." And others, tempting him, sought of him a sign from heaven.

But he, knowing their thoughts, said unto them, "Every kingdom 6 divided against itself is brought to desolation; and a house divided against a house falls. If Satan also be divided against himself, how shall his kingdom stand? because you say that I cast out demons through Beelzebub.

"And if I by Beelzebub cast out demons, by whom do your sons cast 7 them out? therefore shall they be your judges. But if I with the finger of God cast out demons, no doubt the kingdom of God is come upon you.

"When a strong man armed keeps his palace, his goods are in peace: but 8 when a stronger than he shall come upon him, and overcome him, he takes from him all his armor wherein he trusted, and divides his belongings. He that is not with me is against me: and he that gathers not with me scatters."

Again: Unclean Spirits
Luke 11:24-26

"When the unclean spirit is gone out of a man, it walks through dry 9 places, seeking rest; and finding none, it says, 'I will return unto my house from which I came out.' And when it comes, it finds it swept and put in order. Then it goes, and takes to itself seven other spirits more wicked than itself; and they enter in, and dwell there: and the last state of that man is worse than the first."

"Blessed Are They That Hear"
Luke 11:27-28

And it came to pass, as he spoke these things, a certain woman of the 10 company lifted up her voice, and said unto him, "Blessed is the womb that bore you, and the breasts which you have nursed." But he said, "Yes rather, blessed are they that hear the word of God, and keep it."

Again: Seeking a Sign
Luke 11:29-32

And when the people were gathered thickly together, he began to say, 11 "This is an evil generation: they seek a sign; and there shall no sign be given it, but the sign of Jonah the prophet. For as Jonah was a sign unto the Ninevites, so shall also the Son of man be to this generation.

"The queen of the south shall rise up in the judgment with the men of 12 this generation, and condemn them: for she came from the utmost parts of the earth to hear the wisdom of Solomon; and, behold, a greater than Solomon is here."

"The men of Nineveh shall rise up in the judgment with this genera- 13 tion, and shall condemn it: for they repented at the preaching of Jonah; and, behold, a greater than Jonah is here."

Again: Light of the World
Luke 11:33

"No man, when he has lit a lamp, puts it in a secret place, neither under 14 a tub, but on a lampstand, that they which come in may see the light."

Again: Light of the Body
Luke 11:34-36

15 "The light of the body is the eye: therefore when your eye is single, your whole body also is full of light; but when your eye is evil, your body also is full of darkness. Take heed therefore that the light which is in you be not darkness. If your whole body therefore be full of light, having no part dark, the whole shall be full of light, as when the bright shining of a lamp does give you light."

Woe! Pharisees and Lawyers
Luke 11:37-54

16 And as he spoke, a certain Pharisee asked him to dine with him: and he went in, and sat down to eat. And when the Pharisee saw it, he marveled that he had not first washed before dinner. The Lord said unto him, "Now do you Pharisees make clean the outside of the cup and the platter; but your inward part is full of greediness and wickedness. You fools, did not he that made that which is outside make that which is inside also? But rather give charitable deeds of such things as you have; and, behold, all things are clean unto you.

17 "But woe unto you, Pharisees! for you tithe mint and rue and all manner of herbs, and pass over judgment and the love of God: these ought you to have done, and not to leave the others undone.

18 "Woe unto you, Pharisees! for you love the uppermost seats in the synagogues, and greetings in the marketplaces.

19 "Woe unto you, scribes and Pharisees, hypocrites! for you are as graves which are not seen, and the men that walk over them are not aware of them."

20 Then answered one of the lawyers, and said unto him, "Teacher, thus saying you reproach us also." And he said, "Woe unto you also, you lawyers! for you load men with burdens grievous to be borne, and you yourselves do not touch the burdens with one of your fingers.

21 "Woe unto you! for you build the tombs of the prophets, and your fathers killed them. Truly you bear witness that you approve the deeds of your fathers: for they indeed killed them, and you build their tombs. Therefore also said the wisdom of God, I will send them prophets and apostles, and some of them they shall slay and persecute: that the blood of all the prophets, which was shed from the foundation of the world, may be required of this generation; from the blood of Abel unto the blood of Zacharias, which perished between the altar and the temple: yes I say unto you, It shall be required of this generation.

22 "Woe unto you, lawyers! for you have taken away the key of knowledge: you did not enter in yourselves, and them that were entering in you hindered."

23 As he said these things unto them, the scribes and the Pharisees began to urge him strongly, and to provoke him to speak of many things: laying wait for him, and seeking to catch something out of his mouth, that they might accuse him.

CHAPTER 30

THE KEYS OF THE KINGDOM

Beware of Hypocrisy
Luke 12:1-3

In the meantime, when there were gathered together an innumerable 1
multitude of people, insomuch that they trampled one upon another, he
began to say unto his disciples first of all, "Beware of the leaven of the
Pharisees, which is hypocrisy. For there is nothing covered, that shall not be
revealed; neither hidden, that shall not be known. Therefore whatsoever you
have spoken in darkness shall be heard in the light; and that which you have
spoken in the ear in inner rooms shall be proclaimed upon the housetops."

Whom Shall You Fear Most?
Luke 12:4-7

"And I say unto you my friends, Be not afraid of them that kill the 2
body, and after that have no more that they can do. But I will forewarn you
whom you shall fear: Fear him, which after he has killed has power to cast
into hell; yes, I say unto you, Fear him. Are not five sparrows sold for two
copper coins, and not one of them is forgotten before God? But even the
very hairs of your head are all numbered. Fear not therefore: you are of
more value than many sparrows."

Confess Christ Before Men
Luke 12:8-9

"Also I say unto you, Whosoever shall confess me before men, him 3
shall the Son of man also confess before the angels of God: but he that
denies me before men shall be denied before the angels of God."

Again: The One Unforgiven Sin
Luke 12:10-12

"And whosoever shall speak a word against the Son of man, it shall be 4
forgiven him: but unto him that blasphemes against the Holy Ghost it shall

4   not be forgiven. And when they bring you unto the synagogues, and unto magistrates, and authorities, worry not how or what thing you shall answer, or what you shall say: for the Holy Ghost shall teach you in the same hour what you ought to say."

Parable of the Rich Fool
Luke 12:13-21

5   One of the company said unto him, "Teacher, speak to my brother, that he divide the inheritance with me." He said unto him, "Man, who made me a judge or a divider over you?" He said unto them, "Take heed, and beware of covetousness: for a man's life consists not in the abundance of the things which he possesses."

6   And he spoke a parable unto them, saying, "The ground of a certain rich man brought forth plentifully: and he thought within himself, saying, 'What shall I do, because I have no room where to store my fruits?' And he said, 'This will I do: I will pull down my barns, and build greater; and there will I store all my fruits and my goods. And I will say to my soul, "Soul, you have many goods laid up for many years; take your ease, eat, drink, and be merry." ' But God said unto him, 'You fool, this night your soul shall be required of you: then whose shall those things be, which you have provided?' So is he that lays up treasure for himself, and is not rich toward God."

> "BEWARE OF COVETOUSNESS: FOR A MAN'S LIFE CONSISTS NOT IN THE ABUNDANCE OF THE THINGS WHICH HE POSSESSES."

Again: Consider This
Luke 12:22-34

7   He said unto his disciples, "Therefore I say unto you, Be not anxious for your life, what you shall eat; neither for the body, what you shall put on. The life is more than food, and the body is more than clothing. Consider the ravens: for they neither sow nor reap; which neither have storehouse nor barn; and God feeds them: how much more are you better than the birds? And which of you with worrying can add to his stature one cubit?

> "LIFE IS MORE THAN FOOD, AND THE BODY IS MORE THAN CLOTHING."

8   "If you then be not able to do that thing which is least, why be anxious for the rest? Consider the lilies how they grow: they toil not, they spin not; and yet I say unto you, that Solomon in all his glory was not arrayed like one of these. If then God so clothe the grass, which is today in the field, and tomorrow is cast into the oven; how much more will he clothe you, O you of little faith?

9   "And seek not what you shall eat, or what you shall drink, neither be of doubtful mind. For all these things do the nations of the world seek after:

and your Father knows that you have need of these things. But rather seek 9
the kingdom of God; and all these things shall be added unto you.

"Fear not, little flock; for it is your Father's good pleasure to give you 10
the kingdom. Sell that you have, and
give charitable deeds; provide yourselves bags which grow not old, a
treasure in the heavens that fails not,
where no thief approaches, neither
moth corrupts. For where your treasure is, there will your heart be also."

> "WHERE YOUR TREASURE IS, THERE WILL YOUR HEART BE ALSO."

Be as Watchful Servants
Luke 12:35-40

"Let your loins be girded about, and your lamps burning; and you 11
yourselves like men that wait for their master, when he will return from the
wedding; that when he comes and knocks, they may open unto him immediately. Blessed are those servants, whom the master when he comes shall
find watching: truly I say unto you, that he shall dress himself, and make
them to sit down to eat, and will come forth and serve them.

"And if he shall come in the second watch, or come in the third watch, 12
and find them so, blessed are those servants. And this know, that if the
owner of the house had known what hour the thief would come, he would
have watched, and not have allowed his house to be broken into. Be therefore ready also: for the Son of man comes at an hour when you think not."

Faithful and Wise Steward
Luke 12:41-48

Then Peter said unto him, "Lord, do you speak this parable unto us, or 13
even to all?" And the Lord said, "Who then is that faithful and wise steward, whom his master shall make ruler over his household, to give them their
portion of food in due season? Blessed is that servant, whom his master
when he comes shall find so doing. Of a truth I say unto you, that he will
make him ruler over all that he has.

"But and if that servant says in his heart, 'My master delays his com- 14
ing'; and shall begin to beat the men servants and women servants, and to
eat and drink, and to be drunk; the master of that servant will come in a day
when he does not look for him, and at an hour when he is not aware, and will
cut him in pieces, and will appoint him his portion with the unbelievers.

"And that servant, which knew his master's will, and prepared not 15
himself, neither did according to his
will, shall be beaten with many
stripes. But he that knew not, and did
commit things worthy of stripes, shall
be beaten with few stripes. For unto
whomsoever much is given, of him shall be much required: and to whom
men have committed much, of him they will ask the more."

> "UNTO WHOMSOEVER MUCH IS GIVEN, OF HIM SHALL BE MUCH REQUIRED."

"I Have a Baptism"
Luke 12:49-53

16   "I am come to send fire on the earth; and how I wish, that it be already kindled? But I have a baptism to be baptized with; and how I am distressed till it be accomplished!

17   "Do you suppose that I am come to give peace on earth? I tell you, No; but rather division: for from henceforth there shall be five in one house divided, three against two, and two against three. The father shall be divided against the son, and the son against the father; the mother against the daughter, and the daughter against the mother; the mother-in-law against her daughter-in-law, and the daughter-in-law against her mother-in-law."

"Discern This Time"
Luke 12:54-56

18   And he said also to the people, "When you see a cloud rise out of the west, straightway you say,' 'There comes a shower'; and so it is. And when you see the south wind blow, you say, 'There will be heat'; and it comes to pass. You hypocrites, you can discern the face of the sky and of the earth; but how is it that you do not discern this time?"

Again: Reconciliation
Luke 12:57-59

19   "Yes, and why even of yourselves do you not judge what is right? When you go with your adversary to the magistrate, as you are on the way, give diligence that you may be delivered from him; lest he drag you to the judge, and the judge deliver you to the officer, and the officer cast you into prison. I tell you, you shall not depart from there, till you have paid the very last small copper coin."

CHAPTER 31

JESUS ANSWERS HIS ADVERSARIES

Repent or Perish
Luke 13:1-5

There were present at that season some that told him of the Galileans, 1
whose blood Pilate had mingled with their sacrifices. And Jesus answering
said unto them, "Do you suppose that these Galileans were sinners above all
the Galileans, because they suffered such things? I tell you, No: but, except
you repent, you shall all likewise perish.

"Or those eighteen, upon whom the tower in Siloam fell, and killed them, 2
do you think that they were sinners above all men that dwelt in Jerusalem?
I tell you, No: but, except you repent, you shall all likewise perish."

Parable of the Barren Fig Tree
Luke 13:6-9

He spoke also this parable; "A certain man had a fig tree planted in his 3
vineyard; and he came and sought fruit thereon, and found none. Then he
said unto the dresser of his vineyard, 'Behold, these three years I come seeking fruit on this fig tree, and find none: cut it down; why does it use up the
ground?' And he answering said unto him, 'Master, let it alone this year
also, till I shall dig about it, and fertilize it: and if it bears fruit, well: and if
not, then after that you shall cut it down.'"

Healing on the Sabbath
Luke 13:10-17

He was teaching in one of the synagogues on the sabbath. And, behold, 4
there was a woman which had a spirit of infirmity eighteen years, and was
bowed together, and could in no way lift up herself. And when Jesus saw her,
he called her to him, and said unto her, "Woman, you are loosed from your
infirmity." And he laid his hands on her: and immediately she was made
straight, and glorified God.

5   And the ruler of the synagogue answered with indignation, because Jesus had healed on the sabbath day, and said unto the people, "There are six days in which men ought to work: in them therefore come and be healed, and not on the sabbath day." The Lord then answered him, and said, "You hypocrite, does not each one of you on the sabbath loose his ox or his donkey from the stall, and lead it away to watering? And ought not this woman, being a daughter of Abraham, whom Satan has bound, lo, these eighteen years, be loosed from this bond on the sabbath day?"

6   When he had said these things, all his adversaries were ashamed: and all the people rejoiced for all the glorious things that were done by him.

Again: Parable of Mustard Seed
Luke 13:18-19

7   Then he said, "Unto what is the kingdom of God like? and to what shall I compare it? It is like a grain of mustard seed, which a man took, and cast into his garden; and it grew, and became a great tree; and the birds of the air lodged in the branches of it."

Again: Parable of the Leaven
Luke 13:20-21

8   And again he said, "To what shall I liken the kingdom of God? It is like leaven, which a woman took and hid in three measures of meal, till the whole was leavened."

CHAPTER 32

⚬┈ FOURTH MINISTRY AT JERUSALEM ┈⚬

"The Father Is in Me, and I in Him."
John 10:22-38

And it was at Jerusalem the feast of the dedication, and it was winter. 1
Jesus walked in the temple in Solomon's porch. Then came the Jews round
about him, and said unto him, "How long do you make us to doubt? If you
be the Christ, tell us plainly." Jesus answered them, "I told you, and you
believed not: the works that I do in my Father's name, they bear witness of
me. But you do not believe, because you are not of my sheep, as I said unto
you. My sheep hear my voice, and I know them, and they follow me: and I
give unto them eternal life; and they shall never perish, neither shall any
man pluck them out of my hand. My Father, which gave them to me, is
greater than all; and no man is able to pluck them out of my Father's hand.
I and my Father are one."

Then the Jews took up stones again to stone him. Jesus answered 2
them, "Many good works have I shown you from my Father; for which of
those works do you stone me?" The Jews answered him, saying, "For a good
work we do not stone you; but for blasphemy; and because you, being a
man, make yourself God."

Jesus answered them, "Is it not written in your law, 'I said, "You are 3
gods" '? If he called them gods, unto whom the word of God came, and the
scripture cannot be broken; you say of him, whom the Father has sanctified,
and sent into the world, 'You blaspheme'; because I said, 'I am the Son of
God'? If I do not the works of my Father, do not believe me. But if I do,
though you do not believe me, believe the works: that you may know, and
believe, that the Father is in me, and I in him."

Return to Place of John's Baptism
John 10:39-42

Therefore they sought again to take him: but he escaped out of their 4
hand, and went away again beyond Jordan into the place where John at first
baptized; and there he stayed. And many came unto him, and said, "John did
no miracle: but all things that John spoke of this man were true." Many
believed on him there.

PART 8

SERVING AND SERVITUDE

Jesus showed no preference of persons. Understanding that the rich can be poor in spirit, and the poor can be rich in spirit, He taught humility and deference as the true signets of grace. He instructed those who would follow Him to exchange the love of material things for the love of God, knowing that which we serve will become our master. He gave the promise that those who love God will one day be lifted up above those who love the world. In that day, the first shall be last and the last shall be first.

> "THEY SHALL COME FROM THE EAST, AND FROM THE WEST, AND FROM THE NORTH, AND FROM THE SOUTH, AND SHALL SIT DOWN IN THE KINGDOM OF GOD. AND, BEHOLD, THERE ARE LAST WHICH SHALL BE FIRST, AND THERE ARE FIRST WHICH SHALL BE LAST." (LUKE 13:29-30)

CHAPTER 33

THE COST OF SERVING

The Gateway to the Kingdom
Luke 13:22-30

And he went through the cities and villages, teaching, and journeying 1 toward Jerusalem. Then said one unto him, "Lord, are there few that be saved?" He said unto them, "Strive to enter in at the strait gate: for many, I say unto you, will seek to enter in, and shall not be able.

"When once the master of the house is risen up, and has shut the door, 2 and you begin to stand outside, and to knock at the door, saying, 'Lord, Lord, open unto us'; and he shall answer and say unto you, 'I know not from where you are': then shall you begin to say, 'We have eaten and drunk in your presence, and you have taught in our streets.' But he shall say, 'I tell you, I know not from where you are; depart from me, all you workers of iniquity.'

"There shall be weeping and gnashing of teeth, when you shall see 3 Abraham, and Isaac, and Jacob, and all the prophets, in the kingdom of God, and you yourselves thrust out. And they shall come from the east, and from the west, and from the north, and from the south, and shall sit down in the kingdom of God. And, behold, there are last which shall be first, and there are first which shall be last."

Jesus Laments for Jerusalem
Luke 13:31-35

The same day there came certain of the Pharisees, saying unto him, 4 "Get out, and depart from here: for Herod will kill you." And he said unto them, "Go, and tell that fox, 'Behold, I cast out demons, and I do cures today and tomorrow, and the third day I shall be perfected.' Nevertheless I must walk today, and tomorrow, and the day following: for it cannot be that a prophet perish outside of Jerusalem.

"O Jerusalem, Jerusalem, which kill the prophets, and stone them that 5 are sent unto you; how often would I have gathered your children together,

5   as a hen does gather her brood under her wings, and you would not! Behold, your house is left unto you desolate: and truly I say unto you, You shall not see me, until the time comes when you shall say, *Blessed is he that comes in the name of the Lord.*"

Man Healed on the Sabbath Day
Luke 14:1-6

6   And it came to pass, as he went into the house of one of the chief Pharisees to eat bread on the sabbath day, that they watched him. And, behold, there was a certain man before him which had the dropsy. Jesus answering spoke unto the lawyers and Pharisees, saying, "Is it lawful to heal on the sabbath day?" And they held their peace. He took him, and healed him, and let him go; and answered them, saying, "Which of you shall have a donkey or an ox fallen into a pit, and will not straightway pull it out on the sabbath day?" They could not answer him again to these things.

Parable of the Wedding Guest
Luke 14:7-11

7   He put forth a parable to those which were invited, when he noticed how they chose out the chief places; saying unto them, "When you are invited of any man to a wedding, do not sit down in the highest place; lest a more prominent man than you be invited of him; and he that invited you and him come and say to you, 'Give this man your place'; and you begin with shame to take the lowest place.

8   "But when you are invited, go and sit down in the lowest place; that when he that invited you comes, he may say unto you, 'Friend, go up higher': then shall you have honor in the presence of them that sit at the table with you. For whosoever exalts himself shall be humbled; and he that humbles himself shall be exalted."

> "HE THAT HUMBLES HIMSELF SHALL BE EXALTED."

Parable of the Great Repayment
Luke 14:12-14

9   Then he said also to him that invited him, "When you make a dinner or a supper, call not your friends, nor your brethren, neither your relatives, nor your rich neighbors; lest they also invite you in return, and a repayment be made you. But when you make a feast, call the poor, the maimed, the lame, the blind: and you shall be blessed; for they cannot repay you: for you shall be repaid at the resurrection of the just."

Parable of the Great Supper
Luke 14:15-24

10   When one of them that sat at the table with him heard these things, he said unto him, "Blessed is he that shall eat bread in the kingdom of God." Then said he unto him, "A certain man made a great supper, and invited

many: and sent his servant at supper time to say to them that were invited, 10 'Come; for all things are now ready.'

"And they all with one purpose began to make excuses. The first said 11 unto him, 'I have bought a piece of ground, and I must of necessity go and see it: I ask you have me excused.' And another said, 'I have bought five yoke of oxen, and I go to test them: I ask you have me excused.' And another said, 'I have married a wife, and therefore I cannot come.'

"So that servant came, and showed his master these things. Then the 12 master of the house being angry said to his servant, 'Go out quickly into the streets and lanes of the city, and bring in here the poor, and the maimed, and the lame, and the blind.' And the servant said, 'Master, it is done as you have commanded, and yet there is room.' And the master said unto the servant, 'Go out into the highways and country roads, and compel them to come in, that my house may be filled. For I say unto you, That none of those men which were invited shall taste of my supper.'"

Counting the Cost to Follow
Luke 14:25-33

And there went great multitudes with him: and he turned, and said 13 unto them, "If any man comes to me, and does not hate his father, and mother, and wife, and children, and brethren, and sisters, yes, and his own life also, he cannot be my disciple. Whosoever does not bear his cross, and come after me, cannot be my disciple.

> "WHOSOEVER DOES NOT BEAR HIS CROSS, AND COME AFTER ME, CANNOT BE MY DISCIPLE."

"For which of you, intending to build a tower, sits not down first, and 14 counts the cost, whether he has sufficient to finish it? Lest perhaps, after he has laid the foundation, and is not able to finish it, all that behold it begin to mock him, saying, 'This man began to build, and was not able to finish.'

"Or what king, going to make war against another king, sits not down 15 first, and consults whether he be able with ten thousand to meet him that comes against him with twenty thousand? Or else, while the other is yet a great way off, he sends a delegation, and desires conditions of peace. So likewise, whosoever he be of you that forsakes not all that he has, he cannot be my disciple."

Again: Salt of the Earth
Luke 14:34-35

"Salt is good: but if the salt has lost its savor, with what shall it be sea- 16 soned? It is neither fit for the land, nor even for the waste pile; but men cast it out. He that has ears to hear, let him hear."

CHAPTER 34

THE RESPONSIBILITIES OF SERVING

Again: Parable of the Lost Sheep
Luke 15:1-7

1   Then drew near unto him all the tax collectors and sinners to hear him. And the Pharisees and scribes murmured, saying, "This man receives sinners, and eats with them."

2   And he spoke this parable unto them, saying, "What man of you, having a hundred sheep, if he loses one of them, does not leave the ninety and nine in the wilderness, and go after that which is lost, until he finds it? And when he has found it, he lays it on his shoulders, rejoicing. And when he comes home, he calls together his friends and neighbors, saying unto them, 'Rejoice with me; for I have found my sheep which was lost.' I say unto you, that likewise joy shall be in heaven over one sinner that repents, more than over ninety and nine just persons, which need no repentance."

Parable of the Lost Coin
Luke 15:8-10

3   "Or what woman having ten pieces of silver, if she loses one piece, does not light a lamp, and sweep the house, and seek diligently till she finds it? And when she has found it, she calls her friends and her neighbors together, saying, 'Rejoice with me; for I have found the piece which I had lost.' Likewise, I say unto you, there is joy in the presence of the angels of God over one sinner that repents."

Parable of the Prodigal Son
Luke 15:11-32

4   And he said, "A certain man had two sons: and the younger of them said to his father, 'Father, give me the portion of goods that falls to me.' And he divided unto them his livelihood. Not many days afterward the younger son gathered all together, and took his journey into a far country, and there

wasted his possessions with reckless living. When he had spent all, there 4
arose a mighty famine in that land; and he began to be in need. He went and
joined himself to a citizen of that country; and he sent him into his fields to
feed swine. He would gladly have filled his belly with the husks that the
swine did eat: and no man gave unto him.

"And when he came to himself, he said, 'How many hired servants of 5
my father's have bread enough and to spare, and I perish with hunger! I will
arise and go to my father, and will say unto him, "Father, I have sinned
against heaven, and before you, and am no more worthy to be called your
son: make me as one of your hired servants."' He arose, and came to his
father. But when he was yet a great way off, his father saw him, and had
compassion, and ran, and fell on his neck, and kissed him. The son said unto
him, 'Father, I have sinned against heaven, and in your sight, and am no
more worthy to be called your son.'

"But the father said to his servants, 'Bring forth the best robe, and put 6
it on him; and put a ring on his hand, and shoes on his feet: and bring here the
fatted calf, and kill it; and let us eat, and be merry: for this my son was dead,
and is alive again; he was lost, and is found.' And they began to be merry.

"Now his older son was in the field: and as he came and drew near to 7
the house, he heard music and dancing. He called one of the servants, and
asked what these things meant. He said unto him, 'Your brother is come;
and your father has killed the fatted calf, because he has received him safe
and sound.'

"And he was angry, and would not go in: therefore his father came out, 8
and pleaded with him. He answering said to his father, 'Lo, these many
years do I serve you, neither trans-
gressed I at any time your commandment: and yet you never gave me a
young goat, that I might make merry
with my friends: but as soon as this

> SON, YOU ARE EVER WITH ME,
> AND ALL THAT I HAVE IS
> YOURS.

your son was come, which has devoured your livelihood with harlots, you
have killed for him the fatted calf.' And he said unto him, 'Son, you are ever
with me, and all that I have is yours. It was fitting that we should make
merry, and be glad: for this your brother was dead, and is alive again; and
was lost, and is found.'"

Parable of the Shrewd Steward
Luke 16:1-13

He said also unto his disciples, "There was a certain rich man, 9
which had a steward; and the same was accused unto him that he had
wasted his goods. And he called him, and said unto him, 'How is it that
I hear this of you? give an account of your stewardship; for you may be
no longer steward.' Then the steward said within himself, 'What shall I
do? for my master takes away from me the stewardship: I cannot dig; to
beg I am ashamed. I am resolved what to do, that, when I am put out of
the stewardship, they may receive me into their houses.'

10   "So he called every one of his master's debtors unto him, and said unto the first, 'How much do you owe unto my master?' And he said, 'A hundred measures of oil.' He said unto him, 'Take your bill, and sit down quickly, and write fifty.' Then he said to another, 'And how much do you owe?' He said, 'A hundred measures of wheat.' And he said unto him, 'Take your bill, and write eighty.'

11   "And the master commended the unjust steward, because he had done shrewdly: for the children of this world are in their generation more shrewd than the children of light. And I say unto you, Make to yourselves friends of the money of unrighteousness; that, when you fail, they may receive you into everlasting dwellings. He that is faithful in that which is least is faithful also in much: and he that is unjust in the least is unjust also in much.

12   "If therefore you have not been faithful in the unrighteous money, who will commit to your trust the true riches? And if you have not been faithful in that which is another man's, who shall give you that which is your own? No servant can serve two masters: for either he will hate the one, and love the other; or else he will hold to the one, and despise the other. You cannot serve God and money."

The Law and the Prophets
Luke 16:14-17

13   And the Pharisees also, who were covetous, heard all these things: and they scoffed at him. He said unto them, "You are they which justify yourselves before men; but God knows your hearts: for that which is highly esteemed among men is abomination in the sight of God.

14   "The law and the prophets were until John: since that time the kingdom of God is preached, and every man presses into it. And it is easier for heaven and earth to pass, than one little stroke of the law to fail."

Again: Divorce
Luke 16:18

15   "Whosoever puts away his wife, and marries another, commits adultery: and whosoever marries her that is put away from her husband commits adultery."

Rich Man and Beggar Lazarus
Luke 16:19-31

16   "There was a certain rich man, which was clothed in purple and fine linen, and feasted sumptuously every day: and there was a certain beggar named Lazarus, which was laid at his gate, full of sores, and desiring to be fed with the crumbs which fell from the rich man's table: moreover the dogs came and licked his sores.

17   "And it came to pass, that the beggar died, and was carried by the angels into Abraham's bosom: the rich man also died, and was buried; and in Hades he lifted up his eyes, being in torments, and saw Abraham afar off, and Lazarus in his bosom. He cried and said, 'Father Abraham, have mercy

on me, and send Lazarus, that he may dip the tip of his finger in water, and 17
cool my tongue; for I am tormented in this flame.'

"But Abraham said, 'Son, remember that you in your lifetime 18
received your good things, and likewise Lazarus evil things: but now he is
comforted, and you are tormented. And besides all this, between us and
you there is a great gulf fixed: so that they which would pass from here to
you cannot; neither can they pass to us, that would come from there.'

"Then he said, 'I beg you therefore, father, that you would send him to 19
my father's house: for I have five brethren; that he may testify unto them,
lest they also come into this place of torment.' Abraham said unto him,
'They have Moses and the prophets; let them hear them.' And he said, 'No,
father Abraham: but if one went unto them from the dead, they will repent.'

"And he said unto him, 'If they hear not Moses and the prophets, nei- 20
ther will they be persuaded, though one rose from the dead.' "

The Reward for Causing Sin
Luke 17:1-2

Then he said unto the disciples, "It is impossible that no causes to sin 21
will come: but woe unto him, through whom they come! It would be better
for him that a millstone were hung around his neck, and he cast into the sea,
than that he should cause one of these little ones to sin."

Forgiving Those Who Repent of Sin
Luke 17:3-4

"Take heed to yourselves: If your brother trespasses against you, 22
rebuke him; and if he repents, forgive him. And if he trespasses against you
seven times in a day, and seven times in a day turns again to you, saying, 'I
repent'; you shall forgive him."

The Power of Faith
Luke 17:5-6

The apostles said unto the Lord, "Increase our faith." And the Lord 23
said, "If you had faith as a grain of mustard seed, you might say unto this
mulberry tree, 'Be plucked up by the root, and be planted in the sea'; and it
should obey you."

Duties of a Servant
Luke 17:7-10

"But which of you, having a servant plowing or feeding sheep, will say 24
unto him at once, when he is come from the field, 'Go and sit down to eat'?
And will not rather say unto him, 'Make ready with what I may dine, and
dress yourself, and serve me, till I have eaten and drunk'; and afterward you
shall eat and drink'? Does he thank that servant because he did the things
that were commanded him? I think not. So likewise you, when you shall
have done all those things which are commanded you, say, 'We are unprofitable servants: we have done that which was our duty to do.' "

CHAPTER 35

⸱⸱ Lazarus Raised From the Dead ⸱⸱

"Lazarus Is Dead"
John 11:1-16

1   Now a certain man was sick, named Lazarus, of Bethany, the town of Mary and her sister Martha. (It was that Mary which anointed the Lord with ointment, and wiped his feet with her hair, whose brother Lazarus was sick.) Therefore his sisters sent unto him, saying, "Lord, behold, he whom you love is sick." When Jesus heard that, he said, "This sickness is not unto death, but for the glory of God, that the Son of God might be glorified thereby." Now Jesus loved Martha, and her sister, and Lazarus.

2   When he had heard therefore that he was sick, he stayed two days still in the same place where he was. Then after that he said to his disciples, "Let us go into Judea again." His disciples say unto him, "Rabbi, the Jews of late sought to stone you; and do you go there again?" Jesus answered, "Are there not twelve hours in the day? If any man walks in the day, he does not stumble, because he sees the light of this world. But if a man walks in the night, he stumbles, because there is no light in him."

3   These things said he: and after that he said unto them, "Our friend Lazarus sleeps; but I go, that I may awake him out of sleep." Then said his disciples, "Lord, if he sleeps, he shall get well." Howbeit Jesus spoke of his death: but they thought that he had spoken of taking of rest in sleep.

4   Then Jesus said unto them plainly, "Lazarus is dead. And I am glad for your sakes that I was not there, to the intent you may believe; nevertheless let us go unto him." Then said Thomas, which is called Didymus, unto his fellow disciples, "Let us also go, that we may die with him."

"I Am the Resurrection"
John 11:17-27

5   Then when Jesus came, he found that he had lain in the grave four days already. Now Bethany was near unto Jerusalem, about two miles away:

and many of the Jews came to Martha and Mary, to comfort them concern- 5
ing their brother. Then Martha, as soon as she heard that Jesus was coming,
went and met him: but Mary sat still in the house. Then Martha said unto
Jesus, "Lord, if you had been here, my brother would not have died. But I
know, that even now, whatsoever you will ask of God, God will give you."

Jesus said unto her, "Your brother shall rise again." Martha said 6
unto him, "I know that he shall rise again in the resurrection at the last
day." Jesus said unto her, "I am the
resurrection, and the life: he that
believes in me, though he were dead,
yet shall he live: and whosoever lives
and believes in me shall never die.
Do you believe this?" She said unto

> "I AM THE RESURRECTION, AND
> THE LIFE: HE THAT BELIEVES IN
> ME, THOUGH HE WERE DEAD,
> YET SHALL HE LIVE."

him, "Yes, Lord: I believe that you are the Christ, the Son of God, which
should come into the world."

Jesus Weeps
John 11:28-37

And when she had so said, she went her way, and called Mary her sis- 7
ter secretly, saying, "The Teacher is come, and calls for you." As soon as she
heard that, she arose quickly, and came unto him. Now Jesus was not yet
come into the town, but was in that place where Martha met him. The Jews
then which were with her in the house, and comforted her, when they saw
Mary, that she rose up hastily and went out, followed her, saying, "She goes
unto the grave to weep there."

Then when Mary was come where Jesus was, and saw him, she fell 8
down at his feet, saying unto him, "Lord, if you had been here, my brother
would not have died." When Jesus therefore saw her weeping, and the Jews
also weeping which came with her, he groaned in the spirit, and was troubled, and said, "Where have you laid him?" They said unto him, "Lord,
come and see." Jesus wept. Then said the Jews, "Behold how he loved him!"
And some of them said, "Could not this man, which opened the eyes of the
blind, have caused that even this man should not have died?"

Restoring Life to Lazarus
John 11:38-46

Jesus therefore again groaning in himself came to the grave. It was a 9
cave, and a stone lay upon it. Jesus said, "Take away the stone." Martha, the
sister of him that was dead, said unto him, "Lord, by this time he stinks: for
he has been dead four days." Jesus said unto her, "Said I not unto you, that,
if you would believe, you should see the glory of God?"

Then they took away the stone from the place where the dead was laid. 10
And Jesus lifted up his eyes, and said, "Father, I thank you that you have
heard me. And I knew that you hear me always: but because of the people
which stand by I said it, that they may believe that you have sent me." And

10 when he thus had spoken, he cried with a loud voice, "Lazarus, come forth." And he that was dead came forth, bound hand and foot with graveclothes: and his face was bound about with a cloth. Jesus said unto them, "Loose him, and let him go."

11 Then many of the Jews which came to Mary, and had seen the things which Jesus did, believed on him. But some of them went their ways to the Pharisees, and told them what things Jesus had done.

Priests Plot to Kill Jesus
John 11:47-54

12 Then gathered the chief priests and the Pharisees a council, and said, "What do we? for this man does many miracles. If we let him alone like this, all men will believe on him: and the Romans shall come and take away both our place and nation."

13 And one of them, named Caiaphas, being the high priest that same year, said unto them, "You know nothing at all, nor consider that it is expedient for us, that one man should die for the people, and that the whole nation not perish." And this spoke he not of himself: but being high priest that year, he prophesied that Jesus should die for that nation; and not for that nation only, but that also he should gather together in one the children of God that were scattered abroad. Then from that day forth they plotted together to put him to death.

14 Jesus therefore walked no more openly among the Jews; but went from there unto a country near to the wilderness, into a city called Ephraim, and there continued with his disciples.

PART 9

FINAL JOURNEY

Jesus began His last journey to Jerusalem knowing that betrayal and death awaited Him. Still He continued, teaching through healings and parables that the kingdom of heaven is not attained through intellect, riches, and pride—but rather that gratitude, childlike humility, and virtue embody the spiritual essence and power of Christ. Those who possess such qualities are assured that the kingdom of heaven is not a distant hope, but a very present reality here and now.

> THEN HE TOOK UNTO HIM THE TWELVE, AND
> SAID UNTO THEM, "BEHOLD, WE GO UP TO
> JERUSALEM, AND ALL THINGS THAT ARE WRITTEN
> BY THE PROPHETS CONCERNING THE SON OF
> MAN SHALL BE ACCOMPLISHED."   (LUKE 18:31)

CHAPTER 36

LIVING THE KINGDOM LIFE

Jesus Cleanses Ten Lepers
Luke 17:11-19

1   And it came to pass, as he went to Jerusalem, that he passed through the midst of Samaria and Galilee. And as he entered into a certain village, there met him ten men that were lepers, which stood afar off: and they lifted up their voices, and said, "Jesus, Master, have mercy on us." And when he saw them, he said unto them, "Go show yourselves unto the priests." And it came to pass, that, as they went, they were cleansed.

2   One of them, when he saw that he was healed, turned back, and with a loud voice glorified God, and fell down on his face at his feet, giving him thanks: and he was a Samaritan. And Jesus answering said, "Were there not ten cleansed? but where are the nine? There are not found that returned to give glory to God, except this foreigner." And he said unto him, "Arise, go your way: your faith has made you whole."

About the Coming of the Kingdom
Luke 17:20-37

3   When he was asked of the Pharisees, when the kingdom of God should come, he answered them and said, "The kingdom of God comes not with observation: neither shall they say, 'Lo here!' or, 'lo there!' for, behold, the kingdom of God is within you."

4   And he said unto the disciples, "The days will come, when you shall desire to see one of the days of the Son of man, and you shall not see it. And they shall say to you, 'See here'; or, 'see there': go not after them, nor follow them. For as the lightning, that flashes out of the one part under heaven, shines unto the other part under heaven; so shall also the Son of man be in his day. But first he must suffer many things, and be rejected of this generation.

5   "And as it was in the days of Noah, so shall it be also in the days of the Son of man. They did eat, they drank, they married wives, they were

given in marriage, until the day that Noah entered into the ark, and the flood 5
came, and destroyed them all. Likewise also as it was in the days of Lot;
they did eat, they drank, they bought, they sold, they planted, they built; but
the same day that Lot went out of Sodom it rained fire and brimstone from
heaven, and destroyed them all.

"Even thus shall it be in the day when the Son of man is revealed. In 6
that day, he which shall be upon the housetop, and his stuff in the house, let
him not come down to take it away: and he that is in the field, let him likewise not return back. Remember Lot's wife. Whosoever shall seek to save
his life shall lose it; and whosoever shall lose his life shall preserve it.

"I tell you, in that night there shall be two men in one bed; the one 7
shall be taken, and the other shall be left. Two women shall be grinding
together; the one shall be taken, and the other left. Two men shall be in the
field; the one shall be taken, and the other left."

They answered and said unto him, "Where, Lord?" And he said 8
unto them, "Wheresoever the body is, there will the eagles be gathered
together."

Parable of the Persistent Widow
Luke 18:1-8

And he spoke a parable unto them to this end, that men ought always 9
to pray, and not to lose heart; saying, "There was in a city a judge, which
feared not God, neither respected man:
and there was a widow in that city; and

> MEN OUGHT ALWAYS TO PRAY,
> AND NOT TO LOSE HEART.

she came unto him, saying, 'Avenge
me of my adversary.' And he would
not for a while: but afterward he said within himself, 'Though I fear not
God, nor respect man; yet because this widow troubles me, I will avenge
her, lest by her continual coming she wearies me.'"

The Lord said, "Hear what the unjust judge says. And shall not God 10
avenge his own elect, which cry day and night unto him, though he delays
long with them? I tell you that he will avenge them speedily. Nevertheless
when the Son of man comes, shall he find faith on the earth?"

Parable of the Self-Righteous Pharisee
Luke 18:9-14

And he spoke this parable unto certain which trusted in themselves 11
that they were righteous, and despised others: "Two men went up into the
temple to pray; the one a Pharisee, and the other a tax collector.

"The Pharisee stood and prayed thus with himself, 'God, I thank you, 12
that I am not as other men are, extortioners, unjust, adulterers, or even as
this tax collector. I fast twice in the week, I give tithes of all that I possess.'

"And the tax collector, standing afar off, would not lift up so much as 13
his eyes unto heaven, but struck down upon his breast, saying, 'God be merciful to me a sinner.' I tell you, this man went down to his house justified

13 rather than the other: for everyone that exalts himself shall be humbled; and he that humbles himself shall be exalted."

About Marriage and Divorce
Matthew 19:1-9; Mark 10:1-12

14   And it came to pass, that when Jesus had finished these sayings, he departed from Galilee, and came into the region of Judea beyond Jordan; and great multitudes followed him; and he healed them there: and, as he was accustomed, he taught them again.

15   The Pharisees also came unto him, tempting him, and saying unto him, "Is it lawful for a man to put away his wife for every cause?" And he answered and said unto them, "What did Moses command you?" And they said, "Moses gave permission to *write a bill of divorcement, and to put her away*." And Jesus answered and said unto them, "For the hardness of your heart he wrote you this precept."

16   He answered and said unto them, "Have you not read, that God which made them at the beginning of the creation *made them male and female,* and said, '*For this cause shall a man leave father and mother, and shall cleave to his wife: and they two shall be one flesh*'? Therefore they are no more two, but one flesh. What therefore God has joined together, let not man put asunder."

> "WHAT THEREFORE GOD HAS JOINED TOGETHER, LET NOT MAN PUT ASUNDER."

17   They said unto him, "Why did Moses then give permission to *give a writing of divorcement, and to put her away?*" He said unto them, "Moses because of the hardness of your hearts permitted you to put away your wives: but from the beginning it was not so. And I say unto you, Whosoever shall put away his wife, except it be for fornication, and shall marry another, commits adultery: and whoever marries her which is put away does commit adultery."

18   And in the house his disciples asked him again of the same matter. He said unto them, "Whosoever shall put away his wife, and marry another, commits adultery against her. If a woman shall put away her husband, and be married to another, she commits adultery."

About Celibacy
Matthew 19:10-12

19   His disciples said unto him, "If the case of the man be so with his wife, it is not good to marry." But he said unto them, "All men cannot receive this saying, except they to whom it is given. For there are some eunuchs, which were so born from their mother's womb: and there are some eunuchs, which were made eunuchs of men: and there be eunuchs, which have made themselves eunuchs for the kingdom of heaven's sake. He that is able to receive it, let him receive it."

CHAPTER 37

GAINING ETERNAL LIFE

Blessing Little Children
Matthew 19:13-15; Mark 10:13-16; Luke 18:15-17

Then were there brought unto him little children, that he should put his 1
hands on them, and pray: and they brought unto him also infants, that he
would touch them: but when his disciples saw it, they rebuked those that
brought them. But when Jesus saw it, he was much displeased, and said unto
them, "Allow the little children to come unto me, and do not forbid them:
for of such is the kingdom of God." Jesus called them unto him, and said,
"Truly I say unto you, Whosoever shall not receive the kingdom of God as
a little child shall in no way enter therein." And he took them up in his arms,
put his hands upon them, and blessed them, and departed from there.

The Rich Ruler and Eternal Life
Matthew 19:16-22; Mark 10:17-22; Luke 18:18-23

And when he was gone forth into the road, behold, there came a cer- 2
tain ruler running, and kneeled to him, and asked him, saying, "Good
Teacher, what good thing shall I do, that I may inherit eternal life?" Jesus
said unto him, "Why do you call me good? there is none good but one, that
is, God: but if you would enter into life, keep the commandments."

He said unto him, "Which?" Jesus said, "You know the command- 3
ments, '*You shall do no murder, You shall not commit adultery, You shall not
steal, You shall not bear false witness, Defraud not, Honor your father and
your mother: and, You shall love your neighbor as yourself.*'"

The young man answered and said unto him, "Teacher, all these have 4
I observed from my youth: what lack I yet?" Then Jesus beholding him
loved him, and said unto him, "If you would be perfect, one thing you lack:
go your way, sell whatsoever you have, and give to the poor, and you shall
have treasure in heaven: and come, take up the cross, and follow me."

5   But when the young man heard this, he was very sorrowful: for he was very rich. And he was sad at that saying, and went away grieved: for he had great possessions.

All Things Are Possible With God
Matthew 19:23-30; Mark 10:23-31; Luke 18:24-30

6   And when Jesus saw that he was very sorrowful, he looked round about, and said unto his disciples, "How hard shall they that have riches find it to enter into the kingdom of God!" The disciples were astonished at his words. But Jesus answered again, and said unto them, "Children, how hard it is for them that trust in riches to enter into the kingdom of God! It is easier for a camel to go through the eye of a needle, than for a rich man to enter into the kingdom of God."

7   When his disciples heard it, they were astonished out of measure, saying among themselves, "Who then can be saved?" Jesus looking upon them said, "With men it is impossible, but not with God: for the things which are impossible with men are possible with God. For with God all things are possible."

> "THE THINGS WHICH ARE IMPOSSIBLE WITH MEN ARE POSSIBLE WITH GOD."

8   Then Peter answered and said unto him, "Lo, we have left all, and have followed you; what shall we have therefore?" Jesus said unto them, "Truly I say unto you, That you which have followed me, in the regeneration when the Son of man shall sit in the throne of his glory, you also shall sit upon twelve thrones, judging the twelve tribes of Israel.

9   And Jesus answered and said unto them, "Truly I say unto you, everyone that has left house, or brethren, or sisters, or father, or mother, or wife, or children, or lands, for the kingdom of God's sake, for my name's sake, and the gospel's, shall receive many times more in this present time a hundredfold, houses, and brethren, and sisters, and mothers, and children, and lands, with persecutions; and in the world to come, shall inherit life everlasting.

10   "But many that are first shall be last; and the last shall be first."

Parable of the Laborers
Matthew 20:1-16

11   "For the kingdom of heaven is like a man that is a landowner, which went out early in the morning to hire laborers into his vineyard. When he had agreed with the laborers for a silver coin a day, he sent them into his vineyard.

12   "And he went out about the third hour, and saw others standing idle in the marketplace, and said unto them; 'Go also into the vineyard, and whatsoever is right I will give you.' And they went their way. Again he went out about the sixth and ninth hour, and did likewise.

"And about the eleventh hour he went out, and found others standing 13 idle, and said unto them, 'Why do you stand here all the day idle?' They said unto him, 'Because no man has hired us.' He said unto them, 'Go also into the vineyard; and whatsoever is right, that shall you receive.'

"So when evening was come, the owner of the vineyard said unto 14 his steward, 'Call the laborers, and give them their wages, beginning from the last unto the first.' And when they came that were hired about the eleventh hour, they received every man a silver coin. But when the first came, they supposed that they should have received more; and they likewise received every man a silver coin.

"And when they had received it, they murmured against the owner of 15 the land, saying, 'These last have labored but one hour, and you have made them equal unto us, which have borne the burden and heat of the day.' But he answered one of them, and said, 'Friend, I do you no wrong: did not you agree with me for a silver coin?'

" 'Take what is yours, and go your way: I will give unto this last, even 16 as unto you. Is it not lawful for me to do what I will with my own? Is your eye evil, because I am good?' So the last shall be first, and the first last: for many be called, but few chosen."

CHAPTER 38

GAINING SPIRITUAL LIFE

Jesus Again Predicts His Death
Matthew 20:17-19; Mark 10:32-34; Luke 18:31-34

1   Then he took unto him the twelve, and said unto them, "Behold, we go up to Jerusalem, and all things that are written by the prophets concerning the Son of man shall be accomplished."

2   And they were on the road going up to Jerusalem; and Jesus went before them: and they were amazed; and as they followed, they were afraid. He took again the twelve disciples apart on the road, and began to tell them what things should happen unto him, saying, "Behold, we go up to Jerusalem; and the Son of man shall be betrayed unto the chief priests, and unto the scribes; and they shall condemn him to death, and shall deliver him to the Gentiles: and they shall mock him, and shall scourge him, and shall spit upon him, and shall put him to death: and the third day he shall rise again."

3   And they understood none of these things: and this saying was hidden from them, neither knew they the things which were spoken.

Greatness in Serving
Matthew 20:20-28; Mark 10:35-45

4   Then came to him the mother of Zebedee's children with her sons, worshiping him, and desiring a certain thing of him. And he said unto her, "What will you?" She said unto him, "Grant that these my two sons may sit, the one on your right hand, and the other on the left, in your kingdom." James and John, the sons of Zebedee, came unto him, saying, "Teacher, we would that you should do for us whatsoever we shall desire." And he said unto them, "What would you that I should do for you?" They said unto him, "Grant unto us that we may sit, one on your right hand, and the other on your left hand, in your glory."

5   But Jesus answered and said, "You know not what you ask. Are you able to drink of the cup that I shall drink of, and to be baptized with the baptism

that I am baptized with?" They said unto him, "We are able." And Jesus said 5
unto them, "You shall drink indeed of my cup, and be baptized with the baptism that I am baptized with: but to sit on my right hand, and on my left hand, is not mine to give, but it shall be given to them for whom it is prepared of my Father."

And when the ten heard it, they were moved with indignation against 6
the two brethren, James and John. But Jesus called them unto him, and said, "You know that they which are accounted to rule over the Gentiles exercise dominance over them, and they that are great exercise authority upon them.

"But it shall not be so among you: but whosoever will be great among you, let him be your minister; and whosoever will be chief among you, let him be your servant: and

> "EVEN THE SON OF MAN CAME NOT TO BE MINISTERED UNTO, BUT TO MINISTER."

7

whosoever of you will be the first, shall be servant of all. For even the Son of man came not to be ministered unto, but to minister, and to give his life a ransom for many."

Healing the Blind at Jericho
Matthew 20:29-34; Mark 10:46-52; Luke 18:35-43

And it came to pass, that as he was come near unto Jericho, a certain 8
blind man, blind Bartimaeus, the son of Timaeus, sat by the wayside begging: and hearing the multitude pass by, he asked what it meant. They told him, that Jesus of Nazareth passes by. When he heard that it was Jesus of Nazareth, he began to cry out, and say, "Jesus, Son of David, have mercy on me." They which went before warned him, that he should hold his peace: but he cried so much the more, "Son of David, have mercy on me."

Jesus stood still, and commanded him to be called. They called the 9
blind man, saying unto him, "Be of good cheer, rise; he calls you." And he, casting away his garment, rose, and came to Jesus. Jesus answered and said unto him, "What will you that I should do unto you?" The blind man said unto him, "Rabboni, that I might receive my sight." Jesus said unto him, "Receive your sight: go your way; your faith has made you whole." Immediately he received his sight, and followed Jesus on the road, glorifying God: and all the people, when they saw it, gave praise unto God.

And as they departed from Jericho, a great multitude followed him. 10
And, behold, two blind men sitting by the wayside, when they heard that Jesus passed by, cried out, saying, "Have mercy on us, O Lord, Son of David." The multitude warned them, because they should hold their peace: but they cried the more, saying, "Have mercy on us, O Lord, Son of David." And Jesus stood still, and called them, and said, "What will you that I shall do unto you?" They said unto him, "Lord, that our eyes may be opened." So Jesus had compassion on them, and touched their eyes: and immediately their eyes received sight, and they followed him.

A Tax Collector Finds Salvation
Luke 19:1-10

11   Jesus entered and passed through Jericho. And, behold, there was a man named Zacchaeus, which was the chief among the tax collectors, and he was rich. He sought to see Jesus who he was; and could not for the crowd, because he was little of stature. He ran ahead, and climbed up into a sycamore tree to see him: for he was to pass that way.

12   When Jesus came to the place, he looked up, and saw him, and said unto him, "Zacchaeus, make haste, and come down; for today I must stay at your house." And he made haste, and came down, and received him joyfully. When they saw it, they all murmured, saying, "That he was gone to be guest with a man that is a sinner."

13   Zacchaeus stood, and said unto the Lord; "Behold, Lord, the half of my goods I give to the poor; and if I have taken anything from any

> "THE SON OF MAN IS COME TO SEEK AND TO SAVE THAT WHICH WAS LOST."

man by false accusation, I restore him fourfold." And Jesus said unto him, "This day is salvation come to this house, forasmuch as he also is a son of Abraham. For the Son of man is come to seek and to save that which was lost."

Parable of Good Stewardship
Luke 19:11-28

14   As they heard these things, he added and spoke a parable, because he was near to Jerusalem, and because they thought that the kingdom of God should immediately appear. He said therefore, "A certain nobleman went into a far country to receive for himself a kingdom, and to return. And he called his ten servants, and delivered them ten gold coins, and said unto them, 'Conduct business till I come.' But his citizens hated him, and sent a message after him, saying, 'We will not have this man to reign over us.'

15   "And it came to pass, that when he was returned, having received the kingdom, then he commanded these servants to be called unto him, to whom he had given the money, that he might know how much every man had gained by trading. Then came the first, saying, 'Master, your gold coin has gained ten gold coins.' He said unto him, 'Well, good servant: because you have been faithful in a very little, you have authority over ten cities.'

16   "And the second came, saying, 'Master, your gold coin has gained five gold coins.' And he said likewise to him, 'Be you also over five cities.'

17   "And another came, saying, 'Master, behold, here is your gold coin, which I have kept laid up in a cloth: for I feared you, because you are a stern man: you take up that you did not lay down, and reap that you did not sow.' He said unto him, 'Out of your own mouth will I judge you, you wicked servant. You knew that I was a stern man, taking up that I did not lay down, and reaping that I did not sow: why then did you not give my money into the bank, that at my coming I might have collected my own with interest?'

"And he said unto them that stood by, 'Take from him the gold coin, 18 and give it to him that has ten gold coins.' (And they said unto him, 'Master, he has ten gold coins.') 'For I say unto you, That unto everyone which has shall be given; and from him that has not, even that he has shall be taken away from him. But those my enemies, which would not that I should reign over them, bring here, and slay them before me.' "

And when he had thus spoken, he went ahead, ascending up to 19 Jerusalem.

Priests Plot to Kill Jesus
John 11:55-57

And the Jews' passover was near at hand: and many went out of the 20 country up to Jerusalem before the passover, to purify themselves. Then they searched for Jesus, and spoke among themselves, as they stood in the temple, "What do you think, that he will not come to the feast?" Now both the chief priests and the Pharisees had given a commandment, that, if any man knew where he were, he should show it, that they might take him.

Priests Plot to Kill Lazarus
John 12:1, 9-11

Then Jesus six days before the passover came to Bethany, where 21 Lazarus was which had been dead, whom he raised from the dead.

Many people of the Jews therefore knew that he was there: and they 22 came not for Jesus' sake only, but that they might see Lazarus also, whom he had raised from the dead. But the chief priests consulted that they might put Lazarus also to death; because by reason of him many of the Jews went away, and believed on Jesus.

PART 10

LAST SUPPER

Jesus' life had fulfilled the prophecies recorded in the Old Testament, and He had often described the precise manner of His death. His actions proved that He was most assuredly the Christ. During His final journey to Jerusalem, He instructed those who followed Him, and all that would follow thereafter, to be vigilant in their adherence to the Word, even unto the end of days, for in this way only could they hope to enter into the kingdom of heaven. In the twilight of a glorious mission with shadows fast falling around, Jesus broke bread with His disciples and washed their feet, knowing He would soon be betrayed into the hands of sinners for 30 pieces of silver.

"IN MY FATHER'S HOUSE ARE MANY MANSIONS: IF
IT WERE NOT SO, I WOULD HAVE TOLD YOU. I GO
TO PREPARE A PLACE FOR YOU." (JOHN 14:2)

CHAPTER 39

THE FINAL ENTRY

Triumphal Entry of Jesus
Matthew 21:1-9; Mark 11:1-10; Luke 19:29-40; John 12:12-19

On the next day many people that were come to the feast, when they 1
heard that Jesus was coming to Jerusalem, took branches of palm trees, and
went forth to meet him, and cried, "Hosanna: *Blessed is the King of Israel
that comes in the name of the Lord.*"

And it came to pass, when they came near to Jerusalem, unto Beth- 2
phage and Bethany, at the mount called the mount of Olives, he sent forth
two of his disciples, saying unto them, "Go your way into the village opposite you: and as soon as you be entered into it, you shall find a donkey tied,
and a colt with it, whereon yet never man sat: loose them, and bring them
unto me. And if any man says unto you, 'Why do you this?' you shall say,
'The Lord has need of him'; and straightway he will send them here."

All this was done, that it might be fulfilled which was spoken by the 3
prophet, saying, "*Tell the daughter of Zion, Behold, your King comes unto
you, meek, and sitting upon a donkey, and a colt the foal of a donkey.*" The
disciples that were sent went their way, and did as Jesus commanded them,
and found the colt tied by the door outside in a place where two roads met,
even as he had said unto them. And as they were loosing the colt, the own-
ers thereof said unto them, "Why do you loose the colt?" And they said unto
them, "The Lord has need of it," even as Jesus had commanded: and they
let them go. They brought the donkey, and the colt to Jesus, and put on them
their clothes, and they set Jesus thereon.

And as he went, a very great multitude spread their clothes on the 4
road; and others cut down branches from the trees, and spread them on the
road. The multitudes that went before, and that followed, cried, saying,
"Hosanna to the Son of David: *Blessed is he that comes in the name of the
Lord*; Hosanna in the highest. Blessed be the kingdom of our father David,
that comes in the name of the Lord: Hosanna in the highest."

5   And when he was come near, even now at the descent of the mount of Olives, the whole multitude of the disciples began to rejoice and praise God with a loud voice for all the mighty works that they had seen; saying, "Blessed be the King that comes in the name of the Lord: peace in heaven, and glory in the highest."

6   And some of the Pharisees from among the multitude said unto him, "Teacher, rebuke your disciples." He answered and said unto them, "I tell you that, if these should hold their peace, the stones would immediately cry out."

7   These things his disciples did not understand at the first: but when Jesus was glorified, then they remembered that these things were written of him, and that they had done these things unto him.

8   The people therefore that were with him when he called Lazarus out of his grave, and raised him from the dead, bore record. For this cause the people also met him, because they heard that he had done this miracle.

9   The Pharisees therefore said among themselves, "Do you perceive how you prevail nothing? behold, the world is gone after him."

Jesus Laments Jerusalem's Fate
Luke 19:41-44

10   And when he was come near, he beheld the city, and wept over it, saying, "If you had known, even you, at least in this your day, the things which belong unto your peace! but now they are hidden from your eyes. For the days shall come upon you, that your enemies shall cast a trench around you, and circle you round, and close you in on every side, and shall lay you even with the ground, and your children within you; and they shall not leave in you one stone upon another; because you knew not the time of your visitation."

Jesus Enters Jerusalem
Matthew 21:10-11; Mark 11:11

11   When Jesus entered into Jerusalem, all the city was moved, saying, "Who is this?" And the multitude said, "This is Jesus the prophet of Nazareth of Galilee." Jesus entered into the temple: and when he had looked round about upon all things, and now the evening hour was come, he went out unto Bethany with the twelve.

Jesus Condemns Barren Fig Tree
Matthew 21:18-19; Mark 11:12-14

12   Now in the morning as he returned into the city, when they were come from Bethany, he was hungry: and seeing a fig tree afar off having leaves, he came to it, if perhaps he might find anything thereon: and when he came to it, he found nothing but leaves; for the time of figs was not yet. And Jesus said unto it, "Let no fruit grow on you henceforth for ever." At once the fig tree withered away. And Jesus answered and said unto it, "No man shall eat fruit of you hereafter for ever." And his disciples heard it.

Jesus Again Clears the Temple
Matthew 21:12-17; Mark 11:15-19; Luke 19:45-48

And they came to Jerusalem: and Jesus went into the temple of God, 13 and cast out all them that sold and bought in the temple, and overturned the tables of the money changers, and the seats of them that sold doves; and would not allow that any man should carry any vessel through the temple. He taught, saying unto them, "Is it not written, '*My house shall be called of all nations the house of prayer*'? but you have made it '*a den of thieves.*'"

And the blind and the lame came to him in the temple; and he healed 14 them. When the chief priests and scribes saw the wonderful things that he did, and the children crying in the temple, and saying, "Hosanna to the Son of David"; they were very displeased, and said unto him, "Do you hear what these say?" Jesus said unto them, "Yes; have you never read, '*Out of the mouth of babies and nursing infants you have perfected praise*'?" The scribes and chief priests heard it, and sought how they might destroy him: for they feared him, because all the people were astonished at his doctrine.

He taught daily in the temple. But the chief priests and the scribes and 15 the leaders of the people sought to destroy him, and could not find what they might do: for all the people were very attentive to hear him.

And when evening was come, he left them, and went out of the city 16 into Bethany; and he lodged there.

CHAPTER 40

THE FINAL LESSONS

Lesson From Withered Fig Tree
Matthew 21:20-22; Mark 11:20-24

1   And in the morning, as they passed by, they saw the fig tree dried up
from the roots, and when the disciples saw it, they marveled, saying,
"How soon is the fig tree withered away!" And Peter calling to remembrance said unto him, "Rabbi, behold, the fig tree which you cursed is withered away."

2   Jesus answering said unto them, "Have faith in God. For truly I say
unto you, If you have faith, you shall not only do this which is done to the
fig tree, but also if you shall say unto this mountain, 'Be removed, and be
cast into the sea'; and shall not doubt in his heart, but shall believe that
those things which he says shall come to pass; he shall have whatsoever he
says. Therefore I say unto you, Whatsoever things you desire, when you
pray, believe that you receive them, and you shall have them."

"When You Stand Praying, Forgive"
Mark 11:25-26

3   "And when you stand praying, forgive, if you have anything against
any: that your Father also which is in heaven may forgive you your trespasses. But if you do not forgive, neither will your Father which is in
heaven forgive your trespasses."

Authority of Jesus Questioned
Matthew 21:23-27; Mark 11:27-33; Luke 20:1-8

4   They came again to Jerusalem: and it came to pass, that on one of those
days, as he taught the people in the temple, and preached the gospel, the
chief priests and the scribes came upon him with the elders, as he was walking in the temple: and spoke unto him, saying, "Tell us, by what authority do
you these things? and who gave you this authority to do these things?"

And Jesus answered and said unto them, "I also will ask of you one 5 question, which if you answer me, I will tell you by what authority I do these things. The baptism of John, from where was it? from heaven, or of men?" They reasoned with themselves, saying, "If we shall say, 'From heaven'; he will say unto us, 'Why then did you not believe him?' But if we shall say, 'Of men'; we fear the people; all the people will stone us: for all hold John as a prophet."

They answered and said unto Jesus, "We cannot tell from where it 6 was." Jesus answering said unto them, "Neither do I tell you by what authority I do these things."

Parable of the Two Sons
Matthew 21:28-32

He began to speak unto them by parables. "But what do you think? A 7 certain man had two sons; and he came to the first, and said, 'Son, go work today in my vineyard.' He answered and said, 'I will not': but afterward he repented, and went. And he came to the second, and said likewise. And he answered and said, 'I go, sir': and did not go.

"Which of these two did the will of his father?" They said unto him, 8 "The first." Jesus said unto them, "Truly I say unto you, That the tax collectors and the harlots go into the kingdom of God before you. For John came unto you in the way of righteousness, and you did not believe him: but the tax collectors and the harlots believed him: and you, when you had seen it, did not repent afterward, that you might believe him.

Parable of the Vinedressers
Matthew 21:33-46; Mark 12:1-12; Luke 20:9-19

"Hear another parable: There was a certain landowner, which *plant-* 9 *ed a vineyard, and set a hedge around it, and dug a place for the winepress, and built a tower*, and rented it out to vinedressers, and went into a far country for a long time. At the season when the time of the fruit drew near, he sent a servant to the vinedressers, that they should give him of the fruit of the vineyard. They caught him, and beat him, and sent him away empty.

"And again he sent unto them another servant: and they beat him also, 10 and at him they cast stones, and wounded him in the head, and sent him away empty. And again he sent a third: and him they killed, and many others; beating some, and killing some.

"Then said the owner of the vineyard, 'What shall I do? I will send my 11 beloved son: it may be they will respect him when they see him.' Having yet therefore one son, his beloved, he sent him also last unto them, saying, 'They will respect my son.' But when the vinedressers saw him, they reasoned among themselves, saying, 'This is the heir: come, let us kill him, that the inheritance may be ours.'

12   "So they caught him, and cast him out of the vineyard, and killed him. When the owner therefore of the vineyard comes, what will he do unto these vinedressers?" They said unto him, "He will miserably destroy those wicked men, and will rent out his vineyard unto other vinedressers, which shall render him the fruits in their seasons."

13   "What shall therefore the owner of the vineyard do? he will come and destroy the vinedressers, and will give the vineyard unto others." When they heard it, they said, "God forbid."

14   And Jesus beheld them, and said, "What is this then that is written, did you never read in the scriptures, '*The stone which the builders rejected, the same is become the head of the cornerstone: this is the Lord's doing, and it is marvelous in our eyes'?*

15   "Therefore say I unto you, The kingdom of God shall be taken from you, and given to a nation bringing forth the fruits thereof. And whosoever shall fall on this stone shall be broken: but on whomsoever it shall fall, it will grind him to powder."

16   When the chief priests and Pharisees had heard his parables, they perceived that he spoke of them. And they and the scribes the same hour sought to lay hands on him; and they feared the people, because they took him for a prophet: and they left him, and went their way.

CHAPTER 41

WISE ANSWERS TO SLY QUESTIONS

Parable of the Wedding Feast
Matthew 22:1-14

And Jesus answered and spoke unto them again by parables, and said, 1 "The kingdom of heaven is like a certain king, which made a marriage for his son, and sent forth his servants to call them that were invited to the wedding: and they would not come. Again, he sent forth other servants, saying, 'Tell them which are invited, "Behold, I have prepared my dinner: my oxen and my fatlings are killed, and all things are ready: come unto the marriage." '

"But they made light of it, and went their ways, one to his farm, another 2 to his business: and the remaining ones took his servants, and treated them spitefully, and killed them. But when the king heard thereof, he was angry: and he sent forth his armies, and destroyed those murderers, and burned up their city.

"Then he said to his servants, 'The wedding is ready, but they which 3 were invited were not worthy. Go therefore into the highways, and as many as you shall find, invite to the marriage.' So those servants went out into the highways, and gathered together all as many as they found, both bad and good: and the wedding was filled with guests.

"And when the king came in to see the guests, he saw there a man 4 which did not have on a wedding garment: and he said unto him, 'Friend, how came you in here not having a wedding garment?' And he was speechless. Then the king said to the servants, 'Bind him hand and foot, and take him away, and cast him into outer darkness; there shall be weeping and gnashing of teeth.' For many are called, but few are chosen."

Paying Taxes to Caesar
Matthew 22:15-22; Mark 12:13-17; Luke 20:20-26

Then the Pharisees went, and plotted how they might entangle him in 5 his talk. And they watched him, and sent forth spies, which should pretend

5 themselves just men, that they might catch him in his words, that so they might deliver him unto the power and authority of the governor. And they sent out unto him their disciples with the Herodians, saying, "Teacher, we know that you are true, and teach the way of God in truth, neither do you favor any man: for you do not regard the person of men. Tell us therefore, What do you think? Is it lawful to give tribute unto Caesar, or not?

6 "Shall we give, or shall we not give?" But Jesus perceived their wickedness, knowing their hypocrisy, said unto them, "Why do you tempt me, you hypocrites? Show me the trib-

> "RENDER TO CAESAR THE THINGS THAT ARE CAESAR'S, AND TO GOD THE THINGS THAT ARE GOD'S."

ute money. Bring me a silver coin, that I may see it." And they brought unto him a silver coin. "Whose image and superscription has it?" They answered and said, "Caesar's." Jesus answering said unto them, "Render to Caesar the things that are Caesar's, and to God the things that are God's." They could not take hold of his words before the people: and they marveled at his answer, and held their peace, and left him, and went their way.

No Marriage in the Resurrection
Matthew 22:23-33; Mark 12:18-27; Luke 20:27-40

7 The same day came to him certain of the Sadducees, which deny that there is any resurrection; and they asked him, saying, "Teacher, Moses wrote unto us, '*If any man's brother dies, having a wife, and he dies without children, that his brother should marry his wife, and raise up seed unto his brother.*'

8 "Now there were with us seven brethren: and the first took a wife, and died without children, left his wife unto his brother. And the second took her as wife, and he died childless. And the third took her; and in like manner the seven also: and they left no children, and died. And last of all the woman died also.

9 "Therefore in the resurrection, when they shall rise, whose wife shall she be of them? for the seven had her as wife." Jesus answered and said unto them, "You do err, not knowing the scriptures, nor the power of God. For in the resurrection they neither marry, nor are given in marriage, but are as the angels of God in heaven. The children of this world marry, and are given in marriage: but they which shall be accounted worthy to obtain that world, and the resurrection from the dead, neither marry, nor are given in marriage: neither can they die anymore: but are as the angels which are in heaven; and are the children of God, being the children of the resurrection.

10 "But as concerning the resurrection of the dead, have you not read in the book of Moses, how in the bush God spoke unto him, saying, '*I am the God of Abraham, and the God of Isaac, and the God of Jacob*'? He is not the God of the dead, but the God of the living: for all live unto him: you therefore do greatly err." And when the multitude heard this, they were astonished at his doctrine.

Then certain of the scribes answering said, "Teacher, you have well 11 said." And after that they dared not ask him any question at all.

First and Greatest Commandment
Matthew 22:34-40; Mark 12:28-34

But when the Pharisees had heard that he had put the Sadducees to 12 silence, they were gathered together. Then one of them, which was a scribe, came, and having heard them reasoning together, and perceiving that he had answered them well, asked him a question, tempting him, and saying, "Teacher, which is the great commandment in the law? which is the first commandment of all?" And Jesus answered him, "The first of all the commandments is, *'Hear, O Israel; The Lord our God is one Lord: and You shall love the Lord your God with all your heart, and with all your soul, and with all your mind, and with all your strength.'* This is the first and great commandment.

"And the second is like it, namely this, *'You shall love your neighbor 13 as yourself.'* There is no other commandment greater than these. On these two commandments hang all the law and the prophets."

The scribe said unto him, "Well, Teacher, you have said the truth: *for 14 there is one God*; and *there is no other but he*: and to *love him with all the heart, and with all the understanding, and with all the soul, and with all the strength*, and to *love his neighbor as himself*, is more than all the whole of burnt offerings and sacrifices."

When Jesus saw that he answered wisely, he said unto him, "You are 15 not far from the kingdom of God." And no man after that dared ask him any question.

Whose Son Is Christ?
Matthew 22:41-46; Mark 12:35-37; Luke 20:41-44

While the Pharisees were gathered together, Jesus asked them, saying, 16 "What do you think of Christ? whose son is he?" They said unto him, "The Son of David." He said unto them, "How then does David in spirit call him 'Lord'?" Jesus answered and said unto them, while he taught in the temple, "How said the scribes that Christ is the Son of David? for David himself said by the Holy Ghost in the book of Psalms, *'The Lord said unto my Lord, "Sit on my right hand, till I make your enemies your footstool."'*

"If David himself therefore calls him 'Lord,' how is he then his son?" 17 No man was able to answer him a word, neither dared any man from that day forth ask him any more questions. And the common people heard him gladly.

CHAPTER 42

BLUNT WORDS TO THE HYPOCRITES

Beware of Scribes and Pharisees
Matthew 23:1-12; Mark 12:38-40; Luke 20:45-47

1   Then in the audience of all the people he said unto his disciples in his doctrine, "Beware of the scribes, which love to go in long robes, and love greetings in the marketplaces, and the chief seats in the synagogues, and the uppermost rooms at feasts; which devour widows' houses, and for a show make long prayers: the same shall receive greater condemnation."

2   Then Jesus spoke to the multitude, and to his disciples, saying, "The scribes and the Pharisees sit in Moses' seat: all therefore whatsoever they tell you observe, that observe and do; but do not according to their works: for they say, and do not. For they bind heavy burdens grievous to be borne, and lay them on men's shoulders; but they themselves will not move them with one of their fingers. But all their works they do to be seen of men: they make broad their phylacteries (scripture boxes), and enlarge the borders of their garments, and love the uppermost rooms at feasts, and the chief seats in the synagogues, and greetings in the marketplaces, and to be called of men, 'Rabbi, Rabbi.'

3   "But be not called 'Rabbi': for one is your Teacher, even Christ; and all you are brethren. Call no man your father upon the earth: for one is your Father, which is in heaven. Neither be called teachers: for one is your Teacher, even Christ. But he that is greatest among you shall be your servant. And whosoever shall exalt himself shall be humbled; and he that shall humble himself shall be exalted."

Scribes and Pharisees: Hypocrites
Matthew 23:13-36

4   "But woe unto you, scribes and Pharisees, hypocrites! for you shut up the kingdom of heaven against men: for you neither go in yourselves, neither allow them that are entering to go in.

"Woe unto you, scribes and Pharisees, hypocrites! for you devour wid- 5
ows' houses, and for a pretense make long prayers: therefore you shall
receive the greater condemnation.

"Woe unto you, scribes and Pharisees, hypocrites! for you journey sea 6
and land to make one convert, and when he is made, you make him twofold
more the child of hell than yourselves.

"Woe unto you, you blind guides, which say, 'Whosoever shall swear 7
by the temple, it is nothing; but whosoever shall swear by the gold of the
temple, he is a debtor!' You fools and blind: for which is greater, the gold,
or the temple that sanctifies the gold? And, 'Whosoever shall swear by the
altar, it is nothing; but whosoever swears by the gift that is upon it, he is
bound.' You fools and blind: for which is greater, the gift, or the altar that
sanctifies the gift? Whoever therefore shall swear by the altar, swears by it,
and by all things thereon. And whoever shall swear by the temple, swears
by it, and by him that dwells therein. And he that shall swear by heaven,
swears by the throne of God, and by him that sits thereon.

"Woe unto you, scribes and Pharisees, hypocrites! for you pay tithe of 8
mint and anise and cummin, and have omitted the weightier matters of the
law, judgment, mercy, and faith: these ought you to have done, and not to
leave the others undone. You blind guides, which strain out a gnat, and swal-
low a camel.

"Woe unto you, scribes and Pharisees, hypocrites! for you make clean 9
the outside of the cup and of the platter, but inside they are full of extortion
and excess. You blind Pharisee, cleanse first that which is inside the cup and
platter, that the outside of them may be clean also.

"Woe unto you, scribes and Pharisees, hypocrites! for you are like 10
whitewashed tombs, which indeed appear beautiful outwardly, but are
inside full of dead men's bones, and of all uncleanness. Even so you also
outwardly appear righteous unto men, but inside you are full of hypocrisy
and iniquity.

"Woe unto you, scribes and Pharisees, hypocrites! because you build 11
the tombs of the prophets, and decorate the monuments of the righteous,
and say, 'If we had been in the days of our fathers, we would not have been
partakers with them in the blood of the prophets.' Therefore you be witnesses unto yourselves, that you are the children of them which killed the
prophets. Fill up then the measure of your fathers. You serpents, you generation of vipers, how can you escape the condemnation of hell?

"Therefore, behold, I send unto you prophets, and wise men, and 12
scribes: and some of them you shall kill and crucify; and some of them shall
you scourge in your synagogues, and persecute them from city to city: that
upon you may come all the righteous blood shed upon the earth, from the
blood of righteous Abel unto the blood of Zacharias son of Barachiah,
whom you slew between the temple and the altar.

"Truly I say unto you, All these things shall come upon this generation." 13

Jesus Again Laments for Jerusalem
Matthew 23:37-39

14   "O Jerusalem, Jerusalem, you that kill the prophets, and stone them which are sent unto you, how often would I have gathered your children together, even as a hen gathers her chickens under her wings, and you would not! Behold, your house is left unto you desolate. For I say unto you, You shall not see me henceforth, till you shall say, 'Blessed is he that comes in the name of the Lord.'"

The Poor Widow's Two-Coin Offering
Mark 12:41-44; Luke 21:1-4

15   And Jesus sat opposite the treasury, and beheld how the people cast money into the treasury: and many that were rich cast in much. There came a certain poor widow, and she threw in two small copper coins, which make a copper coin.

16   He called unto him his disciples, and said unto them, "Truly I say unto you, That this poor widow has cast more in, than all they which have cast into the treasury: for all these have of their abundance cast in unto the offerings of God: but she of her poverty has cast in all the livelihood that she had, even all her livelihood."

Jesus Invites All Men to Serve Him
John 12:20-26

17   And there were certain Greeks among them that came up to worship at the feast: the same came therefore to Philip, which was of Bethsaida of Galilee, and desired him, saying, "Sir, we would see Jesus." Philip came and told Andrew: and in turn Andrew and Philip told Jesus.

18   Jesus answered them, saying, "The hour is come, that the Son of man should be glorified. Truly, truly, I say unto you, Except a grain of wheat falls into the ground and dies, it remains alone: but if it dies, it brings forth much fruit. He that loves his life shall lose it; and he that hates his life in this world shall keep it unto life eternal.

> "HE THAT LOVES HIS LIFE SHALL LOSE IT."

19   "If any man serves me, let him follow me; and where I am, there shall also my servant be: if any man serves me, him will my Father honor."

"Now Is the Judgment of This World"
John 12:27-36

20   "Now is my soul troubled; and what shall I say? 'Father, save me from this hour': but for this cause came I unto this hour. Father, glorify your name." Then came there a voice from heaven, saying, "I have both glorified it, and will glorify it again."

21   The people therefore, that stood by, and heard it, said that it thundered: others said, "An angel spoke to him." Jesus answered and said, "This voice

came not because of me, but for your sakes. Now is the judgment of this 21
world: now shall the prince of this world be cast out. And I, if I be lifted up
from the earth, will draw all men unto me." This he said, signifying what
death he should die.

The people answered him, "We have heard out of the law that Christ 22
remains for ever: and how do you say, 'The Son of man must be lifted up'?
who is this Son of man?" Then Jesus said unto them, "Yet a little while is
the light with you. Walk while you have the light, lest darkness come upon
you: for he that walks in darkness does not know where he goes. While you
have light, believe in the light, that you may be the children of light." These
things spoke Jesus, and departed, and did hide himself from them.

As a Light Into the World
John 12:37-50

But though he had done so many miracles before them, yet they had 23
not believed on him: that the saying of Isaiah the prophet might be fulfilled,
which he spoke, "*Lord, who has believed our report? and to whom has the
arm of the Lord been revealed?*" Therefore they could not believe, because
Isaiah said again, "*He has blinded their eyes, and hardened their hearts;
that they should not see with their eyes, nor understand with their hearts,
and be converted, and I should heal them.*"

These things said Isaiah, when he saw his glory, and spoke of him. 24
Nevertheless among the chief rulers also many believed on him; but
because of the Pharisees they did not confess him, lest they should be put
out of the synagogue: for they loved the praise of men more than the praise
of God.

Jesus cried and said, "He that believes on me, believes not on me, but 25
on him that sent me. And he that sees
me sees him that sent me. I am come
a light into the world, that whosoever
believes on me should not abide in
darkness. And if any man hears my
words, and does not believe, I do not
judge him: for I came not to judge the world, but to save the world.

> "I AM COME A LIGHT INTO THE
> WORLD, THAT WHOSOEVER
> BELIEVES ON ME SHOULD NOT
> ABIDE IN DARKNESS."

"He that rejects me, and receives not my words, has one that judges 26
him: the word that I have spoken, the same shall judge him in the last day.
For I have not spoken of myself; but the Father which sent me, he gave me
a commandment, what I should say, and what I should speak. And I know
that his commandment is life everlasting: whatsoever I speak therefore,
even as the Father said unto me, so I speak."

CHAPTER 43

THE END TIMES

Signs: The End of the Age
Matthew 24:1-14; Mark 13:1-13; Luke 21:5-19

1   And as he went out of the temple, one of his disciples said unto him, "Teacher, see what manner of stones and what buildings are here!" Jesus answering said unto him, "Do you see these great buildings? there shall not be left one stone upon another, that shall not be thrown down." Jesus went out, and departed from the temple: and his disciples came to him to show him the buildings of the temple. As some spoke of the temple, how it was adorned with beautiful stones and gifts, he said unto them, "Do you not see all these things? truly I say unto you, As for these things which you behold, the days will come, in which there shall not be left one stone upon another, that shall not be thrown down."

2   As he sat upon the Mount of Olives opposite the temple, Peter and James and John and Andrew asked him privately, "Tell us, when shall these things be? and what shall be the sign when all these things shall come to pass?" And they asked him, saying, "Teacher, but what shall be the sign of your coming, and of the end of the world?"

3   And Jesus answering them began to say, "Take heed that no man deceives you. For many shall come in my name, saying, 'I am Christ'; and shall deceive many. And 'the time draws near': go not therefore after them. And you shall hear of wars and rumors of wars: see that you be not troubled: for all these things must first come to pass; but the end is not yet, is not immediately.

4   "For nation shall rise against nation, and kingdom against kingdom: and there shall be great earthquakes in various places, and there shall be famines, and pestilences; and fearful sights and great signs shall there be from heaven. All these are the beginning of sorrows.

"But before all these, take heed to yourselves: for they shall lay their 5
hands on you, and persecute you, and shall kill you: delivering you up to
councils and into prisons. And in the synagogues you shall be beaten: and
you shall be brought before rulers and kings for my sake, for a testimony
against them. And the gospel must first be published among all nations.
And you shall be hated of all nations for my name's sake. And it shall turn
to you for a testimony.

"But when they shall lead you, and deliver you up, settle it in your 6
hearts, worry not beforehand what you
shall speak, neither premeditate what
you shall answer: for I will give you a
mouth and wisdom, which all your
adversaries shall not be able to contra-
dict nor resist: but whatsoever shall be given you in that hour, that speak:
for it is not you that speak, but the Holy Ghost.

> "I WILL GIVE YOU A MOUTH AND WISDOM."

"And then shall many fall away, and shall betray one another, and shall 7
hate one another. Many false prophets
shall rise, and shall deceive many.
Because iniquity shall abound, the
love of many shall grow cold. You
shall be betrayed both by parents, and
brethren, and relatives, and friends;
and some of you shall they cause to be
put to death. Now the brother shall betray the brother to death, and the
father the son; and children shall rise up against their parents, and shall
cause them to be put to death.

> "THIS GOSPEL OF THE KING-DOM SHALL BE PREACHED IN ALL THE WORLD FOR A WIT-NESS UNTO ALL NATIONS."

"And you shall be hated of all men for my name's sake: but he that 8
shall endure unto the end, the same shall be saved. But there shall not a hair
of your head perish. In your patience you possess your souls. And this
gospel of the kingdom shall be preached in all the world for a witness unto
all nations; and then shall the end come."

Signs: The Great Tribulation
Matthew 24:15-28; Mark 13:14-23; Luke 21:20-24

"When you shall see Jerusalem surrounded with armies, then know 9
that the desolation thereof is near. When you therefore shall see the 'abomination of desolation,' spoken of by Daniel the prophet, stand in the holy
place, standing where it ought not, (let him that reads understand). Then let
them that be in Judea flee to the mountains; and let them which are in the
midst of the city depart out; and let not them that are in the country enter
thereinto. Let him that is on the housetop not go down into the house, neither enter therein, to take anything out of his house: neither let him which
is in the field return back to take his clothes. For these be the days of
vengeance, that all things which are written may be fulfilled.

"Woe unto them that are with child, and to them that nurse babies, 10
in those days! for there shall be great distress in the land, and wrath upon
this people. And pray that your flight be not in the winter, neither on the

10   sabbath day: for in those days shall be affliction, then shall be great tribulation, such as was not since the beginning of the world to this time, no, nor ever shall be.

11   "They shall fall by the edge of the sword, and shall be led away captive into all nations: and Jerusalem shall be trampled down of the Gentiles, until the times of the Gentiles be fulfilled.

12   "And except that the Lord had shortened those days, no flesh should be saved: but for the elect's sake, whom he has chosen, he has shortened the days.

13   "Then if any man shall say to you, 'Lo, here is Christ'; or, 'lo, he is there'; do not believe him: for there shall arise false Christs, and false prophets, and shall show great signs and wonders; insomuch that, if it were possible, they shall deceive the very elect. But take heed: behold, I have foretold you all things.

> "BEHOLD, I HAVE FORETOLD YOU ALL THINGS."

14   "Therefore if they shall say unto you, 'Behold, he is in the desert'; go not forth: 'behold, he is in the inner rooms'; do not believe it. For as the lightning comes out of the east, and shines even unto the west; so shall also the coming of the Son of man be. For wheresoever the carcass is, there will the eagles be gathered together."

Signs: Second Coming of the Son
Matthew 24:29-31; Mark 13:24-27; Luke 21:25-28

15   "But in those days, immediately after that tribulation, the sun shall be darkened, and the moon shall not give its light, and the stars shall fall from heaven, and the powers of the heavens shall be shaken. And there shall be signs in the sun, and in the moon, and in the stars; and upon the earth distress of nations, with perplexity; the sea and the waves roaring; men's hearts failing them for fear, and for awaiting those things which are coming on the earth: for the powers of heaven shall be shaken. Then shall appear the sign of the Son of man in heaven: and then shall all the tribes of the earth mourn, and they shall see *the Son of man coming in the clouds of heaven* with power and great glory.

16   "And he shall send his angels with a great sound of a trumpet, and they shall gather together his elect from the four winds, from one end of heaven to the other, from the uttermost part of the earth to the uttermost part of heaven. When these things begin to come to pass, then look up, and lift up your heads; for your redemption draws near."

Signs: Parable of the Fig Tree
Matthew 24:32-35; Mark 13:28-31; Luke 21:29-33

17   And he spoke to them a parable; "Behold the fig tree, and all the trees. Now learn a parable of the fig tree; When its branch is yet tender, and puts forth leaves, you see and know of your own selves that summer is now near at hand. So likewise you, when you shall see all these things come to pass, know that the kingdom of God is near, even at the doors.

"Truly I say unto you, This generation shall not pass away, till all 18 these things be fulfilled. Heaven and earth shall pass away, but my words shall not pass away."

Signs: No One Knows the Hour
Matthew 24:36-44; Mark 13:32-37; Luke 21:34-36

"But of that day and that hour knows no man, no, not the angels which 19 are in heaven, neither the Son, but the Father only. But as the days of Noah were, so shall also the coming of the Son of man be. For as in the days that were before the flood they were eating and drinking, marrying and giving in marriage, until the day that Noah entered into the ark, and knew not until the flood came, and took them all away; so shall also the coming of the Son of man be. Take heed, watch and pray: for you know not when the time is.

> "OF THAT DAY AND THAT HOUR KNOWS NO MAN, NO, NOT THE ANGELS WHICH ARE IN HEAVEN, NEITHER THE SON, BUT THE FATHER ONLY."

"And take heed to yourselves, lest at any time your hearts be weighted 20 down with carousing, and drunkenness, and cares of this life, and so that day come upon you suddenly. For as a snare shall it come on all them that dwell on the face of the whole earth. Then shall two be in the field; the one shall be taken, and the other left. Two women shall be grinding at the mill; the one shall be taken, and the other left.

"Watch therefore: for you know not what hour your Lord does come. 21 But know this, that if the owner of the house had known in what watch the thief would come, he would have watched, and would not have allowed his house to be broken into. Therefore be also ready: for in such an hour as you think not the Son of man comes.

"Watch therefore, and pray always, that you may be accounted worthy 22 to escape all these things that shall come to pass, and to stand before the Son of man.

"For the Son of man is as a man taking a far journey, who left his 23 house, and gave authority to his servants, and to every man his work, and commanded the doorkeeper to watch. Watch therefore: for you know not when the master of the house comes, at evening, or at midnight, or at the cockcrowing, or in the morning: lest coming suddenly he find you sleeping. And what I say unto you I say unto all, Watch."

Signs: Faithful and Wise Servant
Matthew 24:45-51

"Who then is a faithful and wise servant, whom his master has made 24 ruler over his household, to give them food in due season? Blessed is that servant, whom his master when he comes shall find so doing. Truly I say unto you, That he shall make him ruler over all his goods.

"But and if that evil servant shall say in his heart, 'My master delays 25 his coming'; and shall begin to strike his fellow servants, and to eat and drink with the drunkards; the master of that servant shall come in a day

25 when he does not look for him, and in an hour that he is not aware of, and shall cut him to pieces, and appoint him his portion with the hypocrites: there shall be weeping and gnashing of teeth."

Signs: Parable of the Ten Virgins
Matthew 25:1-13

26 "Then shall the kingdom of heaven be likened unto ten virgins, which took their lamps, and went forth to meet the bridegroom. And five of them were wise, and five were foolish. They that were foolish took their lamps, and took no oil with them: but the wise took oil in their vessels with their lamps. While the bridegroom tarried, they all slumbered and slept.

27 "And at midnight there was a cry made, 'Behold, the bridegroom comes; go out to meet him.' Then all those virgins arose, and trimmed their lamps. And the foolish said unto the wise, 'Give us of your oil; for our lamps are gone out.' But the wise answered, saying, 'Not so; lest there be not enough for us and you: but go rather to them that sell, and buy for yourselves.'

28 "And while they went to buy, the bridegroom came; and they that were ready went in with him to the marriage: and the door was shut.

29 "Afterward came also the other virgins, saying, 'Lord, Lord, open to us.' But he answered and said, 'Truly I say unto you, I do not know you.'

30 "Watch therefore, for you know neither the day nor the hour wherein the Son of man comes."

Signs: Parable of the Talents
Matthew 25:14-30

31 "For the kingdom of heaven is as a man traveling into a far country, who called his own servants, and delivered unto them his goods. Unto one he gave five talents, to another two, and to another one; to every man according to his particular ability; and straightway took his journey. Then he that had received the five talents went and traded with the same, and made them another five talents. And likewise he that had received two, he also gained another two. But he that had received one went and dug in the earth, and hid his master's money.

32 "After a long time the master of those servants came, and reckoned with them. And so he that had received five talents came and brought another five talents, saying, 'Master, you delivered unto me five talents: behold, I have gained besides them five talents more.' His master said unto him, 'Well done, good and faithful servant: you have been faithful over a few things, I will make you ruler over many things: enter into the joy of your master.'

33 "He also that had received two talents came and said, 'Master, you delivered unto me two talents: behold, I have gained two other talents besides them.' His master said unto him, 'Well done, good and faithful servant; you have been faithful over a few things, I will make you ruler over many things: enter into the joy of your master.'

34 "Then he which had received the one talent came and said, 'Master, I knew you that you are a hard man, reaping where you have not sown, and gathering where you have not scattered: and I was afraid, and went and hid

your talent in the earth: lo, there you have that is yours.' His master 34
answered and said unto him, 'You wicked and lazy servant, you knew that
I reap where I have not sowed, and gather where I have not scattered: you
ought therefore to have put my money to the exchangers, and then at my
coming I should have received my own with interest.

"Take therefore the talent from him, and give it unto him which has 35
ten talents. For unto everyone that has shall be given, and he shall have
abundance: but from him that has not shall be taken away even that which
he has. And cast the unprofitable servant into outer darkness: there shall be
weeping and gnashing of teeth."

Signs: The Final Judgment
Matthew 25:31-46; Luke 21:37-38

"When the Son of man shall come in his glory, and all the holy angels 36
with him, then shall he sit upon the throne of his glory: and before him shall
be gathered all nations: and he shall separate them one from another, as a
shepherd divides his sheep from the goats: and he shall set the sheep on his
right hand, but the goats on the left.

"Then shall the King say unto them on his right hand, 'Come, you 37
blessed of my Father, inherit the kingdom prepared for you from the foundation of the world: for I was hungry, and you gave me food: I was thirsty,
and you gave me drink: I was a stranger, and you took me in: naked, and
you clothed me: I was sick, and you visited me: I was in prison, and you
came unto me.'

"Then shall the righteous answer him, saying, 'Lord, when did we see 38
you hungry, and fed you? or thirsty, and gave you drink? When did we see you a stranger, and took you in? or naked, and clothed you? Or when did we see you sick, or in prison, and came unto you?' And the King shall

> "INASMUCH AS YOU HAVE DONE IT UNTO ONE OF THE LEAST OF THESE MY BRETHREN, YOU HAVE DONE IT UNTO ME."

answer and say unto them, 'Truly I say unto you, Inasmuch as you have
done it unto one of the least of these my brethren, you have done it unto me.'

"Then shall he say also unto them on the left hand, 'Depart from me, 39
you cursed, into everlasting fire, prepared for the devil and his angels: for I
was hungry, and you gave me no food: I was thirsty, and you gave me no
drink: I was a stranger, and you did not take me in: naked, and you did not
clothe me: sick, and in prison, and you did not visit me.'

"Then shall they also answer him, saying, 'Lord, when did we see you 40
hungry, or thirsty, or a stranger, or naked, or sick, or in prison, and did not
minister unto you?' Then shall he answer them, saying, 'Truly I say unto you,
Inasmuch as you did it not to one of the least of these, you did it not to me.'
And these shall go away into everlasting punishment: but the righteous into
life eternal."

And in the daytime he was teaching in the temple; and at night he went 41
out, and stayed in the mount that is called the Mount of Olives. All the people came early in the morning to him in the temple, to hear him.

CHAPTER 44

THE EVIL PLOT AWAITS

Priests Plot to Kill Jesus
Matthew 26:1-5; Mark 14:1-2; Luke 22:1-2

1   And it came to pass, when Jesus had finished all these sayings, he said unto his disciples, "You know that after two days is the feast of the passover, and the Son of man is betrayed to be crucified."

2   After two days was the feast of the passover, and of unleavened bread, which is called the Passover. And the chief priests and scribes sought how they might take him by deceit, and put him to death. Then assembled together the chief priests and the scribes, and the elders of the people, unto the palace of the high priest, who was called Caiaphas, and plotted that they might take Jesus by deceit, and kill him. But they said, "Not on the feast day, lest there be an uproar of the people"; for they feared the people.

Jesus Anointed at Bethany
Matthew 26:6-13; Mark 14:3-9; John 12:2-8

3   Now when Jesus was in Bethany, in the house of Simon the leper, they made him a supper; and Martha served: but Lazarus was one of them that sat at the table with him. There came unto him a woman having an alabaster jar of very precious ointment, and she broke open the jar, and poured it on his head, as he sat at the table. Then Mary took a pound of ointment of spikenard, very costly, and anointed the feet of Jesus, and wiped his feet with her hair: and the house was filled with the fragrance of the ointment.

4   But when his disciples saw it, there were some that had indignation within themselves, and said, "Why was this waste of the ointment made? To what purpose is this waste?" Then said one of his disciples, Judas Iscariot, Simon's son, which should betray him, "Why was not this ointment sold for three hundred silver coins, and given to the poor?" This he said, not that he cared for the poor; but because he was a thief, and had the bag, and took what was put therein. And they murmured against her. When Jesus

understood it, he said unto them, "Why trouble the woman? for she has 4
wrought a good work upon me."

Then Jesus said, "Let her alone: for the day of my burial has she kept 5
this. For in that she has poured this ointment on my body, she did it for my
burial. For you have the poor with you
always, and whensoever you will you
may do them good: but me you have
not always. She has done what she

> "SHE HAS DONE WHAT SHE
> COULD."

could: she is come beforehand to anoint my body to the burial.

"Truly I say unto you, Wheresoever this gospel shall be preached 6
throughout the whole world, this also that she has done shall be spoken of
for a memorial of her."

Judas Agrees to Betray Jesus
Matthew 26:14-16; Mark 14:10-11; Luke 22:3-6

Then entered Satan into Judas surnamed Iscariot, being of the number 7
of the twelve. He went his way, and went unto the chief priests, and com-
muned with the chief priests and captains, how he might betray him unto
them. And said unto them, "What will
you give me, and I will deliver him
unto you?" When they heard it, they
were glad, and promised to give him
money. They bargained with him for

> AND THEY BARGAINED WITH
> HIM FOR THIRTY PIECES OF
> SILVER.

thirty pieces of silver. He promised, and from that time, he sought opportunity to betray him unto them in the absence of the multitude.

CHAPTER 45

THE LAST SUPPER

Passover: Preparation
Matthew 26:17-19; Mark 14:12-16; Luke 22:7-13

1   Then came the day of unleavened bread, when the passover must be killed. Now the first day of the feast of unleavened bread the disciples came to Jesus, saying unto him, "Where will you that we go and prepare that you may eat the passover?"

2   And he said, "Go into the city to such a man, and say unto him, 'The Teacher says, "My time is at hand; I will keep the passover at your house with my disciples."'" And he sent Peter and John, saying, "Go and prepare us the passover, that we may eat." And they said unto him, "Where?" And he said unto them, "Behold, when you are entered into the city, there shall a man meet you, bearing a pitcher of water; follow him into the house where he enters in. And you shall say unto the owner of the house, 'The Teacher says unto you, "Where is the guest room, where I shall eat the passover with my disciples?"' And he will show you a large upper room furnished and prepared: there make ready for us."

3   His disciples did as Jesus had appointed them, and came into the city, and found as he had said unto them: and they made ready the passover.

Passover: Observance Begins
Matthew 26:20; Mark 14:17; Luke 22:14-18; John 13:1-4

4   Now before the feast of the passover, when Jesus knew that his hour was come that he should depart out of this world unto the Father, having loved his own which were in the world, he loved them unto the end.

5   In the evening he came with the twelve. And when the hour was come, he sat down, and the twelve apostles with him. He said unto them, "With desire I have desired to eat this passover with you before I suffer: for I say unto you, I will not eat thereof anymore, until it be fulfilled in the kingdom of God."

And he took the cup, and gave thanks, and said, "Take this, and divide 6
it among yourselves: for I say unto you, I will not drink of the fruit of the
vine, until the kingdom of God shall come."

And supper being ended, the devil having now put into the heart of 7
Judas Iscariot, Simon's son, to betray him; Jesus knowing that the Father
had given all things into his hands, and that he was come from God, and
went to God; he rose from supper, and laid aside his garments; and took
a towel, and girded himself.

Passover: Washing Disciples' Feet
John 13:5-17

After that he poured water into a basin, and began to wash the disci- 8
ples' feet, and to wipe them with the towel with which he was girded. Then
he came to Simon Peter: and Peter said unto him, "Lord, do you wash my
feet?" Jesus answered and said unto him, "What I do you know not now; but
you shall know hereafter."

Peter said unto him, "You shall never wash my feet." Jesus answered 9
him, "If I do not wash you, you have no part with me." Simon Peter said
unto him, "Lord, not my feet only, but also my hands and my head." Jesus
said to him, "He that is bathed needs not except to wash his feet, but is clean
every bit: and you are clean, but not all." For he knew who should betray
him; therefore he said, "You are not all clean."

So after he had washed their feet, and had taken his garments, and 10
was seated again, he said unto them,
"Do you know what I have done to | "I HAVE GIVEN YOU AN EXAM-
you? You call me Teacher and Lord: | PLE, THAT YOU SHOULD DO AS
and you say well; for so I am. If I | I HAVE DONE TO YOU."
then, your Lord and Teacher, have
washed your feet; you also ought to wash one another's feet. For I have
given you an example, that you should do as I have done to you.

"Truly, truly, I say unto you, The servant is not greater than his mas- 11
ter; neither he that is sent greater than he that sent him. If you know these
things, happy are you if you do them.

Passover: Prediction of Betrayal
John 13:18-20

"I speak not of you all: I know whom I have chosen: but that the scrip- 12
ture may be fulfilled, '*He that eats
bread with me has lifted up his heel* | "HE THAT RECEIVES WHOMSO-
against me.' Now I tell you before it | EVER I SEND RECEIVES ME;
comes, that, when it is come to pass, | AND HE THAT RECEIVES ME
you may believe that I am he. Truly, | RECEIVES HIM THAT SENT ME."
truly, I say unto you, He that receives
whomsoever I send receives me; and he that receives me receives him that
sent me."

Passover: Betrayer Revealed
Matthew 26:21-25; Mark 14:18-21; Luke 22:21-23; John 13:21-30

13   When Jesus had said these things, and as they sat and did eat, he was troubled in spirit, and testified, and said, "Truly, truly, I say unto you, One of you which eats with me shall betray me." Then the disciples looked one on another, doubting of whom he spoke. And they began to be exceedingly sorrowful, and to say unto him one by one, "Is it I?" and another said, "Is it I?" And he answered and said unto them, "It is one of the twelve," and said, "He that dips his hand with me in the dish, the same shall betray me. But, behold, the hand of him that betrays me is with me on the table.

> "ONE OF YOU WHICH EATS WITH ME SHALL BETRAY ME."

14   "And truly the Son of man goes, as it was determined, as it is written of him: but woe unto that man by whom he is betrayed! it had been good for that man if he had never been born." Then Judas, which betrayed him, answered and said, "Rabbi, is it I?" He said unto him, "You have said."

15   And they began to inquire among themselves, which of them it was that should do this thing. Now there was leaning on Jesus' bosom one of his disciples, whom Jesus loved. Simon Peter therefore beckoned to him, that he should ask who it should be of whom he spoke. He then lying on Jesus' breast said unto him, "Lord, who is it?"

16   Jesus answered, "He it is, to whom I shall give a piece of bread, when I have dipped it." And when he had dipped the piece of bread, he gave it to Judas Iscariot, the son of Simon. And after the piece of bread Satan entered into him. Then said Jesus unto him, "That you do, do quickly."

17   Now no man at the table knew for what intent he spoke this unto him. For some of them thought, because Judas had the bag, that Jesus had said unto him, "Buy those things that we have need of for the feast"; or, that he should give something to the poor.

18   He then having received the piece of bread went immediately out: and it was night.

Passover: Greatest Is He Who Serves
Luke 22:24-30

19   And there was also a dispute among them, which of them should be considered the greatest. He said unto them, "The kings of the Gentiles exercise dominance over them; and they that exercise authority upon them are called benefactors.

20   "But you shall not be so: but he that is greatest among you, let him be as the younger; and he that is leader, as he that does serve. For which is greater, he that sits at the table, or he that serves? is not he that sits at the table ? but I am among you as he that serves.

21   "You are they which have continued with me in my temptations. And I appoint unto you a kingdom, as my Father has appointed unto me; that you

may eat and drink at my table in my kingdom, and sit on thrones judging 21
the twelve tribes of Israel."

Passover: The Last Supper
Matthew 26:26-29; Mark 14:22-25; Luke 22:19-20

And as they were eating, Jesus took bread, and blessed it, and broke it, 22
and gave it to the disciples, and said, "Take, eat: this is my body which is
given for you: this do in remembrance of me."

Likewise also the cup after supper, saying, "This cup is the new testament in my blood, which is shed for
you." And he took the cup, and when
he had given thanks, he gave it to
them, saying, "Drink it all of you; for

> "THIS IS MY BLOOD OF THE
> NEW TESTAMENT, WHICH IS
> SHED FOR MANY FOR THE
> REMISSION OF SINS."

23

this is my blood of the new testament, which is shed for many for the remission of sins." And they all drank of it.

"Truly I say unto you, I will drink no more of the fruit of the vine, until 24
that day when I drink it new with you in my Father's kingdom."

CHAPTER 46

WHAT MUST BE WILL BE

Passover: The New Commandment
John 13:31-35

1   Therefore, when he was gone out, Jesus said, "Now is the Son of man glorified, and God is glorified in him. If God be glorified in him, God shall also glorify him in himself, and shall straightway glorify him. Little children, yet a little while I am with you. You shall seek me: and as I said unto the Jews, Where I go, you cannot come; so now I say to you.

2   "A new commandment I give unto you, That you love one another; as I have loved you, that you also love one another. By this shall all men know that you are my disciples, if you have love one to another."

Passover: Prediction of Denials
Matthew 26:31-35; Mark 14:27-31; Luke 22:31-34; John 13:36-38

3   Simon Peter said unto him, "Lord, where do you go?" Jesus answered him, "Where I go, you cannot follow me now; but you shall follow me afterward."

4   And the Lord said, "Simon, Simon, behold, Satan has desired to have you, that he may sift you as wheat: but I have prayed for you, that your faith not fail: and when you are converted, strengthen your brethren."

5   Then Jesus said unto them, "All you shall fall away because of me this night: for it is written, '*I will strike the shepherd, and the sheep of the flock shall be scattered abroad.*' But after I am risen again, I will go before you into Galilee."

6   Peter answered and said unto him, "Though all men shall fall away because of you, yet will I never fall away." And Jesus said unto him, "Truly I say unto you, That this day, even in this night, before the cock crows twice, you shall deny me three times." Peter said unto him, "Lord, why cannot I follow you now? I will lay down my life for your sake. Lord, I am ready to

go with you, both into prison, and to death." Jesus answered him, "Will you 6 lay down your life for my sake? Truly, truly, I say unto you, Peter, the cock shall not crow this day, before that you shall three times deny that you know me."

But Peter spoke the more emphatically, "Though I should die with 7 you, yet will I not deny you in any way." Likewise also said all the disciples.

Passover: What Is Written Must Be
Luke 22:35-38

And he said unto them, "When I sent you without purse, and bag, and 8 shoes, did you lack anything?" And they said, "Nothing." Then he said unto them, "But now, he that has a purse, let him take it, and likewise his bag: and he that has no sword, let him sell his garment, and buy one.

"For I say unto you, that this that is written must yet be accomplished 9 in me, '*And he was numbered among the transgressors*': for the things concerning me have an end." And they said, "Lord, behold, here are two swords." And he said unto them, "That is enough."

CHAPTER 47

THE PRECIOUS PROMISES

Passover: In My Father's House
John 14:1-14

1   "Let not your heart be troubled: you believe in God, believe also in me. In my Father's house are many mansions: if it were not so, I would have told you. I go to prepare a place for you. And if I go and prepare a place for you, I will come again, and receive you unto myself; that where I am, there you may be also. And where I go you know, and the way you know."

2   Thomas said unto him, "Lord, we know not where you go; and how can we know the way?" Jesus said unto him, "I am the way, the truth, and the life: no man comes unto the Father, but by me. If you had known me, you should have known my Father also: and from henceforth you know him, and have seen him."

3   Philip said unto him, "Lord, show us the Father, and it suffices us." Jesus said unto him, "Have I been so long time with you, and yet have you not known me, Philip? he that has seen me has seen the Father; and how do you say then, 'Show us the Father'? Do you not believe that I am in the Father, and the Father in me? the words that I speak unto you I speak not of myself: but the Father that dwells in me, he does the works. Believe me that I am in the Father, and the Father in me: or else believe me for the very works' sake.

4   "Truly, truly, I say unto you, He that believes on me, the works that I do shall he do also; and greater works than these shall he do; because I go unto my Father. And whatsoever you shall ask in my name, that will I do, that the Father may be glorified in the Son. If you shall ask anything in my name, I will do it."

Passover: Promise of a Comforter
John 14:15-24

5   "If you love me, keep my commandments. And I will ask the Father, and he shall give you another Comforter, that he may be with you for ever;

even the Spirit of truth; whom the world cannot receive, because it sees him 5
not, neither knows him: but you know
him; for he dwells with you, and shall

> "I WILL NOT LEAVE YOU COM-
> FORTLESS."

be in you. I will not leave you com-
fortless: I will come to you.

"Yet a little while, and the world sees me no more; but you see me: 6
because I live, you shall live also. At that day you shall know that I am in
my Father, and you in me, and I in you. He that has my commandments, and
keeps them, he it is that loves me: and he that loves me shall be loved of my
Father, and I will love him, and will manifest myself to him."

Judas said unto him, not Iscariot, "Lord, how is it that you will mani- 7
fest yourself unto us, and not unto the world?" Jesus answered and said unto
him, "If a man loves me, he will keep my words: and my Father will love
him, and we will come unto him, and make our home with him. He that
does not love me does not keep my sayings: and the word which you hear
is not mine, but the Father's which sent me."

Passover: "Peace I Leave With You"
Matthew 26:30; Mark 14:26; John 14:25-31

"These things have I spoken unto you, being yet present with you. But 8
the Comforter, which is the Holy Ghost, whom the Father will send in my
name, he shall teach you all things, and bring all things to your remembrance, whatsoever I have said unto you.

"Peace I leave with you, my peace I give unto you: not as the world 9
gives, give I unto you. Let not your heart be troubled, neither let it be afraid.
You have heard how I said unto you, 'I go away, and come again unto you.'
If you loved me, you would rejoice, because I said, 'I go unto the Father':
for my Father is greater than I.

"And now I have told you before it comes to pass, that, when it is come 10
to pass, you might believe. Hereafter I will not talk much with you: for the
prince of this world comes, and has nothing in me. But that the world may
know that I love the Father; and as the Father gave me commandment, even
so I do. Arise, let us go from here."

And when they had sung a hymn, they went out into the Mount of Olives. 11

CHAPTER 48

THE ETERNAL CONNECTION

"Abide in Me, and I in You"
John 15:1-10

1   "I am the true vine, and my Father is the vinedresser. Every branch in me that bears no fruit he takes away: and every branch that bears fruit, he prunes it, that it may bring forth more fruit. Now you are clean through the word which I have spoken unto you.

2   "Abide in me, and I in you. As the branch cannot bear fruit of itself, except it remains in the vine; no more can you, except you abide in me. I am the vine, you are the branches: He that abides in me, and I in him, the same brings forth much fruit: for without me you can do nothing. If a man does not abide in me, he is cast forth as a branch, and is withered; and men gather them, and cast them into the fire, and they are burned.

3   "If you abide in me, and my words abide in you, you shall ask what you will, and it shall be done unto you. Herein is my Father glorified, that you bear much fruit; so shall you be my disciples. As the Father has loved me, so have I loved you: continue in my love. If you keep my commandments, you shall abide in my love; even as I have kept my Father's commandments, and abide in his love."

"Love One Another"
John 15:11-17

4   "These things have I spoken unto you, that my joy might remain in you, and that your joy might be full. This is my commandment, That you love one another, as I have loved you.

5   "Greater love has no man than this, that a man lay down his life for his friends. You are my friends, if you do whatsoever I command you. Henceforth I do not call you servants; for the servant does not know what his master does: but I have called you friends; for all things that I

have heard of my Father I have made known unto you. You have not cho- 5
sen me, but I have chosen you, and ordained you, that you should go and bring forth fruit, and that your fruit should remain: so that whatsoever you shall ask of the Father in my

> "GREATER LOVE HAS NO MAN THAN THIS, THAT A MAN LAY DOWN HIS LIFE FOR HIS FRIENDS."

name, he may give it you. These things I command you, that you love one another."

"You Also Shall Bear Witness"
John 15:18-27

"If the world hates you, you know that it hated me before it hated you. 6
If you were of the world, the world would love its own: but because you are not of the world, but I have chosen you out of the world, therefore the world hates you. Remember the word that I said unto you, 'The servant is not greater than his master.' If they have persecuted me, they will also persecute you; if they have kept my saying, they will keep yours also. But all these things will they do unto you for my name's sake, because they know not him that sent me.

"If I had not come and spoken unto them, they would have no sin: but 7
now they have no excuse for their sin. He that hates me hates my Father also. If I had not done among them the works which no other man did, they would have no sin: but now they have both seen and hated both me and my Father. But this comes to pass, that the word might be fulfilled that is written in their law, 'They hated me without a cause.'

"But when the Comforter is come, whom I will send unto you from 8
the Father, even the Spirit of truth, which proceeds from the Father, he shall testify of me: and you also shall bear witness, because you have been with me from the beginning."

CHAPTER 49

THE PROMISE TO RETURN

"These Things Have I Told You"
John 16:1-4

1   "These things have I spoken unto you, that you should not fall away. They shall put you out of the synagogues: yes, the time comes, that whosoever kills you will think that he does God service. And these things will they do unto you, because they have not known the Father, nor me.

2   "But these things have I told you, that when the time shall come, you may remember that I told you of them. And these things I have not said unto you at the beginning, because I was with you."

The Spirit of Truth Will Come
John 16:5-15

3   "But now I go my way to him that sent me; and none of you asks me, 'Where do you go?' But because I have said these things unto you, sorrow has filled your hearts. Nevertheless I tell you the truth; It is expedient for you that I go away: for if I do not go away, the Comforter will not come unto you; but if I depart, I will send him unto you. And when he is come, he will expose the world of sin, and of righteousness, and of judgment: of sin, because they do not believe on me; of righteousness, because I go to my Father, and you see me no more; of judgment, because the prince of this world is judged.

4   "I have yet many things to say unto you, but you cannot bear them now. Howbeit when he, the Spirit of truth, is come, he will guide you into all truth: for he shall not speak of himself; but whatsoever he shall hear, that shall he speak: and he will show you things to come. He shall glorify me: for he shall receive of mine, and shall show it unto you. All things that the Father has are mine: therefore said I, that he shall take of mine, and shall show it unto you."

Your Sorrow Will Become Joy
John 16:16-33

"A little while, and you shall not see me: and again, a little while, and 5 you shall see me, because I go to the Father." Then said some of his disciples among themselves, "What is this that he says unto us, 'A little while, and you shall not see me: and again, a little while, and you shall see me': and, 'Because I go to the Father'? They said therefore, "What is this that he says, 'A little while'? we cannot know what he says." Now Jesus knew that they were desirous to ask him, and said unto them, "Do you inquire among yourselves of that I said, 'A little while, and you shall not see me: and again, a little while, and you shall see me'?

"Truly, truly, I say unto you, That you shall weep and lament, but the 6 world shall rejoice: and you shall be sorrowful, but your sorrow shall be turned into joy. A woman when she is in labor has sorrow, because her hour is come: but as soon as she is delivered of the child, she remembers no more the anguish, for joy that a child is born into the world. And you now therefore have sorrow: but I will see you again, and your heart shall rejoice, and your joy no man takes from you. And in that day you shall ask me nothing. Truly, truly, I say unto you, Whatsoever you shall ask the Father in my name, he will give you. Until now have you asked nothing in my name: ask, and you shall receive, that your joy may be full.

"These things have I spoken unto you in figures of speech: but the 7 time comes, when I shall no more speak unto you in figures of speech, but I shall show you plainly of the Father. At that day you shall ask in my name: and I say not unto you, that I will ask the Father for you: for the Father himself loves you, because you have loved me, and have believed that I came out from God. I came forth from the Father, and am come into the world: again, I leave the world, and go to the Father."

His disciples said unto him, "Lo, now you speak plainly, and speak no 8 figure of speech. Now are we sure that you know all things, and need not that any man should ask you: by this we believe that you came forth from God." Jesus answered them, "Do you now believe?

"Behold, the hour comes, yes, is now come, that you shall be scattered, every man to his own, and shall leave me alone: and yet I am not alone, because the Father is with me. These things I have spoken unto

> "IN THE WORLD YOU SHALL HAVE TRIBULATION: BUT BE OF GOOD CHEER; I HAVE OVERCOME THE WORLD."

9

you, that in me you might have peace. In the world you shall have tribulation: but be of good cheer; I have overcome the world."

CHAPTER 50

THE INTERCESSORY PRAYER

Jesus Prays for Himself
John 17:1-5

1   These words spoke Jesus, and lifted up his eyes to heaven, and said, "Father, the hour is come; glorify your Son, that your Son also may glorify you: as you have given him authority over all flesh, that he should give eternal life to as many as you have given him. And this is life eternal, that they might know you the only true God, and Jesus Christ, whom you have sent.

2   "I have glorified you on the earth: I have finished the work which you gave me to do. And now, O Father, glorify me with your own self with the glory which I had with you before the world was."

Jesus Prays for All Disciples
John 17:6-19

3   "I have manifested your name unto the men which you gave me out of the world: yours they were, and you gave them to me; and they have kept your word. Now they have known that all things whatsoever you have given me are of you. For I have given unto them the words which you gave me; and they have received them, and have known surely that I came out from you, and they have believed that you did send me.

4   "I pray for them: I pray not for the world, but for them which you have given me; for they are yours. And all mine are yours, and yours are mine; and I am glorified in them. And now I am no more in the world, but these are in the world, and I come to you. Holy Father, keep through your own name those whom you have given me, that they may be one, as we are. While I was with them in the world, I kept them in your name: those that you gave me I have kept, and none of them is lost, but the son of perdition; that the scripture might be fulfilled.

"And now I come to you; and these things I speak in the world, that 5 they might have my joy fulfilled in themselves. I have given them your word; and the world has hated them, because they are not of the world, even as I am not of the world.

"I pray not that you should take them out of the world, but that you 6 should keep them from the evil. They are not of the world, even as I am not of the world. Sanctify them through your truth: your word is truth. As you have sent me into the world, even so have I also sent them into the world. And for their sakes I sanctify myself, that they also might be sanctified through the truth."

Jesus Prays for All Believers
John 17:20-26

"Neither pray I for these alone, but for them also which shall believe 7 on me through their word; that they all may be one; as you, Father, are in me, and I in you, that they also may be one in us: that the world may believe that you have sent me. And the glory which you gave me I have given them; that they may be one, even as we are one: I in them, and you in me, that they may be made perfect in one; and that the world may know that you have sent me, and have loved them, as you have loved me.

"Father, I desire that they also, whom you have given me, be with me 8 where I am; that they may behold my glory, which you have given me: for you loved me before the foundation of the world.

"O righteous Father, the world has not known you: but I have known 9 you, and these have known that you have sent me. And I have declared unto them your name, and will declare it: that the love with which you have loved me may be in them, and I in them."

PART 11

BETRAYAL, TRIAL, AND DEATH

In anticipation of His final hour, Jesus withdrew to the Mount of Olives to pray. In speechless agony He pleaded with His Father to spare Him from this trial. Yet He knew that there was a cross to be borne before He could make the supreme demonstration of God's power over evil, of joy over sorrow, of life over death. Embracing His divine mission with renewed faith, He asserted His oneness with the Father in the face of His adversaries. For this He was about to suffer violence and offer up the final vestige of His mortal soul. This final act of faith proved the all-encompassing power of God's love for all mankind and for all time.

THERE APPEARED AN ANGEL UNTO HIM FROM
HEAVEN, STRENGTHENING HIM. AND BEING IN
AGONY HE PRAYED MORE EARNESTLY.

(LUKE 22:43-44)

CHAPTER 51

THE TRIAL BEFORE DAWN

Gethsemane: Jesus Prays in Agony
Matthew 26:36-46; Mark 14:32-42; Luke 22:39-46; John 18:1

When Jesus had spoken these words, he came out, and went forth over 1
the brook Cedron, where was a garden, as he was accustomed, to the Mount
of Olives; and his disciples also followed him. And they came to a place
which was named Gethsemane, into which he entered, and his disciples.
When he was at the place, he said unto them, "Pray that you enter not into
temptation." And he said to his disciples, "Sit here, while I go and pray yonder." He took with him Peter and the two sons of Zebedee, James and John,
and began to be sorrowful and very heavy.

Then said he unto them, "My soul is exceedingly sorrowful, even unto 2
death: tarry here, and watch with me." And he went forward about a stone's
cast, and kneeled down, and fell on his face, and prayed that, if it were possible, the hour might pass from him. He said, "Abba, Father, all things are
possible unto you; take away this cup from me: nevertheless not my will,
but yours, be done."

He came unto the disciples, and found them asleep, and said unto 3
Peter, "Simon, do you sleep? What, could you not watch with me one hour?
Watch and pray, that you enter not into temptation: the spirit indeed is will-
ing, but the flesh is weak."

He went away again the second time, and prayed, saying, "O my 4
Father, if this cup may not pass away from me, unless I drink it, your will
be done." And there appeared an angel unto him from heaven, strengthening him. Being in agony he prayed more earnestly: and his sweat was as it
were great drops of blood falling down to the ground.

When he rose up from prayer, and was come to his disciples, he found 5
them asleep again, sleeping for sorrow, for their eyes were heavy. And said
unto them, "Why do you sleep? rise and pray, lest you enter into temptation." And neither knew they what to answer him.

6   And he left them, and went away again, and prayed the third time, saying the same words. He came to his disciples the third time, and said unto them, "Sleep on now, and take your rest: it is enough, the hour is come; behold, the Son of man is betrayed into the hands of sinners. Rise up, let us go; lo, he that betrays me is at hand."

Judas Betrays Jesus
Matthew 26:47-56; Mark 14:43-52; Luke 22:47-53; John 18:2-11

7   Immediately, while he yet spoke, lo, Judas, one of the twelve, came, and with him a great multitude with swords and staves, from the chief priests and the scribes and the elders of the people. And Judas also, which betrayed him, knew the place: for Jesus often met there with his disciples. Judas then, having received a band of men and officers from the chief priests and Pharisees, came there with lanterns and torches and weapons.

8   Jesus therefore, knowing all things that should come upon him, went forth, and said unto them, "Whom do you seek?" They answered him, "Jesus of Nazareth." Jesus said unto them, "I am he." And Judas also, which betrayed him, stood with them. As soon then as he had said unto them, "I am he," they went backward, and fell to the ground.

9   Then he asked them again, "Whom do you seek?" And they said, "Jesus of Nazareth." Jesus answered, "I have told you that I am he: if therefore you seek me, let these go their way": that the saying might be fulfilled, which he spoke, "Of them which you gave me have I lost none."

10   And while he yet spoke, he that was called Judas, one of the twelve, went before them, and drew near unto Jesus to kiss him. Now he that betrayed him had given them a sign, saying, "Whomsoever I shall kiss, that same is he; take him, and lead him away under guard." But Jesus said unto him, "Judas, do you betray the Son of man with a kiss?" And forthwith he came to Jesus, and said, "Hail, Rabbi"; and kissed him. And Jesus said unto him, "Friend, for what purpose are you come?" Then they came, and laid hands on Jesus, and took him.

11   When they which were about him saw what would follow, they said unto him, "Lord, shall we strike with the sword?" Then Simon Peter having a sword drew it, and struck the high priest's servant, and cut off his right ear. The servant's name was Malchus.

12   Then Jesus said unto Peter, "Resist no more." And he touched his ear, and healed him. "Put up your sword into the sheath: for all they that take the sword shall perish with the sword. Do you think that I cannot now appeal to my Father, and he shall at once give me more than twelve legions of angels? But how then shall the scriptures be fulfilled, that thus it must be? The cup which my Father has given me, shall I not drink it?"

> "THEY THAT TAKE THE SWORD SHALL PERISH WITH THE SWORD."

Then Jesus said unto the chief priests, and captains of the temple, and 13 the elders, which were come to him, "Are you come out, as against a thief, with swords and staves to take me? When I sat daily with you teaching in the temple, you stretched forth no hands against me: but this is your hour, and the power of darkness. But all this was done, that the scriptures of the prophets might be fulfilled." Then all the disciples forsook him, and fled.

And there followed him a certain young man, having a linen cloth cast 14 about his naked body; and the young men laid hold on him: and he left the linen cloth, and fled from them naked.

Jesus Is Seized and Taken Away
Matthew 26:57-58; Mark 14:53-54; Luke 22:54-55; John 18:12-16

Then the band and the captain and officers of the Jews took Jesus, and 15 bound him, and led him away to Annas first; for he was father-in-law to Caiaphas, which was the high priest that same year. Now Caiaphas was he, which gave advice to the Jews, that it was expedient that one man should die for the people.

And they that had laid hold on Jesus led him away to Caiaphas the 16 high priest, and brought him into the high priest's house, where the chief priests and the scribes and the elders were assembled. And Simon Peter followed Jesus afar off unto the high priest's palace, and so did another disciple: that disciple was known unto the high priest, and went in with Jesus into the palace of the high priest. But Peter stood at the door outside. Then went out that other disciple, which was known unto the high priest, and spoke unto her that kept the door, and brought in Peter. And when they had kindled a fire in the midst of the hall, and were seated together, Peter sat down among the servants, and warmed himself at the fire, to see the end.

Council: Questioned and Struck
John 18:19-24

The high priest then asked Jesus of his disciples, and of his doctrine. 17 Jesus answered him, "I spoke openly to the world; I ever taught in the synagogues, and in the temple, where the Jews always meet; and in secret have I said nothing. Why do you ask me? ask them which heard me, what I have said unto them: behold, they know what I said."

And when he had thus spoken, one of the officers which stood by 18 struck Jesus with the palm of his hand, saying, "Do you answer the high priest so?" Jesus answered him, "If I have spoken evil, bear witness of the evil: but if well, why do you strike me?" Now Annas had sent him bound unto Caiaphas the high priest.

Council: The False Witnesses
Matthew 26:59-62; Mark 14:55-60

Now the chief priests, and elders, and all the council, sought for wit- 19 ness against Jesus to put him to death; but found none. For many bore false

19 witness against him, but their witness had not agreed together. At the last came two false witnesses, and said, "This fellow said, 'I am able to destroy the temple of God, and to build it in three days.'" And saying, "We heard him say, 'I will destroy this temple that is made with hands, and within three days I will build another made without hands.'" But neither so did their witness agree together.

20 And the high priest stood up in the midst, and asked Jesus, saying, "Do you answer nothing? what is it which these witness against you?"

Council: Questioned and Beaten
Matthew 26:63-68; Mark 14:61-65; Luke 22:63-65

21 But Jesus held his peace, and answered nothing. And the high priest answered and said unto him, "I charge you by the living God, that you tell us whether you be the Christ, the Son of God." Jesus said unto him, "You have said: nevertheless I say unto you, Hereafter shall you see *the Son of man sitting on the right hand of power, and coming in the clouds of heaven.*" Again the high priest asked him, and said unto him, "Are you the Christ, the Son of the Blessed?" And Jesus said, "I am."

22 Then the high priest tore his clothes, saying, "He has spoken blasphemy; what further need have we of witnesses? behold, now you have heard his blasphemy. What do you think?" They answered and said, "He is guilty of death." And they all condemned him to be guilty of death.

23 And the men that held Jesus mocked him, and struck him. And some began to spit in his face, and the servants did strike him with the palms of their hands. And when they had blindfolded him, they struck him on the face, and asked him, saying, "Prophesy unto us, you Christ, Who is it that struck you?" And many other things blasphemously spoke they against him.

Council: Outside Peter Denies Jesus
Matthew 26:69-75; Mark 14:66-72; Luke 22:56-62; John 18:17-18, 25-27

24 Now Peter sat outside in the palace. And the servants and officers stood there, who had made a fire of coals; for it was cold: and they warmed themselves: and Peter stood with them, and warmed himself. There came one of the servant girls of the high priest that kept the door. And when she saw Peter warming himself, she closely looked upon him, and said, "Are not you also one of this man's disciples? You also were with Jesus of Galilee." But he denied him before them all, saying, "I know not, neither do I understand what you say." And he went out into the porch; and the cock crowed.

25 When he was gone out into the porch, after a little while, another girl saw him, and said unto them that were there, "This fellow was also with Jesus of Nazareth." They said therefore unto him, "Are not you also one of his disciples?" And again he denied with an oath, "I do not know the man."

26 And about the space of one hour later, one of the servants of the high priest, being his relative whose ear Peter cut off, said, "Did not I see you in

the garden with him? Surely you also are one of them: for you are a 26 Galilean; for your speech betrays you." But he began to curse and to swear, saying, "Man, I know not what you say. I know not this man of whom you speak." And immediately, while he yet spoke, the cock crowed the second time. And the Lord turned, and looked upon Peter. And Peter called to mind the word that Jesus said unto him, "Before the cock crows twice, you shall deny me three times." And when he thought thereon, Peter went out, and wept bitterly.

Council: Condemned to Pilate
Matthew 27:1-2; Mark 15:1; Luke 22:66-71; 23:1

When the morning was come, all the chief priests and elders of the 27 people and the scribes plotted against Jesus to put him to death: and led him into their council, saying, "Are you the Christ? tell us." And he said unto them, "If I tell you, you will not believe: and if I also ask you, you will not answer me, nor let me go. Hereafter shall *the Son of man sit on the right hand of the power of God.*" Then said they all, "Are you then the Son of God?" And he said unto them, "You say that I am." They said, "What need we any further witness? for we ourselves have heard of his own mouth." The whole multitude of them arose, and when they had bound Jesus, they led him away, and delivered him to Pontius Pilate the governor.

Judas Hangs Himself
Matthew 27:3-10

Then Judas, which had betrayed him, when he saw that he was con- 28 demned, repented himself, and brought back the thirty pieces of silver to the chief priests and elders, saying, "I have sinned in that I have betrayed the innocent blood." And they said, "What is that to us? you see to that." And he cast down the pieces of silver in the temple, and departed, and went and hanged himself.

And the chief priests took the silver pieces, and said, "It is not lawful 29 to put them into the treasury, because it is the price of blood." And they conferred, and bought with them the potter's field, to bury foreigners in. Therefore that field was called, The Field of Blood, unto this day. Then was fulfilled that which was spoken by Jeremiah the prophet, saying, *"And they took the thirty pieces of silver, the price of him that was valued, whom they of the children of Israel did value; and gave them for the potter's field, as the Lord appointed me."*

CHAPTER 52

THE ROMAN TRIAL

Before Pilate: Accusations
Luke 23:2; John 18:28-32

1   Then they led Jesus from Caiaphas unto the hall of judgment: and it was early; and they themselves went not into the judgment hall, lest they should be defiled; but that they might eat the passover. Pilate then went out unto them, and said, "What accusation do you bring against this man?"

2   They answered and said unto him, "If he were not an evildoer, we would not have delivered him up unto you." Then said Pilate unto them, "Take him, and judge him according to your law." The Jews therefore said unto him, "It is not lawful for us to put any man to death": that the saying of Jesus might be fulfilled, which he spoke, signifying what death he should die.

3   And they began to accuse him, saying, "We found this fellow perverting the nation, and forbidding to give tribute to Caesar, saying that he himself is Christ a King."

Before Pilate: King of the Jews?
Matthew 27:11-14; Mark 15:2-5; Luke 23:3-7; John 18:33-38

4   And Jesus stood before the governor: and the governor asked him, saying, "Are you the King of the Jews?" Jesus said unto him, "You say it." And the chief priests and elders accused him of many things: but he answered nothing. Pilate asked him again, saying, "Do you answer nothing? behold how many things they witness against you." But Jesus answered him to never a word; insomuch that the governor marveled greatly.

5   Then Pilate entered into the judgment hall again, and called Jesus, and said unto him, "Are you the King of the Jews?" Jesus answered him, "Do you say this thing of yourself, or did others tell you it of me?" Pilate answered, "Am I a Jew? Your own nation and the chief priests have delivered you unto me: what have you done?"

Jesus answered, "My kingdom is not of this world: if my kingdom 6 were of this world, then would my servants fight, that I should not be delivered to the Jews: but now is my kingdom not from here."

Pilate therefore said unto him, "Are you a king then?" Jesus answered, 7 "You say that I am a king. To this end was I born, and for this cause came I into the world, that I should bear witness unto the truth. Everyone that is of the truth hears my voice." Pilate said unto him, "What is truth?" And when he had said this, he went out again

> "TO THIS END WAS I BORN, AND FOR THIS CAUSE CAME I INTO THE WORLD, THAT I SHOULD BEAR WITNESS UNTO THE TRUTH."

unto the Jews, and said to the chief priests and to the people, "I find no fault in this man at all."

And they were the more fierce, saying, "He stirs up the people, teach- 8 ing throughout all Judea, beginning from Galilee to this place."

When Pilate heard of Galilee, he asked whether the man were a 9 Galilean. And as soon as he knew that he belonged unto Herod's jurisdiction, he sent him to Herod, who himself also was at Jerusalem at that time.

Before Pilate: Sent to Herod
Luke 23:8-12

And when Herod saw Jesus, he was exceedingly glad: for he was 10 desirous to see him of a long time, because he had heard many things of him; and he hoped to have seen some miracle done by him. Then he questioned with him in many words; but he answered him nothing. And the chief priests and scribes stood and strongly accused him.

Herod with his men of war rejected him, and mocked him, and arrayed 11 him in a gorgeous robe, and sent him again to Pilate.

The same day Pilate and Herod were made friends together: for before 12 they were at hostility between themselves.

Before Pilate: Whom to Release?
Matthew 27:15-16; Mark 15:6-7; Luke 23:13-17

And Pilate, when he had called together the chief priests and the rulers 13 and the people, said unto them, "You have brought this man unto me, as one that perverts the people: and, behold, I, having examined him before you, have found no fault in this man concerning those things whereof you accuse him: no, nor Herod: for I sent you to him; and, lo, nothing deserving of death is done by him. I will therefore chastise him, and release him."

Now at that feast the governor was accustomed to release unto the 14 people one prisoner, whomsoever they desired. And there was then a notorious prisoner, named Barabbas, which lay bound with them that had made insurrection with him, who had committed murder in the insurrection.

Before Pilate: "Crucify Him!"
Matthew 27:17-23; Mark 15:8-14; Luke 23:18-23; John 18:39-40

15   And the multitude crying aloud began to desire him to do as he had ever done unto them. Therefore when they were gathered together, Pilate answered them, saying, "Whom will you that I release unto you? Barabbas, or Jesus which is called Christ? For you have a custom, that I should release unto you one at the passover: will you therefore that I release unto you the King of the Jews?" For he knew that the chief priests had delivered him for envy.

16   When he was seated on the judgment seat, his wife sent unto him, saying, "Have nothing to do with that just man: for I have suffered many things this day in a dream because of him."

17   But the chief priests and elders persuaded the multitude that he should rather release Barabbas unto them, and destroy Jesus. The governor answered and said unto them, "Which of the two will you that I release unto you?" They said, "Barabbas." And they all cried out at once, saying, "Away with this man, and release unto us Barabbas": (who for a certain insurrection made in the city, and for murder, was cast into prison). Then they all cried again, saying, "Not this man, but Barabbas." Now Barabbas was a robber.

18   And Pilate answered and said again unto them, "What will you then that I shall do with Jesus which is called Christ, whom you call the King of the Jews?" They all said unto him, "Let him be crucified." And they cried out again, "Crucify him."

19   Then Pilate said unto them, "Why, what evil has he done?" And they cried out the more, saying, "Let him be crucified." Pilate therefore, willing to release Jesus, spoke again to them. But they cried, saying, "Crucify him, crucify him."

20   Then Pilate the governor said unto them the third time, "Why, what evil has he done? I have found no cause of death in him: I will therefore chastise him, and let him go." And they were insistent with loud voices, requiring that he might be crucified. And the voices of them and of the chief priests prevailed.

Before Pilate: Jesus Is to Die
Matthew 27:24-26; Mark 15:15; Luke 23:24-25; John 19:1

21   When Pilate saw that he could prevail nothing, but that rather a tumult was made, he took water, and washed his hands before the multitude, saying, "I am innocent of the blood of this just person: you see to it." Then answered all the people, and said, "His blood be on us, and on our children."

22   Pilate gave sentence that it should be as they required. He released unto them him that for insurrection and murder was cast into prison, whom they had desired; but he delivered Jesus to their will. And so Pilate, willing to satisfy the people, released Barabbas unto them, and when he had scourged Jesus, he delivered Jesus to be crucified.

Before Pilate: Crown of Thorns
Matthew 27:27-30; Mark 15:16-19; John 19:2-3

Then the soldiers of the governor led Jesus away into the common 23 hall, called Praetorium; and gathered unto him the whole band of soldiers. They stripped him, and they clothed him with a purple robe. And when they had twisted a crown of thorns, they put it upon his head, and a reed in his right hand: and they bowed the knee before him, and mocked him, and said, "Hail, King of the Jews!" and they struck him with their hands. They spit upon him, and took the reed, and struck him on the head.

Before Pilate: Final Decision
John 19:4-16

Pilate therefore went forth again, and said unto them, "Behold, I bring 24 him forth to you, that you may know that I find no fault in him." Then came Jesus forth, wearing the crown of thorns, and the purple robe. And Pilate said unto them, "Behold the man!"

When the chief priests therefore and officers saw him, they cried out, 25 saying, "Crucify him, crucify him." Pilate said unto them, "Take him, and crucify him: for I find no fault in him." The Jews answered him, "We have a law, and by our law he ought to die, because he made himself the Son of God."

When Pilate therefore heard that saying, he was the more afraid; and 26 went again into the judgment hall, and said unto Jesus, "From where are you?" But Jesus gave him no answer. Then said Pilate unto him, "Do you not speak unto me? know you not that I have power to crucify you, and have power to release you?"

Jesus answered, "You could have no power at all against me, except it 27 were given you from above: therefore he that delivered me unto you has the greater sin." And from then on Pilate sought to release him: but the Jews cried out, saying, "If you let this man go, you are not Caesar's friend: whosoever makes himself a king speaks against Caesar."

When Pilate therefore heard that saying, he brought Jesus forth, and 28 sat down in the judgment seat in a place that is called the Pavement, but in the Hebrew, Gabbatha. And it was the preparation of the passover, and about the sixth hour: and he said unto the Jews, "Behold your King!"

But they cried out, "Away with him, away with him, crucify him." 29 Pilate said unto them, "Shall I crucify your King?" The chief priests answered, "We have no king but Caesar." Then he delivered him therefore unto them to be crucified. And they took Jesus, and led him away.

Before Pilate: Jesus Is Mocked
Matthew 27:31; Mark 15:20

And when they had mocked him, they took off the purple robe from 30 him, and put his own clothes on him, and led him out to crucify him.

CHAPTER 53

THE DARKEST DAY

The Son of God Is Crucified
Matthew 27:32-44; Mark 15:21-32; Luke 23:26-43; John 19:17-24

1   And as they came out, they found a man of Cyrene, Simon by name, coming out of the country, the father of Alexander and Rufus: him they compelled to bear his cross. And as they led him away, on him they laid the cross, that he might bear it after Jesus.

2   There followed him a great company of people, and of women, which also bewailed and lamented him. But Jesus turning unto them said, "Daughters of Jerusalem, weep not for me, but weep for yourselves, and for your children. For, behold, the days are coming, in which they shall say, 'Blessed are the barren, and the wombs that never bore, and the breasts which never nursed babies.' Then shall they begin *'to say to the mountains, "Fall on us"; and to the hills, "Cover us."'* For if they do these things in a green tree, what shall be done in the dry?"

3   And there were also two others, criminals, led with him to be put to death.

4   They bring him bearing his cross unto a place called Golgotha in the Hebrew, that is to say, a place of a skull, which is called Calvary: where they crucified him, and the two criminals, one on the right hand, and the other on the left, and Jesus in the middle. And they gave him to drink wine, sour wine mingled with myrrh, gall: and when he had tasted thereof, he would not drink. Then Jesus said, "Father, forgive them; for they know not what they do."

5   It was the third hour, and they crucified him. Then the soldiers, when they had crucified Jesus, took his garments, and made four parts, and parted his garments, to every soldier a part; and also his coat: now the coat was without seam, woven from the top throughout. They said therefore among themselves, "Let us not tear it, but cast lots for it, whose it shall be": that the scripture might be fulfilled, which says, *"They parted my garments*

among them, and for my clothing they did cast lots." These things therefore 5
the soldiers did.

Sitting down they watched him there. And Pilate wrote a title, and put 6
it on the cross. The writing was, JESUS OF NAZARETH THE KING OF
THE JEWS. This title then read many of the Jews: for the place where Jesus
was crucified was near to the city: and it was written in Hebrew, and Greek,
and Latin. Then said the chief priests of the Jews to Pilate, "Write not, 'The
King of the Jews'; but that 'he said, "I am King of the Jews." ' " Pilate
answered, "What I have written I have written."

Then there were two thieves crucified with him, one on the right hand, 7
and another on the left. And the scripture was fulfilled, which says, *"And he
was numbered with the transgressors."* They that passed by hurled insults
on him, wagging their heads, and saying, "Ah, you that destroy the temple,
and build it in three days, save yourself, and come down from the cross. If
you be the Son of God, come down from the cross."

And the people stood beholding. The rulers also with them scoffed at 8
him, saying, "He saved others; let him save himself, if he be Christ, the chosen of God." The soldiers also mocked him, coming to him, and offering him
sour wine, and saying, "If you be the king of the Jews, save yourself."

Likewise also the chief priests mocking him, with the scribes and eld- 9
ers, said among themselves, "He saved others; himself he cannot save. If he
be the King of Israel, let him now come down from the cross, that we may
see, and we will believe him. He trusted in God; let him deliver him now, if
he will have him: for he said, 'I am the Son of God.'" The thieves also,
which were crucified with him, hurled insults on him.

And one of the criminals which were hanged hurled insults on him, 10
saying, "If you be Christ, save yourself and us." But the other answering
rebuked him, saying, "Do you not fear God, seeing you are in the same condemnation? And we indeed justly; for we receive the due reward of our
deeds: but this man has done nothing wrong." He said unto Jesus, "Lord,
remember me when you come into your kingdom." Jesus said unto him,
"Truly I say unto you, Today shall you be with me in paradise."

Jesus Provides for His Mother
John 19:25-27

Now there stood by the cross of Jesus his mother, and his mother's sis- 11
ter, Mary the wife of Clopas, and Mary Magdalene. When Jesus therefore saw
his mother, and the disciple standing by, whom he loved, he said unto his
mother, "Woman, behold your son!" Then he said to the disciple, "Behold
your mother!" And from that hour that disciple took her unto his own home.

Jesus Dies on the Cross
Matthew 27:45-56; Mark 15:33-41; Luke 23:44-49; John 19:28-37

It was about the sixth hour, and from the sixth hour there was darkness 12
over the whole land until the ninth hour.

13 And at about the ninth hour Jesus cried with a loud voice, saying, "Eloi, Eloi, lama sabachthani?" which is, being interpreted, *"My God, my God, why have you forsaken me?"* Some of them that stood there, when they heard that, said, "Behold, he calls for Elijah."

> "MY GOD, MY GOD, WHY HAVE YOU FORSAKEN ME?"

14 After this, Jesus knowing that all things were now accomplished, that the scripture might be fulfilled, said, "I thirst." Now there was set a vessel full of sour wine: and straightway one of them ran, and took a sponge, and filled it with sour wine, and put it on a hyssop reed, and put it to his mouth, and gave him to drink, saying "Let alone; let us see whether Elijah will come to take him down."

15 The rest said, "Let him be, let us see whether Elijah will come to save him."

16 When Jesus therefore had received the sour wine, he said, "It is finished": and when Jesus had cried again with a loud voice, he said, *"Father, into your hands I commend my spirit"*: and having said thus, he bowed his head, and gave up the ghost.

> "IT IS FINISHED"…"FATHER, INTO YOUR HANDS I COMMEND MY SPIRIT."

17 And the sun was darkened, and, behold, the veil of the temple was torn in two, in the middle, from the top to the bottom; and the earth did quake, and the rocks split; and the graves were opened; and many bodies of the saints which slept arose, and came out of the graves after his resurrection, and went into the holy city, and appeared unto many.

18 Now when the centurion, and they that were with him, watching Jesus, saw the earthquake, and those things that were done, they feared greatly. And when the centurion, which stood opposite him, saw that he so cried out, and gave up the ghost, he glorified God, saying, "Certainly this was a righteous man. Truly this man was the Son of God."

19 And all the people that came together to that sight, beholding the things which were done, struck down their breasts, and returned. And all his acquaintances, and the women that followed him from Galilee, stood afar off, beholding these things: among whom was Mary Magdalene, and Mary the mother of James the less and of Joses, and Salome, the mother of Zebedee's children; (who also, when he was in Galilee, followed him, and ministered unto him); and many other women which came up with him unto Jerusalem.

20 The Jews therefore, because it was the preparation, that the bodies should not remain upon the cross on the sabbath day, (for that sabbath day was a high day), besought Pilate that their legs might be broken, and that they might be taken away. Then came the soldiers, and broke the legs of the first, and of the other which was crucified with him. But when they came to Jesus, and saw that he was dead already, they did not break his legs: but one of the soldiers with a spear pierced his side, and at once came there out blood and water.

And he that saw it bore witness, and his witness is true: and he knows 21 that he says true, that you might believe. For these things were done, that the scripture should be fulfilled, "*A bone of him shall not be broken.*" And again another scripture says, "*They shall look on him whom they pierced.*"

Burial of Jesus
Matthew 27:57-61; Mark 15:42-47; Luke 23:50-56; John 19:38-42

After this when the evening was come, because it was the preparation, 22 that is, the day before the sabbath, behold, there was a rich man of Arimathea, a city of the Jews, named Joseph, a prominent council member, a good man, and just: (the same had not consented to the purpose and deed of them); who also himself waited for the kingdom of God. And being a disciple of Jesus, but secretly for fear of the Jews, came, and went in boldly unto Pilate, and asked for the body of Jesus. And Pilate marveled that he were already dead: and calling unto him the centurion, he asked him whether he had been already dead. And when he knew it of the centurion, Pilate gave him permission. Then Pilate commanded the body to be delivered to Joseph. He came therefore, and took the body of Jesus.

Now in the place where he was crucified there was a garden; and in 23 the garden a new tomb, wherein was never man yet laid. And he bought fine linen, and when Joseph had taken the body down, he wrapped it in a clean linen cloth: and laid it in his own new tomb, which he had hewn out in the rock. There came also Nicodemus, which at the first came to Jesus by night, and brought a mixture of myrrh and aloes, about a hundred pounds in weight. Then they took the body of Jesus, and wound it in linen clothes with the spices, as the manner of the Jews is to bury. There they laid Jesus; for the tomb was near at hand: and rolled a great stone unto the door of the tomb, and departed.

That day was the preparation, and the sabbath drew on. There was 24 Mary Magdalene, and the other Mary the mother of Joses, sitting opposite the tomb, and beheld where he was laid. And the women also, which came with him from Galilee, followed after, and beheld the tomb, and how his body was laid. They returned, and prepared spices and ointments; and rested the sabbath day according to the commandment.

Pilate Places a Watch at the Tomb
Matthew 27:62-66

Now the next day, that followed the day of the preparation, the chief 25 priests and Pharisees came together unto Pilate, saying, "Sir, we remember that that deceiver said, while he was yet alive, 'After three days I will rise again.' Command therefore that the tomb be made sure until the third day, lest his disciples come by night, and steal him away, and say unto the people, 'He is risen from the dead': so the last error shall be worse than the first."

Pilate said unto them, "You have a guard: go your way, make it as 26 secure as you can." So they went, and made the tomb secure, sealing the stone, and setting a guard.

PART 12

RESURRECTION AND ASCENSION

Just three days past the pain, humiliation, and sorrow of His death on the cross, Jesus rose from the dead in radiant glory, victorious over the grave. He rolled away the stone of doubt from the hearts of all mankind and wiped the tears of sorrow from their eyes. With one divine act He vanquished evil and overcame the last enemy, called death. Then He revealed Himself—as He does today—to all prepared to accept the infinite possibilities of God.

> FOR, BEHOLD, THERE WAS A GREAT EARTHQUAKE:
> FOR THE ANGEL OF THE LORD DESCENDED FROM
> HEAVEN, AND CAME AND ROLLED BACK THE
> STONE FROM THE DOOR. (MATTHEW 28:2)

CHAPTER 54

THE BRIGHTEST DAWN

Jesus Is Raised From the Dead
Matthew 28:1-8; Mark 16:1-8; Luke 24:1-7; John 20:1-2

1 Now when the sabbath was past, upon the first day of the week when it was yet dark, Mary Magdalene, and the other Mary the mother of James, and Salome, had bought sweet spices, that they might come and anoint him. And very early in the morning as it began to dawn at the rising of the sun, they came unto the tomb, bringing the spices which they had prepared, and certain others with them. And they said among themselves, "Who shall roll us away the stone from the door of the tomb?" And when they looked, they saw that the stone was rolled away: for it was very great.

2 For, behold, there was a great earthquake: for the angel of the Lord descended from heaven, and came and rolled back the stone from the door, and sat upon it. His countenance was like lightning, and his clothing white as snow: and for fear of him the guards did shake, and became as dead men.

3 And the angel answered and said unto the women, "Fear not: for I know that you seek Jesus, which was crucified. He is not here: for he is risen, as he said. Come, see the place where the Lord lay. Go quickly, and tell his disciples that he is risen from the dead; and, behold, he goes before you into Galilee; there shall you see him: lo, I have told you."

4 And they entered into the tomb, and did not find the body of the Lord Jesus. They saw a young man sitting on the right side, clothed in a long white robe; and they were alarmed. He said unto them, "Be not alarmed: You seek Jesus of Nazareth, which was crucified: he is risen; he is not here: behold the place where they laid him."

5 And it came to pass, as the women were much perplexed about this, behold, two men stood by them in shining clothes: and as the women were afraid, and bowed down their faces to the earth, they said unto them, "Why do you seek the living among the dead? He is not here, but is risen:

5   remember how he spoke unto you when he was yet in Galilee, saying, 'The Son of man must be delivered into the hands of sinful men, and be crucified, and the third day rise again.'

6   "But go your way, tell his disciples and Peter that he goes before you into Galilee: there shall you see him, as he said unto you." And they went out quickly, and fled from the tomb; for they trembled and were amazed: neither said they anything to any man; for they were afraid.

7   Then Mary Magdalene ran, and came to Simon Peter, and to the other disciple, whom Jesus loved, and said unto them, "They have taken away the Lord out of the tomb, and we know not where they have laid him."

8   And they departed from the tomb with fear and great joy; and did run to bring his disciples word.

John and Peter See Empty Tomb
Luke 24:12; John 20:3-10

9   Peter therefore went forth, and that other disciple, and came to the tomb. So they ran both together: and the other disciple did outrun Peter, and came first to the tomb. And he stooping down, and looking in, saw the linen clothes lying; yet he went not in.

10   Then came Simon Peter following him unto the tomb; and stooping down, he beheld the linen clothes laid by themselves, and went into the tomb, and saw the linen clothes lie, and the cloth, that was about his head, not lying with the linen clothes, but wrapped together in a place by itself, wondering in himself at that which was come to pass.

11   Then went in also that other disciple, which came first to the tomb, and he saw, and believed. For as yet they knew not the scripture, that he must rise again from the dead. Then the disciples went away again unto their own homes.

Jesus Appears to Mary Magdalene
Mark 16:9-11; John 20:11-18

12   But Mary stood outside at the tomb weeping: and as she wept, she stooped down, and looked into the tomb, and saw two angels in white sitting, the one at the head, and the other at the feet, where the body of Jesus had lain. And they said unto her, "Woman, why do you weep?" She said unto them, "Because they have taken away my Lord, and I do not know where they have laid him."

13   And when she had thus said, she turned herself around, and saw Jesus standing, and knew not that it was Jesus. Now when Jesus was risen early the first day of the week, he appeared first to Mary Magdalene, out of whom he had cast seven demons.

14   Jesus said unto her, "Woman, why do you weep? whom do you seek?" She, supposing him to be the gardener, said unto him, "Sir, if you have

carried him from here, tell me where you have laid him, and I will take him 14
away."

Jesus said unto her, "Mary." She turned herself, and said unto him, 15
"Rabboni"; which is to say, Teacher. Jesus said unto her, "Do not touch me;
for I am not yet ascended to my Father: but go to my brethren, and say unto
them, 'I ascend unto my Father, and your Father; and to my God, and your
God.'"

Mary Magdalene came and told the disciples that had been with him, 16
as they mourned and wept, that she had seen the Lord, and that he had spoken these things unto her. And they, when they had heard that he was alive,
and had been seen of her, did not believe her.

Jesus Appears to the Women
Matthew 28:9-10

As they (the women) went to tell his disciples, behold, Jesus met them, 17
saying, "All hail." And they came and held him by the feet, and worshiped
him. Then said Jesus unto them, "Be not afraid: go tell my brethren that they
go into Galilee, and there shall they see me."

Women Give Witness to Resurrection
Luke 24:8-11

And they remembered his words, and told all these things unto the 18
eleven, and to all the rest. It was Mary Magdalene, and Joanna, and Mary
the mother of James, and other women that were with them, which told
these things unto the apostles. Their words seemed to them as idle tales, and
they did not believe them.

Report of the Watch Made False
Matthew 28:11-15

Now when they were going, behold, some of the guard came into the 19
city, and showed unto the chief priests all the things that were done. And
when they were assembled with the elders, and had conferred, they gave a
large sum of money unto the soldiers, saying, "You say, 'His disciples came
by night, and stole him away while we slept.' And if this comes to the governor's ears, we will persuade him, and secure you." So they took the
money, and did as they were instructed: and this saying is commonly
reported among the Jews until this day.

Jesus Appears to Two on the Road
Mark 16:12-13; Luke 24:13-35

After that he appeared in another form unto two of them, as they 20
walked, and went into the country. And, behold, two of them went that same
day to a village called Emmaus, which was from Jerusalem about seven
miles. And they talked together of all these things which had happened.

And it came to pass, that, while they talked together and reasoned, Jesus 21
himself drew near, and went with them. But their eyes were constrained that

21 they should not know him. And he said unto them, "What manner of communications are these that you have one to another, as you walk, and are sad?"

22 And the one of them, whose name was Cleopas, answering said unto him, "Are you only a visitor in Jerusalem, and have not known the things which are come to pass there in these days?" And he said unto them, "What things?" And they said unto him, "Concerning Jesus of Nazareth, which was a prophet mighty in deed and word before God and all the people: and how the chief priests and our rulers delivered him to be condemned to death, and have crucified him. But we trusted that it had been he which should have redeemed Israel: and besides all this, today is the third day since these things were done.

23 "Yes, and certain women also of our company made us astonished, which were early at the tomb; and when they did not find his body, they came, saying, that they had also seen a vision of angels, which said that he was alive.

24 "And certain of them which were with us went to the tomb, and found it even so as the women had said: but him they did not see." Then he said unto them, "O fools, and slow of heart to believe all that the prophets have spoken: ought not Christ to have suffered these things, and to enter into his glory?" And beginning at Moses and all the prophets, he explained unto them in all the scriptures the things concerning himself.

25 They drew near unto the village, where they went: and he made as though he would have gone farther. But they stopped him, saying, "Stay with us: for it is toward evening, and the day is far spent." And he went in to tarry with them.

26 And it came to pass, as he sat at the table with them, he took bread, and blessed it, and broke, and gave to them. And their eyes were opened, and they knew him; and he vanished out of their sight. And they said one to another, "Did not our heart burn within us, while he talked with us on the road, and while he opened to us the scriptures?"

27 They rose up the same hour, and returned to Jerusalem, and found the eleven gathered together, and them that were with them, saying, "The Lord is risen indeed, and has appeared to Simon." They told what things were done on the road, and how he was known of them in breaking of bread: neither did they believe them.

Jesus Appears to Disciples
Mark 16:14; Luke 24:36-43; John 20:19-25

28 Then the same day at evening, being the first day of the week, when the doors were shut where the disciples were assembled for fear of the Jews, he appeared unto the eleven as they sat at the table, and rebuked them with their unbelief and hardness of heart, because they had not believed them which had seen him after he was risen. And as they thus spoke, Jesus himself stood in the midst of them, and said unto them, "Peace be unto you."

But they were terrified and frightened, and supposed that they had 29
seen a spirit. And he said unto them, "Why are you troubled? and why do
thoughts arise in your hearts? Behold my hands and my feet, that it is I
myself: handle me, and see; for a spirit has not flesh and bones, as you see
me have."

When he had thus spoken, he showed them his hands and his feet and 30
his side. And while they yet had not believed for joy, and wondered, he said
unto them, "Have you here any food?" And they gave him a piece of a
broiled fish, and of a honeycomb. And he took it, and did eat before them.
Then were the disciples glad, when they saw the Lord.

Then Jesus said to them again, "Peace be unto you: as my Father has 31
sent me, even so I send you." And
when he had said this, he breathed on   "RECEIVE THE HOLY GHOST."
them, and said unto them, "Receive
the Holy Ghost: those whose sins you forgive, they are forgiven unto them;
and those whose sins you retain, they are retained."

But Thomas, one of the twelve, called Didymus, was not with them 32
when Jesus came. The other disciples therefore said unto him, "We have
seen the Lord." But he said unto them, "Unless I shall see in his hands the
print of the nails, and put my finger into the print of the nails, and thrust my
hand into his side, I will not believe."

CHAPTER 55

THE GREAT COMMISSION

Jesus Appears to Thomas
John 20:26-29

1   And after eight days again his disciples were inside, and Thomas with them: then Jesus came, the doors being shut, and stood in the midst, and said, "Peace be unto you." Then he said to Thomas, "Reach here your finger, and behold my hands; and reach here your hand, and thrust it into my side: and be not faithless, but believing."

2   Thomas answered and said unto him, "My Lord and my God." Jesus said unto him, "Thomas, because you have seen me, you have believed: blessed are they that have not seen, and yet have believed."

Jesus Appears at the Sea of Galilee
John 21:1-14

3   After these things Jesus showed himself again to the disciples at the sea of Galilee; and in this way he showed himself. There were together Simon Peter, and Thomas called Didymus, and Nathanael of Cana in Galilee, and the sons of Zebedee, and two others of his disciples. Simon Peter said unto them, "I go fishing." They said unto him, "We also go with you." They went forth, and entered into a ship immediately; and that night they caught nothing. But when the morning was now come, Jesus stood on the shore: but the disciples did not know that it was Jesus.

4   Then Jesus said unto them, "Children, have you any fish?" They answered him, "No." And he said unto them, "Cast the net on the right side of the ship, and you shall find." They cast therefore, and now they were not able to draw it for the multitude of fishes.

5   Therefore that disciple whom Jesus loved said unto Peter, "It is the Lord." Now when Simon Peter heard that it was the Lord, he wrapped his fisher's coat unto him, (for he was naked), and did cast himself into the sea.

And the other disciples came in a little ship; (for they were not far from 5
land, but as it were three hundred feet), dragging the net with fishes.

As soon then as they were come to land, they saw a fire of coals there, 6
and fish laid thereon, and bread. Jesus said unto them, "Bring of the fish
which you have now caught." Simon Peter went up, and drew the net to land
full of great fishes, a hundred and fifty and three: and although there were
so many, yet the net was not broken.

Jesus said unto them, "Come and have breakfast." And none of the 7
disciples dared ask him, "Who are you?" knowing that it was the Lord.
Jesus then came, and took bread, and gave them, and fish likewise. This is
now the third time that Jesus showed himself to his disciples, after that he
was risen from the dead.

Jesus Counsels Peter
John 21:15-24

So when they had finished breakfast, Jesus said to Simon Peter, 8
"Simon, son of Jonah, do you totally love me more than these?" He said unto
him, "Yes, Lord; you know that I love you." He said unto him, "Feed my
lambs." He said to him again the second time, "Simon, son of Jonah, do you
totally love me?" He said unto him, "Yes, Lord; you know that I love you."
He said unto him, "Tend my sheep." He said unto him the third time, "Simon,
son of Jonah, do you love me?" Peter was grieved because he said unto him
the third time, "Do you love me?" And he said unto him, "Lord, you know
all things; you know that I love you." Jesus said unto him, "Feed my sheep.

"Truly, truly, I say unto you, When you were young, you dressed your- 9
self, and walked where you would: but when you shall be old, you shall
stretch forth your hands, and another shall dress you, and carry you where
you would not." This he spoke, signifying by what death he should glorify
God. And when he had spoken this, he said unto him, "Follow me."

Then Peter, turning about, saw the disciple whom Jesus loved follow- 10
ing; which also leaned on his breast at supper, and said, "Lord, which is he
that betrays you?" Peter seeing him said to Jesus, "Lord, and what shall this
man do?" Jesus said unto him, "If I will that he tarry till I come, what is that
to you? You follow me."

Then went this saying abroad among the brethren, that that disciple 11
should not die: yet Jesus did not say unto him, "He shall not die"; but, "If I
will that he tarry till I come, what is that to you?" This is the disciple which
testifies of these things, and wrote these things: and we know that his testimony is true.

Jesus Appears to Give Commission
Matthew 28:16-20; Mark 16:15-18

Then the eleven disciples went away into Galilee, into a mountain 12
where Jesus had appointed them. And when they saw him, they worshiped
him: but some doubted.

13   And Jesus came and spoke unto them, saying, "All authority is given unto me in heaven and on earth. Go therefore, and teach all nations, baptizing them in the name of the Father, and of the Son, and of the Holy Ghost: teaching them to observe all things whatsoever I have commanded you: and, lo, I am with you always, even unto the end of the world."

14   He said unto them, "Go into all the world, and preach the gospel to every creature. He that believes and is baptized shall be saved; but he that believes not shall be condemned. And these signs shall follow them that believe: In my name shall they cast out demons; they shall speak with new tongues; they shall take up serpents; and if they drink any deadly thing, it shall not hurt them; they shall lay hands on the sick, and they shall recover."

Await the Promise of the Father
Luke 24:44-49

15   And he said unto them, "These are the words which I spoke unto you, while I was yet with you, that all things must be fulfilled, which were written in the law of Moses, and in the prophets, and in the psalms, concerning me. Then he opened their minds, that they might understand the scriptures, and said unto them, Thus it is written, and thus it behooved Christ to suffer, and to rise from the dead the third day: and that repentance and remission of sins should be preached in his name among all nations, beginning at Jerusalem. And you are witnesses of these things.

16   "And, behold, I send the promise of my Father upon you: but tarry in the city of Jerusalem, until you be endued with power from on high."

Jesus Ascends to Heaven
Mark 16:19; Luke 24:50-51

17   He led them out as far as to Bethany, and he lifted up his hands, and blessed them. And it came to pass, while he blessed them, he was parted from them, and carried up into heaven, and sat on the right hand of God.

Disciples Obey Jesus' Commission
Mark 16:20; Luke 24:52-53

18   They worshiped him, and returned to Jerusalem with great joy: and were continually in the temple, praising and blessing God.

19   They went forth, and preached everywhere, the Lord working with them, and confirming the word with signs following.

Written That You Might Believe
John 20:30-31; 21:25

20   Many other signs truly did Jesus in the presence of his disciples, which are not written in this book: but these are written, that you might believe that Jesus is the Christ, the Son of God; and that believing you might have life through his name.

21   There are also many other things which Jesus did, which, if they should be written every one, I suppose that even the world itself could not contain the books that should be written. Amen.

CHAPTER 56

GENEALOGY OF JESUS

The Two Genealogies of Jesus
Matthew 1:1-17; Luke 3:23-38

The book of the genealogy of Jesus Christ, the son of David, the son 1
of Abraham. Abraham begot Isaac; and Isaac begot Jacob; and Jacob begot
Judah and his brethren; and Judah begot Perez and Zerah by Tamar; and
Perez begot Hezron; and Hezron begot Ram; and Ram begot Amminadab;
and Amminadab begot Nahshon; and Nahshon begot Salmon; and Salmon
begot Boaz of Rahab; and Boaz begot Obed by Ruth; and Obed begot Jesse;
and Jesse begot David the king; and David the king begot Solomon by her
who had been the wife of Uriah; and Solomon begot Rehoboam; and
Rehoboam begot Abijah; and Abijah begot Asa; and Asa begot Jehoshaphat;
and Jehoshaphat begot Joram; and Joram begot Uzziah; and Uzziah begot
Jotham; and Jotham begot Ahaz; and Ahaz begot Hezekiah; and Hezekiah
begot Manasseh; and Manasseh begot Amon; and Amon begot Josias; and
Josias begot Jeconiah and his brethren, about the time they were carried
away to Babylon: and after they were brought to Babylon, Jeconiah begot
Shealtiel; and Shealtiel begot Zerubbabel; and Zerubbabel begot Abiud;
and Abiud begot Eliakim; and Eliakim begot Azor; and Azor begot Zadok;
and Zadok begot Achim; and Achim begot Eliud; and Eliud begot Eleazar;
and Eleazar begot Matthan; and Matthan begot Jacob; and Jacob begot
Joseph the husband of Mary, of whom was born Jesus, who is called Christ.

So all the generations from Abraham to David are fourteen genera- 2
tions; and from David until the carrying away into Babylon are fourteen
generations; and from the carrying away into Babylon unto Christ are fourteen generations.

And Jesus himself began to be about thirty years of age, being (as was 3
supposed) the son of Joseph, which was the son of Heli, which was the son
of Matthat, which was the son of Levi, which was the son of Melchi, which

3 was the son of Janna, which was the son of Joseph, which was the son of Mattathiah, which was the son of Amos, which was the son of Nahum, which was the son of Esli, which was the son of Naggai, which was the son of Maath, which was the son of Mattathiah, which was the son of Semei, which was the son of Joseph, which was the son of Judah, which was the son of Joannas, which was the son of Rhesa, which was the son of Zerubbabel, which was the son of Shealtiel, which was the son of Neri, which was the son of Melchi, which was the son of Addi, which was the son of Cosam, which was the son of Elmodam, which was the son of Er, which was the son of Jose, which was the son of Eliezer, which was the son of Jorim, which was the son of Matthat, which was the son of Levi, which was the son of Simeon, which was the son of Judah, which was the son of Joseph, which was the son of Jonan, which was the son of Eliakim, which was the son of Melea, which was the son of Menan, which was the son of Mattathah, which was the son of Nathan, which was the son of David, which was the son of Jesse, which was the son of Obed, which was the son of Boaz, which was the son of Salmon, which was the son of Nahshon, which was the son of Amminadab, which was the son of Ram, which was the son of Hezron, which was the son of Perez, which was the son of Judah, which was the son of Jacob, which was the son of Isaac, which was the son of Abraham, which was the son of Terah, which was the son of Nahor, which was the son of Serug, which was the son of Reu, which was the son of Peleg, which was the son of Eber, which was the son of Shelah, which was the son of Cainan, which was the son of Arphaxad, which was the son of Shem, which was the son of Noah, which was the son of Lamech, which was the son of Methuselah, which was the son of Enoch, which was the son of Jared, which was the son of Mahalalel, which was the son of Cainan, which was the son of Enos, which was the son of Seth, which was the son of Adam, which was the son of God.

About the Compiler

Developed more by Providence than by plan, *The Seamless Bible* represents the culmination of a spiritual journey by the compiler, Charles Roller, that took him through a quarter century of study and searching.

Born in Tulsa, Oklahoma, at the beginning of the Great Depression, he spent his younger years without a father. Between the ages of six and eleven he was raised by his grandparents on a farm near Vinita, Oklahoma, as his mother was unable to work and care for the young boy. The King James Bible that lay on end table in the living room of his grandparents' house was one of the few books they had in the house. During this time was his first remembrance of the Scriptures, for at the church in their town where two railroads crossed in the middle, the preacher talked of the book of Jesus and told the congregation that not everyone believed that Jesus was the Son of God. Young Charles wondered how this could be. So he took his grandparents Bible, big in his small hands, and began to read. It was filled with many words, and he knew but a few. This was his first venture into the book that was to become a central part of his life, summoning a deep calling that would remain with him throughout his years.

Eventually he and his mother reunited and returned to Tulsa, where he attended public schools. He went on to attend Northeastern State University in Oklahoma, where he worked his way through college at part-time jobs. He received a BS Degree in Business Administration in 1954, and in doing so became the first in his family to receive a college degree. As an adult he attended a variety of Protestant churches and in time came to develop an abiding love of the Scripture. He retained a silent yearning to understand more and would often awaken at night with a deep sense that he had not yet done what he was put here to do—yet knew that he should.

Over the years, his longing to understand more of the New Testament became focused on the fragmented compilation of the Bible and the beautiful but archaic language used by the King James Version. Studying a single event carefully across many pages would sometimes cause him to lose track of the story. One day he tried to locate a passage of Scripture that he had been reading the previous evening, but was unable to find it again. The story of unequal wages paid to workers in the field was one he wanted to reread. Frustrated in his search, he asked a friend to help him sort through the myriad of biblical accounts of the event.

This rather ordinary episode turned into the seed of an extraordinary idea that would occupy the next 25 years of Charles' life. He realized he needed a book for someone like himself—an ordinary person looking for a Bible that would lift the story of Jesus out of the darkness of ancient translations and into the light of today.

Searching through the shelves of libraries and bookstores for such a book, but finding none, he set out to compile his own personal edition of the New Testament based on his grandparents' beloved King James text, as it remains today the most beautiful and purest English translation of the bible ever written. His work would tell the story of the life of Christ chronologically, in one single thread of events, blending the many accounts of Jesus' life into one story that all could easily read and understand. It would tell an uninterrupted story of the life of Christ, from his birth through his death and resurrection, and continuing through the works of his followers. Above all else, it would be a Bible compiled *by* a layperson *for* the layperson, built on the work of the religious scholars who had come before, yet unencumbered by the outdated language of the early theologians.

To accomplish this, he first called a friend and asked if she would consent to cut up the King James New Testament and paste it back together again in order. She was horrified. And so Charles labor began, in a small rented apartment in 1976 with a pair of scissors and a commitment to himself and his Maker. Over the years, others joined in the endeavor, each adding their time, treasure, and their sense of the Scripture. The collective effort of ministers, learned religious professionals, and everyday seekers of Truth added immensely to the result. With every precious detail of the King James text intact, it was molded into a form that those of all ages and backgrounds could apply to their own lives and from which those who had wandered from the Bible might gather fresh meaning.

With care and precision the many separate accounts of Jesus' journey given in the King James, Gospels were blended into one single interwoven story that would allow the reader witness the chronological unfolding of events much the same as the disciples had done so many years before. Christian editors and religious advisors edited the work for accuracy and suitability for today's reader. The last half of the New Testament, containing the Acts and Letters, followed in a blended continuum of the first, undergoing the same careful attention. As the work came to fruition, the unique new presentation of this ageless story would astonish even those who had been closely involved.

After a quarter-century of arduous labor requiring the review of over 400 Bibles, references, and biblical studies, there lay before them a spiritual compilation of immense proportion. Charles had believed in his vision of the Scripture as a child and had never wavered from that belief.

Heartfelt thanks go to Timothy Disney, Sherry Jackson, Danny Lynchard, and Gail Runnels, who each gave freely of their time and skills to make compilation of *The Seamless Gospels* a joy of love fulfilled.

Cross-Reference Index